ALEXANDER OSTROVSKY

EASY MONEY
AND TWO OTHER PLAYS

ALEXANDER OSTROVSKY

EASY MONEY
AND TWO OTHER PLAYS

Even a Wise Man Stumbles
and
Wolves and Sheep

Translated with Introduction
and Notes by
DAVID MAGARSHACK

GREENWOOD PRESS, PUBLISHERS
WESTPORT, CONNECTICUT

Originally published in 1944
by George Allen & Unwin, Ltd., London

First Greenwood Reprinting 1970

Library of Congress Catalogue Card Number 78-110861

SBN 8371-4532-5

Printed in the United States of America

CONTENTS

INTRODUCTION
Page 6

EVEN A WISE MAN STUMBLES
Page 13

EASY MONEY
Page 95

WOLVES AND SHEEP
Page 187

NOTES
Page 291

INTRODUCTION

ALEXANDER NIKOLAYEVICH OSTROVSKY was born on the 31st of March, 1823. His grandfather was a priest who, on settling in Moscow, turned monk and entered a monastery, and his father was educated at a church seminary, but became a lawyer and was for some years a member of the Moscow Senate. His mother died when he was only a boy of eight and his father, being too busy to bother about his numerous family, allowed him the run of his large library as well as of the streets, of both of which Ostrovsky availed himself freely. Neither at one of Moscow's grammar schools nor at the university, where he studied law, did Ostrovsky excel himself. He left the university in the third year of his studies after a quarrel with one of the professors. But even as a student he was more often to be found at a pub than in the lecture room.

The next five years of his life, from 1843 to 1848, Ostrovsky spent as a clerk in the Moscow Juvenile Court (the "Court of Conscience" instituted by the Empress Catherine II in 1775) and the Moscow Commercial Court, where, no doubt, the foundations of his realistic outlook on life were laid.

He wrote his first play, *Scenes of Family Happiness, being Scenes of Moscow Life*, in 1847 and a year later he became famous as the author of the play *The Bankrupt* or, as later renamed, *It's All A Family Affair*. The public outcry which this play produced because of its too realistic exposure of bogus bankruptcy cases among a certain section of Moscow's business population, caused his dismissal from the Civil Service and his being placed under police supervision for many years. The play, incidentally, was banned from the stage by Czar Nicholas I himself, who caused the head of the Moscow Department of the Ministry of Education to summon Ostrovsky and read him a lecture (prepared by an Extraordinary State Commission) on the iniquity of playwrights who, while exposing human wickedness on the stage, refuse to sugar the pill by punishing the criminal. The ban on the play was only removed thirteen years later under the more

INTRODUCTION

benignant reign of Alexander II, but it became widely known through private readings.

Both at the house of his father, who had a large legal practice among the members of Moscow's merchant community, and in the courts Ostrovsky gained a deep insight into the domestic life of the middle classes, and his first cycle of plays deals exclusively with it. In 1856 Ostrovsky took part in a grandiose survey of literary documents in different parts of Russia, undertaking himself to study the literary treasures of the Upper Volga region. As a result of this study, Ostrovsky turned to the writing of historical plays. Only in the later part of his life did Ostrovsky begin to write plays of general interest, plays which deal with the impact of the industrial revolution on the Russian middle classes, the disintegration of the feudal class and the evolution of the modern business man.

Between 1847 and 1886, the year of his death, Ostrovsky wrote about fifty original plays, mostly comedies, but also some of the finest tragedies in the Russian language as well as a number of historical plays and a famous fantasy in verse, *The Snow Maiden*.

Ostrovsky's services to the Russian theatre were not, however, limited to the writing of original plays. He was a great translator of the classics. His translations include two plays by Shakespeare, *The Taming of the Shrew* and *Antony and Cleopatra* (translated in the last year of his life), as well as plays by Plautus, Terence, Machiavelli, Cervantes, Goldoni and others.

But in spite of his great popularity and his feverish output of plays, Ostrovsky never made enough money to live in comparative comfort.* He was always in dire need and his whole life was one long fight against the managers of the Imperial Theatres, who, while making enormous profits from his plays, used their monopolistic position to pay him beggarly royalties. This experience led Ostrovsky to start an agitation for the establishment of a National Theatre in Moscow, an idea which was never realized.

* According to the great Russian critic Byelinsky, there were only three plays of note in the Russian repertory before Ostrovsky began to write, namely, Pushkin's *Boris Godunov*, which was not written for the stage, Gogol's *Government Inspector* and Griboyedov's *The Misfortune of Being Too Clever*.

INTRODUCTION

Towards the end of his life Ostrovsky became the acknowledged head of the Russian stage and the founder of the Society of Russian Playwrights.

He died at the age of sixty-three on the 28th of May, 1886, leaving a widow (his second wife) and four children, who were provided for by a special State pension of 3,000 roubles a year.

Ostrovsky is generally considered the greatest representative of the Russian realistic drama. Stanislavsky praises his "grand epic serenity," but the Russian playgoer has chosen him as one of his most favourite dramatists for the simpler reason that he is a master of stage technique and an inexhaustible fount of entertainment.

The author of an anonymous review of Ostrovsky's plays in the July number of the *Edinburgh Review* for the year 1868, one of the most comprehensive appreciations of Ostrovsky yet published in English, remarked on the strange fact that Ostrovsky was completely unknown in England and that "we have never seen or heard of a translation of his plays into English." Since that time only five of Ostrovsky's fifty plays (from his merchant cycle) have been published in an English translation, one of them, the tragedy *The Storm*, in England and four in the United States.

These translations have done nothing to make Ostrovsky known to the English-speaking world and much less to make him popular on the English and American stage. This is only partly due to the fact that the five plays deal exclusively with the life of the Russian merchant class in the middle years of the last century, whose traditions, patriarchal customs and dark superstitions are unintelligible outside Russia.

For even this great difficulty could have been overcome (after all, the customs and superstitions of ancient Greece are no more intelligible to a modern audience), if there were not other, even greater, difficulties. One of these is the marvellous vitality and colour of the language used by Ostrovsky which does not easily lend itself to translation.

"If Western European literature contains no translations of Ostrovsky's works, and if the Western European stage has so far failed to make a success of the production of any of his

INTRODUCTION

plays," a modern Russian critic writes, "it is due mainly to the almost untranslatable language, so full of colour and idiom, in which Ostrovsky's plays are written." Another modern Russian critic expresses the same view. "A translator of Ostrovsky's plays," he writes, "is faced with immense difficulties, first, because of the peculiar local colour which pervades his work and, secondly, because his prose abounds in untranslatable words, turns of speech and idioms."

Ostrovsky, in short, wrote exclusively for the stage and, being a supreme master of stage technique, his dramatic prose is the speech of living men and women and not the artificial prose of literature.

The three famous comedies of Ostrovsky's last period published in this volume have been translated primarily with an eye to the English stage and an attempt has been made to overcome the many difficulties of Ostrovsky's style by a re-casting and remoulding of his prose rather than a direct translation of it. The main difficulty of translating so vital a playwright as Ostrovsky consists in conveying to the English reader and playgoer the emotional tension which he produces. An English audience reacts differently to certain emotional moments from a Russian audience. The words used by Ostrovsky to produce this emotional atmosphere would, therefore, be either too strong or too inadequate. The dialogue has therefore also been re-created in such a way that the emotional undercurrent may at once be perceived and responded to by an English audience. This was done by occasionally compressing the dialogue or, more rarely, by expanding it somewhat.

In these three plays Ostrovsky's realism assumes a wider and deeper significance.

Ostrovsky never really submitted to the romantic conventions of the theatre according to which crime must find its fit punishment before the final curtain. He saw life too clearly and with too unbiassed an eye to believe that any dramatist could reform it.

While in his earlier plays of the merchant cycle he occasionally allowed the long arm of coincidence to bring about a happy ending and even went so far as to have recourse to

INTRODUCTION

sudden conversions of the villain, he steadfastly refused to compromise on this issue in his later plays.

In none of the three plays of this volume, for instance, does right triumph over wrong or virtue over vice. In *Even a Wise Man Stumbles*, the hero Glumov does not recant after his exposure and expulsion from the set of Moscow society he hoped to exploit; on the contrary, the other characters, whose villainy is no less obvious for going unpunished though exposed, decide to give Glumov another chance, not with a view to making a better man of him, but because they cannot carry on without him. In *Easy Money*, which is one of the finest comedies of its kind, the rake Telyatev remains both unconverted and unimpressed by the triumph of Vassilkov, the only really honest character in any of these plays, and the taming of Lydia leaves the reader and playgoer very much in doubt whether her change of heart is either real or permanent. While in the third play, *Wolves and Sheep*, no attempt is even made by Ostrovsky to exact punishment for the criminal acts of the two principal characters. All that happens is merely that the man who exposes and brings to naught their misdeeds carries off the spoils himself.

It would seem that in a drama where realism is allowed to go to such length there is little that could appeal to the innate decency and sense of fair play of the average playgoer and even less to rouse his pity or indignation. Actually, the opposite is true. With such mastery are the secret places of the hearts of the characters exposed, so comic are the situations in which their own folly lands them, so witty is the dialogue and so supremely alive is every character, that the moral effect produced by these plays is much deeper than the one produced by the more conventional play where virtue triumphs in the end and the punishment fits the crime. Life is not only more uncompromising than fiction, its very cruelty and injustice help to produce in the human heart the necessary reaction towards good. These three great plays have exactly the same effect on the reader or spectator.

The plays in this volume belong to that period of Ostrovsky's life when his art emerged from the narrow confines of the merchant caste and when he turned to the production of

INTRODUCTION

masterpieces with a universal appeal. They contain the essence of his great art and have proved a perennial source of entertainment to many generations of Russians. They should help to dissipate the impenetrable fog which has for so long hung over the works of this great genius of the Russian theatre and gain him the respect and even the popularity that so great a classic deserves.

D. M.

EVEN A WISE MAN STUMBLES
A Comedy in Five Acts

By
ALEXANDER OSTROVSKY

Translated by
DAVID MAGARSHACK

CHARACTERS

Yegor Dmitrich Glúmov (George), a young man about town.
Glafíra Klimovna Glúmova, his mother.
Nil Fyedoseyich Mamáyev, a very rich gentleman, a distant relative of Glúmov.
Cleopatra Lvovna Mamáyeva, his wife.
Krutítzky, an old man, a gentleman of great importance.
Ivan Ivanych Gorodúlin, young, a gentleman of importance.
Sofia Ignatyevna Turússina, a rich widow.
Mary, her niece.
Yegor Vassilyevich Kurcháyev, a hussar.
Golútvin, a man without a profession.
Manéfa, a fortune-teller.
1st Poor Relation.
2nd Poor Relation.
Mamáyev's Footman.
Krutítzky's Footman.
Grigóry, Turusina's Footman.

ACT ONE

[*A tidy, well-furnished room, writing desk, mirror; one door leads to inner rooms; to the right—entrance door.*]

GLÚMOV. [*Behind the scenes*] Well, what about it? It is important. Go straight ahead and it's in the bag. [*Enters from side-door*] Do as you're told and don't argue!
GLÚMOVA. [*Enters from side-door*] Why do you force me to write these letters? I can't. I really can't.
GLÚMOV. Do as I tell you. Get on with it!
GLÚMOVA. But what's the good of it? They won't let you marry her. Mary Turussina has a dowry of two hundred thousand roubles, she is of good birth, she has excellent connections, she is fit to be the bride of a prince or of a general. They won't let her marry even Kurchayev; why should I be made to write all sorts of abusive and slanderous letters against the poor man?
GLÚMOV. Who are you more sorry for, me or that hussar Kurchayev? What does he want money for? He'd lose it at cards, anyway. You don't seem to care a rap for me, and yet you are always snivelling: "I brought you into the world!"
GLÚMOVA. If it were of any use!
GLÚMOV. That's my business!
GLÚMOVA. Have you even a ghost of a chance?
GLÚMOV. I have. Mother, you know me. I'm clever, spiteful and envious. In fact, an exact copy of yourself. What have I been doing with myself so far? I've kept on losing my temper and writing epigrams against the whole of Moscow, wasting my time. No, I've had enough of that! It is profitless to laugh at fools, one must know how to make use of their weaknesses. Of course, here it is impossible to make a career. A career can be made only in Petersburg. In Moscow people just talk. But even here it should be possible to get a cushy job and a rich bride. That's all I want. How do people make their way in the world? Not always through the pursuit of some business or profession, more often than not simply by talk. We in Moscow like to talk. And do you really think that I shan't

succeed in this huge talking shop? That's just silly. I shall make friends with the big men and I shall find some really influential people who'll be glad to push me. You'll see. It's silly to tread on their corns, one must flatter them, one must lay it on thick, one must have no conscience at all about that. For that's the whole secret of success. I intend to start with the less important ones, with the circle of Mrs. Turussina. I'll squeeze out all I want from her, and afterwards I'll climb a little higher. Go on, write those letters. We'll discuss it later.

GLÚMOVA. Heaven help you! [*Goes out*]

GLÚMOV. [*Sits down at writing desk*] Away with epigrams! That kind of poetry brings nothing but trouble to the author. Let's turn to panegyrics. [*Takes out notebook from pocket*] All the bile in me I'll jot down in this diary, but on my lips there shall henceforth be nothing but honey. Alone, in the dead of night, I shall chronicle the history of human meanness. This manuscript is not intended for the public. I shall be its only author and reader, unless, in the fullness of time, when I'm firmly on my feet, I decide to publish some well-chosen extracts from it.

[KURCHÁYEV *and* GOLÚTVIN *enter;* GLÚMOV *gets up and hides notebook in pocket.*]

KURCHÁYEV. Good morning.

GLÚMOV. How d'you do? What can I do for you?

KURCHÁYEV. [*Sitting down at writing desk*] We've come on business. [*Pointing at* GOLÚTVIN] Allow me to introduce ...

GLÚMOV. Why introduce him? I've known him a long time.

GOLÚTVIN. I, somehow, don't like the way you talk of me, old man.

GLÚMOV. I don't very much care whether you do or not. I suppose, gentlemen, you've had a good breakfast?

KURCHÁYEV. Yes, thanks. [*He picks up a pencil and begins to draw something on a piece of paper.*]

GLÚMOV. Yes. I can see you have. Well, gentlemen, I haven't much time. What do you want? [*He sits down,* GOLÚTVIN *follows suit.*]

KURCHÁYEV. Have you any verses lying about?

GLÚMOV. What kind of verses? I'm afraid, you've come to the wrong address.

GOLÚTVIN. Not at all, old man. We've come to the right place all right.
GLÚMOV. [*To* KURCHÁYEV] Please, don't spoil my paper.
KURCHÁYEV. We want epigrams. I know you've got them.
GLÚMOV. I haven't.
KURCHÁYEV. That's a damn lie, old man, if you don't mind my saying so. Everyone in town knows you've got them. You have one for every man and woman of consequence in Moscow. [*Pointing to* GOLÚTVIN] He wants to become a contributor to the comic papers.
GLÚMOV. [*To* GOLÚTVIN] Is that so? Have you written anything?
GOLÚTVIN. I have.
GLÚMOV. What?
GOLÚTVIN. Every damn thing: novels, short stories, tragedies, comedies . . .
GLÚMOV. Well?
GOLÚTVIN. Well, I can't get a darned thing published. No publisher will so much as touch my stuff, not for anything in the world. I've begged and begged, but they refuse to publish it even for nothing. I now want to start as a gossip writer.
GLÚMOV. No one will publish that, either.
GOLÚTVIN. There's no harm in trying, old man.
GLÚMOV. But it's dangerous!
GOLÚTVIN. Dangerous? Will I get beaten up?
GLÚMOV. You may.
GOLÚTVIN. Well, you know, old man, the truth is that in certain out-of-the-way places they do beat one up, but I've never heard of its happening here.
GLÚMOV. All right. Go ahead then.
GOLÚTVIN. Go ahead, old man? But who am I to write about? I don't know anyone in town.
KURCHÁYEV. I understand you keep a diary in which you record faithfully the failings of every man and woman prominent in society.
GOLÚTVIN. Exactly. Let's have it, old man. Let's have it.
GLÚMOV. To be sure. Why not?
GOLÚTVIN. And we'll publish it all over the blasted place.
GLÚMOV. [*Firmly*] I have no such diary!

KURCHÁYEV. Go on, tell me another! I know some people who have seen it.
GOLÚTVIN. Look at him, behaving as though he wasn't one of us!
GLÚMOV. I am not one of you!
GOLÚTVIN. But think of the shekels it would net, old man!
KURCHÁYEV. [*To* GLÚMOV] He does want money very badly. "I'm sick of people always standing me drinks," he says, "I want to turn an honest penny by honest work!" He calls gossip writing honest work. How do you like that?
GLÚMOV. I see, I see.
GOLÚTVIN. But I can't write my gossip column because I have no copy, old man!
KURCHÁYEV. You see, the poor lad has no copy. Supply him with the right kind of copy and let him get on with his work.
GLÚMOV. [*Getting up*] Stop scribbling on my paper!
KURCHÁYEV. To hell with your paper!
GLÚMOV. Drawing cockerels, I see!
KURCHÁYEV. Pardon me, this isn't a cockerel. This is my highly respected uncle, Mamayev. Look [*He puts the finishing touch to the caricature*] Isn't it a good likeness? Even to the tuft of hair on the top of his head!
GOLÚTVIN. Is your uncle an amusing bloke, I mean for my purpose?
KURCHÁYEV. He's amusing all right! He's firmly convinced that he's by far the cleverest man alive and he's consequently constantly preaching at people. Treat him to a good meal, and he'll hardly thank you, but ask him for his advice, and he'll fall over himself to be nice to you!
GOLÚTVIN. Well, then, why not write under the cockerel: "Universal Educator?" [KURCHÁYEV *writes*] Now, let's send it off to a comic paper.
KURCHÁYEV. No, you don't! He's my uncle, after all, and I'm his sole heir! [*He drops the paper.* GLÚMOV *picks it up and puts it in his pocket.*]
GOLÚTVIN. Has your uncle any other ambitions?
KURCHÁYEV. Plenty more. He's been flat-hunting for the past three years. Not that he wants a flat. All he wants is to

sit about and talk. He pretends to keep himself busy that way. He leaves his own flat in the morning, has himself driven to about ten different flats, looks them over carefully, has a long chat with their owners and caretakers, then goes on to pay his daily visits to various shops where he proceeds to taste caviare and other titbits. He takes them at a leisurely stride, sits down and begins his interminable talk again. The shopkeepers hate the sight of him, but he's as pleased as Punch. You see, he has managed not to waste another morning! [*To* GLÚMOV] By the way, there's something I forgot to tell you.

GLÚMOV. Oh?

KURCHÁYEV. My aunt has fallen head over ears in love with you!

GLÚMOV. Your aunt? How's that?

KURCHÁYEV. She saw you at the play. The old girl nearly twisted her neck off looking at you. She kept on asking me: "Who's that young man? Who's that young man?" Don't laugh. It's no joke.

GLÚMOV. I'm not laughing. You're the one who laughs at everything.

KURCHÁYEV. All right, have it your own way. Were I in your shoes, though, I'd . . . So you won't let us have your verses?

GLÚMOV. No, sir.

GOLÚTVIN. Don't let's waste any more time on him. Let's go have lunch.

KURCHÁYEV. All right. Come on. So long . . .

[*Bows and follows* GOLÚTVIN *out of the room.*]

GLÚMOV. [*Stops* KURCHÁYEV *at the door*] Why are you dragging him about with you?

KURCHÁYEV. Because I like the company of clever people.

GLÚMOV. You've found a clever man!

KURCHÁYEV. He'll do. You see, really clever men wouldn't dream of wasting their time with me!

[*Goes out.*]

GLÚMOV. [*Calls after him*] You'd better watch your step! Mother!

[GLÚMOVA *enters and he shows her* KURCHÁYEV's *caricature.*]

Look at it. That's the man I'd like to meet.

GLÚMOVA. Who's that?
GLÚMOV. A distant relative of ours, Nil Mamayev.
GLÚMOVA. And who drew the picture?
GLÚMOV. His dearly beloved nephew, the hussar. I'd better hold on to this picture. It may come in useful. [*Puts it away in his pocket*] The trouble is that Mamayev doesn't like relations. He has about thirty nephews and, from time to time, he picks one out and makes him his heir. As for the rest, they'd better not cross his path. When he gets tired of his favourite, he turns him out, chooses another of his nephews and changes his will accordingly. At present, Kurchayev is his favourite.
GLÚMOVA. Ah, if only you . . .
GLÚMOV. It's not so easy, mother, but I'm going to have a shot at it. Mamayev doesn't even suspect that I exist.
GLÚMOVA. It would be worth your while to get to know him. In the first place, there's the inheritance, then, there is his fine establishment, his large circle of friends and, last but not least, his very influential connections.
GLÚMOV. Yes, indeed. There's something else, mother. I seem to have made a hit with his wife. She's seen me somewhere. You'd better make a note of that, in case . . . The first thing, however, is to get on friendly terms with Mamayev. It's the first step towards my goal. Uncle will introduce me to Krutitzky and Gorodulin. They are both men of influence and intimate friends of Mrs. Turussina. Let me once step inside her house and I shall marry that niece of hers!
GLÚMOVA. That may be, son, but don't forget that the first step is the most difficult one.
GLÚMOV. Don't you worry about that, mother. It has been taken already. Mamayev will be here soon.
GLÚMOVA. How did that happen?
GLÚMOV. It didn't happen. It was carefully arranged by me. Mamayev likes to look for flats. I caught him on that hook.
[*Enter* MAMÁYEV'S FOOTMAN.]
MAMÁYEV'S FOOTMAN. Mr. Mamayev is here, sir.
GLÚMOV. Splendid. Here . . . [*He tips the* FOOTMAN] Show your master in here.
MAMÁYEV'S FOOTMAN. But he'll be in the devil of a temper, sir. I told him your flat was a large flat.

GLÚMOV. Don't you worry about that, my man. I shall take the responsibility upon myself. Mother, you'd better go to your room now. I'll call you when necessary.

[GLÚMOVA *leaves by door to the left.* MAMÁYEV's FOOTMAN *goes out by door to the right.* GLÚMOV *sits down at desk and pretends to be absorbed in writing.* MAMÁYEV *enters, followed by* FOOTMAN.]

MAMÁYEV. [*Looks round without taking off his hat*] This is a bachelor's flat.

GLÚMOV. [*Bows and goes on writing*] Yes, sir.

MAMÁYEV. [*Without paying any attention to him*] I say this is not a bad flat, but it is a bachelor's flat. [*To the* FOOTMAN] What do you mean by bringing me here?

GLÚMOV. [*Gets up, offers* MAMÁYEV *a chair and goes back to his writing*] Won't you sit down, sir?

MAMÁYEV. [*Sits down*] Thank you. [*To* FOOTMAN] What do you mean by bringing me here, I ask you?

MAMÁYEV's FOOTMAN. I'm very sorry, sir.

MAMÁYEV. Don't you know, my dear fellow, what kind of flat I want? Haven't you realized yet that I am a State Councillor, that my wife, your mistress, likes to keep open house? We want a large drawing-room, we want two large drawing-rooms! Where's the large drawing-room, I ask you?

MAMÁYEV's FOOTMAN. I'm very sorry, sir.

MAMÁYEV. Where is the large drawing-roon? [*To* GLÚMOV] I beg your pardon, sir.

GLÚMOV. Don't mind me. Carry on. You're not interfering in the least with me.

MAMÁYEV. [*To* FOOTMAN] You see, we're interfering with this gentleman. Of course, he doesn't say so, but that's merely out of politeness. You're to blame for everything, you silly fool!

GLÚMOV. Don't scold him, sir. It isn't his fault at all, but mine. When he was inquiring after a flat on the stairs, I told him mine was a very good flat. I didn't know you were a family man.

MAMÁYEV. Are you the owner of this flat?

GLÚMOV. Yes, sir.

MAMÁYEV. Why are you letting it?

GLÚMOV. Because I can't afford it.

MAMÁYEV. Why did you rent it, if you can't afford it? Who compelled you? Did anyone take you by the scruff of the neck and shove you into it? People always take flats they can't afford. I suppose you're also behind with your rent, aren't you? And I shouldn't wonder if your landlord has already taken out an order for distraint! Of course. Naturally. What else is one to expect? Now you'll have to give up this nice, big flat and move into one room. You won't like that, sir, will you?

GLÚMOV. No, sir. I shouldn't like it at all. In fact, I'm about to move into a bigger flat.

MAMÁYEV. A bigger flat? You can't afford this one and you're about to move into a bigger one! What's the sense of that, sir?

GLÚMOV. No sense at all. Just sheer stupidity.

MAMÁYEV. Sheer stupidity? What nonsense is that, sir?

GLÚMOV. No nonsense, I assure you. I'm just naturally stupid.

MAMÁYEV. Naturally stupid! Good heavens, man, what do you mean by that?

GLÚMOV. It's really very simple. I have no brains. What's there unusual about it?

MAMÁYEV. Well, this certainly is interesting. Here's a man who confesses he's a fool.

GLÚMOV. What else do you expect me to do? Wait till other people tell me I'm one. Doesn't it come to the same thing? You can't hide it, can you?

MAMÁYEV. Well, of course, a thing like that can't very well be hidden.

GLÚMOV. Exactly. I'm not hiding it, then.

MAMÁYEV. I am sorry.

GLÚMOV. Thank you.

MAMÁYEV. I don't suppose you know anyone who can give you some good advice?

GLÚMOV. I'm afraid not. There isn't anyone.

MAMÁYEV. But you realize, don't you? that there are people whose advice is worth listening to? Somehow, however, no one seems to pay any attention to them. Such are the times we're living in. The old ones don't even dream of asking anyone for advice. They think that because they're old they must be wise. However, as even the young don't want to listen to you, what can you expect of the old? Let me tell you of one case, sir. The other day I saw a schoolboy running like mad home from school. I, of course, stopped him and was about to reprimand him, just for a joke, you understand. "See here, my boy," I said, "why aren't you in a hurry on your way to school? Why do you run on your way home?" Anyone else would have thanked me for my words. Think of it, sir. An important person like myself stops a young puppy in the street to teach him good manners. Don't I deserve a word of thanks for that? But no, not that ragamuffin, not he . . .

GLÚMOV. Teaching, sir, is not to-day what . . .

MAMÁYEV. Not he. "We're sick to death of being preached at at school," he says. "If you like to preach, try to get our headmaster's job. And now mind your own business, I'm hungry!" How do you like that, sir, and from a schoolboy, too!

GLÚMOV. That boy is certainly on the downward path, sir. A great pity.

MAMÁYEV. And where does that path lead to? Do you know that, sir?

GLÚMOV. I do, sir. I do.

MAMÁYEV. And another thing. Have you noticed how the servants are getting out of hand? Why? Because it is no longer considered to be their duty to listen to their master's admonitions. In the old days I used to enter into every detail of my servants' private lives. I admonished them all, big and small. I used to spend hours talking to them of their duty to themselves and their master. At times I'd even talk philosophy to them. There they would be, standing in front of me, gradually getting more and more overcome, sighing and moaning their thanks. You know, sir, they'd get tired from moaning alone. But they derived a great advantage from it, and I, too, felt that I wasn't wasting my time, but was engaged in something that was useful to them and which, as it were, conferred a certain honour upon me. But to-day, sir, to-day after all this. . . You follow me?

GLÚMOV. I do, I do.

MAMÁYEV. To-day, sir, you just start trying it on the servants! Read them a lecture once or twice and they come to you with their notice. What have we done to deserve this, they seem to imply, what have we done to deserve this?

GLÚMOV. It's positively immoral! That's what it is!

MAMÁYEV. And, mind you, sir, not that I am a strict man. I just want to talk things over with a fellow. Shopkeepers and suchlike behave very stupidly. They just get hold of a servant's hair and pull it. A word and a pull. "That'll larn you, me lad," they say, "that'll knock some sense into your thick skull." But all I ask is to have a heart-to-heart talk with them and they object even to that!

GLÚMOV. I quite realize, sir, how unpleasant all this must be for you.

MAMÁYEV. I can't bear to talk of it, sir. Take that boy, for instance. You can't imagine how his ingratitude hurt me. [*Pointing to his chest*] It went through me like a knife, right here. Even now I feel as though . . .

GLÚMOV. There?

MAMÁYEV. A little higher!

GLÚMOV. There?

MAMÁYEV. [*Angrily*] Higher, I say.

GLÚMOV. Forgive me, sir. Please, don't be angry with me. I warned you I was a fool.

MAMÁYEV. Yes, sir. You are a fool. That's bad. That is to say, there wouldn't be anything to worry about if you had an old, experienced relative or friend . . .

GLÚMOV. Ah, sir, that's the trouble. I haven't a friend or relation in the world. I have a mother, but she's even a bigger fool than I.

MAMÁYEV. Your position, sir, is certainly desperate. I'm sorry for you, young man.

GLÚMOV. I believe I have an uncle, sir, but it's as if he didn't even exist.

MAMÁYEV. How's that?

GLÚMOV. He doesn't know me and I don't want particularly to meet him.

MAMÁYEV. I am really sorry to hear you say that. No, young man, I don't think I can approve of that.

GLÚMOV. But, my dear sir, were he a poor man I'd be too glad to seek his advice, but he is so very rich. If I came to him for advice, he'd think I'd come for his money. How do you expect me to convince him that I don't want a penny of his, that all I want is his advice, that I'm simply dying to have him admonish me. I'm told he's a very brainy chap. I'd be glad to listen to him day and night.

MAMÁYEV. You know, you're not such a fool, after all.

GLÚMOV. At times I seem to get an inspiration, sir. Everything seems suddenly to become clear, but soon I relapse into my former state of hopeless stupidity. Most of the time I hardly know what I'm doing, that's when I'm so badly in need of some advice.

MAMÁYEV. And who is your uncle?

GLÚMOV. I'm not sure I even know his name. I believe it is Mamayev, Nil Mamayev.

MAMÁYEV. And what's your name?

GLÚMOV. Glumov.

MAMÁYEV. Son of Dimitry Glumov?

GLÚMOV. Yes!

MAMÁYEV. Well, then, really! It's I who am that Mamayev!

GLÚMOV. Good Heavens! Is that possible? No, no. It can't be, it can't be! Sir, let me shake your hand. [*Almost in tears*] But, uncle, I understand you don't like your relations. However, don't be afraid, we can remain as distant as before. I shan't presume to visit you without your permission. I am quite satisfied to have been given the chance of meeting you and enjoying the conversation of a clever man.

MAMÁYEV. Not at all, not at all, my dear boy. Come and see me any time you want to ask my advice.

GLÚMOV. Any time I want to ask your advice! Why, sir, I require advice continually, every minute. I feel I shall be undone without a counsellor.

MAMÁYEV. Very well, come and see me this evening.

GLÚMOV. Thank you very much, sir. Please, let me introduce you to my mother. She may be a bit simple-minded, but she's a very, very good woman.

MAMÁYEV. Well, why not?

GLÚMOV. [*Aloud*] Mother! [GLÚMOVA *comes in*] Mother,

darling, look. [*Pointing at* MAMÁYEV] Please, don't cry! A happy chance has brought my uncle, whom you were so anxious to meet, to see us.

GLÚMOVA. Yes, yes, indeed, sir. I've wanted to meet you for a long time, but you don't seem to be anxious to know your relatives.

GLÚMOV. Don't, mother, don't. Uncle has his own reasons for that.

MAMÁYEV. There are relatives and relatives.

GLÚMOVA. Let me have a good look at you, sir. [*Whispers to her son*] It isn't at all like him, George!

GLÚMOV. [*Pulling at her skirt*] Really, mother, hold your tongue, will you?

GLÚMOVA. Why should I hold my tongue? It isn't like him, I say, not at all like him!

MAMÁYEV. [*Severely*] What are you whispering to each other? Who is not like me? I am like myself!

GLÚMOV. [*To his mother*] What are you talking about?

MAMÁYEV. Well, as you've started it, you may as well finish.

GLÚMOVA. I was saying that that picture was not at all like you.

MAMÁYEV. What picture? Where did you get the picture?

GLÚMOVA. You see, Kurchayev sometimes comes to see us. I believe he's some relation of yours, too, isn't he?

GLÚMOV. Such a fine, merry fellow!

MAMÁYEV. Yes, yes. What about it?

GLÚMOVA. He's always drawing pictures of you. George, show your uncle that picture!

GLÚMOV. But, really, mother, I can't remember where I put it?

GLÚMOVA. Have a good look, dear. He drew it only just now, remember? He had a friend with him. Who was it? What do you call the people who write criticisms in verse? Kurchayev said, "I'll draw you my uncle and you write something under the picture." I heard him myself.

MAMÁYEV. Show me that picture! At once, do you hear?

GLÚMOV. [*Handing him the picture*] Mother, you must never say things which might hurt anyone.

MAMÁYEV. Indeed, sir! Teach your mother to be a hypocrite. Don't listen to him, my dear. Keep your simplicity of mind. It is better to be simple. [*Examining the picture*] I must say, I certainly have a fine nephew!

GLÚMOV. Throw it away, uncle. It's not at all like you and the inscription hardly applies to you, either: "Universal Educator!"

MAMÁYEV. I don't know. It's like me all right and the inscription, too, applies. Well, that's not your business, anyway. It's my business. [*Hands back the picture to* GLÚMOV *and gets up*] You won't draw caricatures of me, will you?

GLÚMOV. Heaven forbid, sir. What are you taking me for? Would I do such a thing?

MAMÁYEV. Well, all right. You . . . er . . . you'd better come and see me this very evening. Yes, do come, and you, too, please.

GLÚMOVA. Leave me out, sir. I'm afraid, I shall bore you with my silly chatter.

[MAMÁYEV *goes out,* GLÚMOV *seeing him off.*]

It's beginning to work, but, I suppose George will still have quite a lot to do. What an uphill struggle it is, to be sure, to make your way in the world.

[GLÚMOV *returns.*]

GLÚMOV. Mother, Manefa is on her way up. Do be nice to her, won't you? And try not only to be nice to her, but to flatter her as much as possible.

GLÚMOVA. Do you want me to humble myself before that silly old countrywoman?

GLÚMOV. You like to play the lady, don't you? But can you afford it, mother? Were it not for my ingenuity, you'd go a-begging. You must help me, I tell you, you must help me.

[*Hearing steps, runs into the hall and comes back with* MANÉFA.]

MANÉFA. [*To* GLÚMOV] Shun vanity, my son, shun vanity!

GLÚMOV. [*Assumes a sanctimonious expression, sighing*] I shun it. I shun it.

MANÉFA. Be not covetous!

GLÚMOV. I'm not guilty of that sin.

MANÉFA. [*Sits down and doesn't pay any attention to* GLÚMOVA *who keeps on bowing to her*] I've been running about, I've been running about and here I am.
GLÚMOVA. Indeed, we're grateful.
MANÉFA. I've just been to see some God-fearing folk and they gave me ten roubles for charity. Through my hands charity is dispensed. It's more meet through holy than sinful hands.
GLÚMOV. [*Producing money*] Accept fifteen roubles from your servant George.
MANÉFA. Blessed are those that give.
GLÚMOV. Remember me in your prayers.
MANÉFA. In that God-fearing house I partook of tea and coffee.
GLÚMOVA. Come on, my dear. I've everything ready for you.

    [MANÉFA *gets up and is led out by* GLÚMOV *and his mother.*
    GLÚMOV *returns and sits down at the desk.*]

GLÚMOV. I must make a note of it. To Mamayev's footman three roubles, to Manefa fifteen roubles. I'd better also make a note of the whole of my conversation with uncle.

    [KURCHÁYEV *enters.*]

KURCHÁYEV. Listen, old man, was my uncle here?
GLÚMOV. Yes.
KURCHÁYEV. Did he mention me?
GLÚMOV. You? Why should he? He didn't even know where he'd come to. He looked in, as usual, to see a flat.
KURCHÁYEV. This is a plot, an infernal plot!
GLÚMOV. What are you talking about?
KURCHÁYEV. Just imagine . . .
GLÚMOV. Imagine what?
KURCHÁYEV. He's forbidden me to visit his house any more. Think of it!
GLÚMOV. What about it?
KURCHÁYEV. I went to see Mrs. Turussina next and she doesn't want to know me any more, either. She sent out some silly old women to tell me they were not receiving any visitors. What do you make of that?
GLÚMOV. What do you expect me to make of that?

KURCHÁYEV. Can you explain it?

GLÚMOV. What right have you to ask me for any explanation?

KURCHÁYEV. Well, you're clever. You can see things that I don't.

GLÚMOV. Very well. Just look at yourself. What kind of life are you leading?

KURCHÁYEV. I don't know. I suppose the kind of life everybody else is leading. If they're not to blame, why should I be blamed? They can't rob me of my inheritance, deprive me of my fiancée, humiliate me—just for that?

GLÚMOV. And what about your friends? Take that Golutvin, for example.

KURCHÁYEV. What's wrong with Golutvin?

GLÚMOV. What's wrong with him? He's a pest. Men like him are capable of anything. Here's your explanation! By the way, what on earth induced you to bring him here? I'm very particular about the people I'm seen about with. I take jolly good care of myself. That's why I'd like to ask you not to come here again.

KURCHÁYEV. Have you gone off your head?

GLÚMOV. Our dear uncle doesn't want to know you any more and I desire to follow the example of that, in every way, exemplary man.

KURCHÁYEV. I get you now. I'm beginning to understand everything.

GLÚMOV. Well, everything's perfect, then.

KURCHÁYEV. Look here, it's you who started it all, isn't it? If what I suspect is true, you'd better look out. Such things are not easily forgotten. You . . . You'd better look out!

GLÚMOV. I shall look out when I find it expedient, but at the moment I'm not aware that I am in any particular danger. Good-bye.

KURCHÁYEV. Good-bye!

[*Goes out.*]

GLÚMOV. Uncle has booted him out. The first step is made.

ACT TWO

[*A big room, one door at the back, one at either side.*]
[MAMÁYEV *and* KRUTÍTZKY *enter from a side-door.*]

MAMÁYEV. Yes, indeed, we seem to be going somewhere, we seem to be led somewhere, but we don't know whither we are going or where we are being led. And what will be the end of it all?

KRUTÍTZKY. You know, I look upon it all as a matter of trial and error and I can't for the life of me see anything particularly evil in it. Our age is essentially an age of experiment. Everything is still so young, so tentative. Let's do this, let's do that. Let's change this, let's change that. Let's, say, put all this furniture upside-down. There's change for you. But where, I ask you, is eternal wisdom, where is eternal knowledge which has put the furniture on its feet and only on its feet? Take this table. It's standing on its four legs and it's standing good and firm, isn't it?

MAMÁYEV. It is.

KRUTÍTZKY. Firm as a rock?

MAMÁYEV. Firm as a rock.

KRUTÍTZKY. Well, someone comes along and says, let's put it upside-down. All right, they put it upside-down.

MAMÁYEV. [*With a scornful wave of the hand*] They do. They do.

KRUTÍTZKY. Well, they'll see . . .

MAMÁYEV. But will they, my dear sir, will they?

KRUTÍTZKY. What do you mean? Of course, they will. After all, there are some sane men left in the world.

MAMÁYEV. There are, there are. Of course! Indeed, there are, without a doubt there are, but who pays any attention to them? No one. There's the rub: they don't listen to men of proved wisdom, they don't listen to you or me, sir.

KRUTÍTZKY. And whose fault is it if they don't listen to us, sir? It's all our own fault: we can't speak, we can't express ourselves. Who does all the writing to-day? Who makes all the noise to-day? Some whipper-snappers! And what do we do?

We keep mum, we keep on complaining that nobody wants to listen to us. We must write, sir. We must keep on writing!

MAMÁYEV. Easier said than done. To be able to write one must have the knack for it. An aptitude for writing may not be of any great importance, but it is necessary all the same. Take myself, for instance. I can get up and make a speech any time, but let me sit down at my desk and try to write and God alone knows what will come of it. Not that I am a fool, either. And look at yourself. How can you be expected to be able to write?

KRUTÍTZKY. Why, not at all, not at all! Please, don't bring me into it. I can write. In fact, I do write and I write quite a lot.

MAMÁYEV. Oh, do you? I didn't know that. But, all the same, you can't expect everyone to be able to write.

KRUTÍTZKY. Ah, but why not? The time has gone by, my dear fellow, when people could afford not to be able to write. If you want to be of any use to-day, you must know how to wield a pen.

MAMÁYEV. But not everyone can do that!

KRUTÍTZKY. By the way, do you know of a young man, on the modest side, and, of course, educated, who could express in writing different thoughts, as it were, schemes, etc.?

MAMÁYEV. Yes, sir. I know the very man.

KRUTÍTZKY. He's not a windbag, is he? Not one of our modern sneering deriders of everything sane and decent?

MAMÁYEV. Not at all, not at all, my dear sir. Only say the word and he'll be as mute as a fish.

KRUTÍTZKY. You see, I've just finished writing a certain project, or memorandum, if you wish, but, you understand, as a man of the old school . . .

MAMÁYEV. Infinitely more stable, my dear sir, infinitely more stable.

KRUTÍTZKY. Quite, quite. But, you see, I express myself in a rather old-fashioned style, more, how shall I put it? in the style of our great Lomonossov.

MAMÁYEV. The old style is so much more vigorous, sir. You can't compare it with the modern style of writing.

KRUTÍTZKY. I quite agree with you, but, all the same, to go on writing in the style of Lomonossov or Sumarokov is, how shall I put it? rather asking for it. I mean, they'll be sure to chaff you about it. So could he, do you think, I mean could that young friend of yours give my work, how shall I put it? . . . I mean, could he revise its style?

MAMÁYEV. Why, certainly, certainly, certainly.

KRUTÍTZKY. Very well. I shall naturally pay him the usual fee.

MAMÁYEV. Not at all, my dear sir, not at all. If you offer him money he may feel offended. He'll be too glad to do it without any fee.

KRUTÍTZKY. Ah, indeed? But why should I be in debt to him? Who is he, by the way?

MAMÁYEV. A nephew of mine, a dear, dear nephew of mine.

KRUTÍTZKY. Very well. Will you tell him to call on me as early as possible, say, about eight o'clock?

MAMÁYEV. All right, all right. Have no fear. He'll be there.

KRUTÍTZKY. But don't forget to warn him: mum's the word! I don't want to set people talking about it yet: it may weaken the effect.

MAMÁYEV. Heaven forbid! I quite understand. I shall impress it on him, I shall impress it on him.

KRUTÍTZKY. Well, good-bye.

MAMÁYEV. I'll bring him to you to-morrow myself.

KRUTÍTZKY. Do, do.

[KRUTÍTZKY *goes out, seen off by* MAMÁYEV. MAMÁYEVA *and* GLÚMOVA *come in.*]

MAMÁYEVA. Young and handsome, educated and well-bred! Ah-h-h!

GLÚMOVA. And for all his fine qualities he might have ended his days in utter obscurity.

MAMÁYEVA. And who asked him to live in obscurity, pray? Isn't he both young and handsome?

GLÚMOVA. How can you expect to know the right people if you don't belong to a good family, or if you haven't got the right connections, or if you don't find anyone able to appreciate your talents?

MAMÁYEVA. He shouldn't have kept away from society. We should have noticed him, we should certainly have noticed him.

GLÚMOVA. To be noticed, a man must have brains; for a common or garden person it is difficult, ever so difficult.

MAMÁYEVA. You do your son an injustice, my dear. There's nothing wrong with his brains. Besides, it isn't very necessary that he should have more than his share of brains: it is quite enough that he is handsome. What does he want brains for? He doesn't want to be a professor, does he? Believe me, people will help a handsome young man to become a useful member of society almost out of sheer pity and they'll provide him with the necessary means to make a good living. When you see a man of intellect badly dressed, living in some dirty attic, riding in a hired cab, you don't feel at all surprised, you don't seem to resent it in the least. For it should be so, that is how a brainy man should live, there is no obvious contradiction there. But to see a handsome young man badly dressed gives you a real pain, for that must not be and it shall not be, it shall never be.

GLÚMOVA. What a heart of gold you have!

MAMÁYEVA. But, of course, not! We shall not allow it, we women won't allow it. We shall rouse our husbands, our friends, all the powers that be, and they'll get him a good job. For it is important that nothing should stand in the way of our admiration of him. Poverty! Fie! We shan't spare anything to . . . to . . . No, never. Handsome young men are so few and far between. . . .

GLÚMOVA. If only everyone thought like you!

MAMÁYEVA. But everyone does, everyone does, my dear. Generally speaking, we must pity the poor, it is our duty, our obligation to do so and there is nothing more to be said about it. But whose heart does not bleed to see a handsome man poverty stricken, and a young one at that? To see his elbows protruding through his torn sleeves or his wrists showing out of a coat that is too short for him, or his collars dirty and frayed. Why, that's too, too horrible! Besides, poverty kills easy manners, it humbles a person so, it deprives him of his dashing look, of his masterfulness, all of which go so well with the face of a handsome man and is so easily forgiven him.

GLÚMOVA. Too, too true!

[MAMÁYEV *enters.*]

MAMÁYEV. Ah, good morning.
GLÚMOVA. I hardly know what to say to you!
MAMÁYEV. To me? Why, what's the matter?
GLÚMOVA. You've robbed me of my son, sir. He has completely stopped caring for me. He just raves about you. He talks of nothing else but your wonderful brains and your clever conversation. He is simply overcome with admiration for you.
MAMÁYEV. He's a good boy, a good boy!
GLÚMOVA. Even as a child he was a wonder.
MAMÁYEVA. But he still is only a child.
GLÚMOVA. He was so quiet, so quiet, it was uncanny. He never forgot to kiss his father's or his mother's hand. He even kissed the hands of his grannies and of all his aunties. Sometimes I even considered it desirable to forbid him to do it, for I was afraid they might think I had told him to kiss their hands on purpose, but he would go up to an aunt of his so quietly, ever so quietly, so that she shouldn't notice it, and kiss her hand! And once, he was only five then, he gave us all such a surprise. He comes down to breakfast and says, "You know, mummy, I dreamt a marvellous dream last night. I dreamt that I saw angels flying down to my bed and they told me, love your daddy and your mummy and don't forget to do what they tell you. And when you grow up and are a big man, don't forget to love all your superiors. I told them," the little darling said, "Dear angels, I shall obey everybody! . . ." He did so surprise us and made us so happy! I just can't forget that dream. . . .
MAMÁYEV. Well, yes. . . . I must go, I've something more important to do. I am pleased with your son. You can tell him that I am very pleased with him. [*Puts on his hat*] Wait, there's another thing. I know, of course, that you aren't too well off, so just call on me one morning and I'll . . . I'll give you . . .
GLÚMOVA. Thank you ever so much, sir.
MAMÁYEV. Oh, no, no, no. I don't mean money. I'll give you something that's much better than money. I'll give you some sound advice about balancing your family budget!
[*He goes out.*]

GLÚMOVA. He's pleased! Well, Heaven be praised. No one can be as grateful as my George.
MAMÁYEVA. I'm glad to hear that.
GLÚMOVA. With George it is not just a matter of being grateful. He just adores his patrons!
MAMÁYEVA. Adores? Isn't that a bit too much?
GLÚMOVA. Not at all. It's in him, it's the way he's made. Of course, a mother ought not to praise her son too much. Besides, he doesn't like me to talk about him.
MAMÁYEVA. Ah, my dear, do talk about him! I shan't tell him anything.
GLÚMOVA. He's just charmed by his patrons. He thinks there isn't anyone better in the whole world. About your husband he says that there isn't a better brain in the whole of Moscow, and the things he says about your beauty could be put into a book, yes, into a book.
MAMÁYEVA. Really?
GLÚMOVA. The things he compares you with!
MAMÁYEVA. Indeed?
GLÚMOVA. Has he seen you anywhere before?
MAMÁYEVA. I don't know. I saw him for the first time at the play.
GLÚMOVA. He must have seen you somewhere.
MAMÁYEVA. Why?
GLÚMOVA. Why? He only knows you such a short time and suddenly such a . . .
MAMÁYEVA. Well, say it. Such a what?
GLÚMOVA. He's suddenly conceived such a . . . such an intimate feeling for you.
MAMÁYEVA. Ah, the dear boy!
GLÚMOVA. It's quite beyond me. Uncle, he says, is ever so clever, but auntie, he says, auntie is such an angel.
MAMÁYEVA. Go on, go on. Please, I'm so curious.
GLÚMOVA. But don't be angry with me for my silly talk.
MAMÁYEVA. No, no.
GLÚMOVA. Auntie, he says, is an angel, an angel, and he hides his dear head in my bosom and bursts into tears.
MAMÁYEVA. Does he now? I must say this is strange.
GLÚMOVA. [*Changing her tone*] You see, he's so grateful that

you've been so good to him, an orphan. He cried out of sheer gratitude.

MAMÁYEVA. Yes, yes. The boy has sentiment.

GLÚMOVA. Why, of course, he has sentiment. He has such an impulsive nature.

MAMÁYEVA. At his age that is understandable and forgivable.

GLÚMOVA. Yes, please, please, forgive him. He is so young.

MAMÁYEVA. But why should *I* forgive him? He hasn't offended me.

GLÚMOVA. Well, you know, this is perhaps the first time in his life that he has met such a beautiful woman. The poor boy, he can't help himself. You've been so nice to him, so . . . obliging. Of course, I mean as one relation to another. And he's so impulsive. No wonder he quite lost his head.

MAMÁYEVA. [*Reflectively*] He's very nice, very nice.

GLÚMOVA. Of course, his feelings are entirely those of a nephew for his aunt. But, say what you will, the proximity of such a ravishingly beautiful woman like yourself at his tender age . . . You know, the poor boy can't sleep any more. When he comes back from you, he's quite beside himself, quite beside himself.

MAMÁYEVA. Does he confide in you at all? He doesn't conceal his feelings from you, does he?

GLÚMOVA. Of course not. Besides, his feelings are as innocent as a child's.

MAMÁYEVA. Quite. He needs someone to guide him. Under the guidance of a clever woman he might with time . . .

GLÚMOVA. Do be his guide! He'll need your guidance all his life. You're so good. . . .

MAMÁYEVA. [*Laughs*] That's quite true. I am good. But, you know, this . . . this may be very dangerous. I may even be carried away myself!

GLÚMOVA. Yes, you are good.

MAMÁYEVA. I can see you love him very much.

GLÚMOVA. He's my only child. Can I help loving him?

MAMÁYEVA. [*Languorously*] Let us love him together!

GLÚMOVA. You'll make me jealous of my own son. Yes, indeed, he has found happiness in your family. However, it's time I was going. Please, don't be angry with me for my silly chatter. And, please, don't give me away. If my son finds out what I've been telling you, I'm undone. At times, you know, he feels so ashamed that I'm such a silly woman. Quite often he ought really to say to me, "Mummy, don't be so silly," but he never does. He even avoids using that word out of respect for his mother. As for me, I should gladly forgive him if only he'd stop me from making a fool of myself. Good-bye. . . .

MAMÁYEVA. [*Embracing her*] Good-bye, my dear. I shall come to see you soon and we shall have another talk about George.

[*She sees her off to the door and returns.*]

MAMÁYEVA. What a chatterbox! If her son had heard her, he wouldn't have thanked her. He is so aloof, approaches me with such cold politeness, and at home he's crazy about me. This means that I can still fire a man's heart with real passion. Well, that's as it should be. For some time I was rather beginning to be aware of a certain falling off in the number of my admirers, but that's because the men round me have grown so old and are so used up. Ah, at last, at last! Ah, my dear! How I shall cherish you! However shy he may be, true passion will out! It's so exciting to know beforehand that a man is in love with you!

[GLÚMOV *comes in and stops at a respectful distance.*]

MAMÁYEVA. Come here, come here. [GLÚMOV *approaches her shyly*] What are you standing like that for? Do all nephews behave like that?

GLÚMOV. [*Kissing her hand*] Good morning.

MAMÁYEVA. Bravo! Bravo, my dear. How did you pluck up the courage to do it, I wonder.

GLÚMOV. I'm afraid I am rather shy.

MAMÁYEVA. Well, don't be too shy. What are you afraid of? Do confide your dearest secrets to me. Don't forget I'm your aunt.

GLÚMOV. I'd be glad to be more frank with you, if . . .

MAMÁYEVA. If what?

GLÚMOV. If you were an old lady.

MAMÁYEVA. Don't be silly! I don't want to be old.

GLÚMOV. I don't want you to be old, either. May you keep your youth for ever. I merely mean that I shouldn't be so shy then, that I should feel more free with you.

MAMÁYEVA. But why? Come sit beside me and tell me everything frankly. Tell me why would you be more free with me if I were an old lady?

GLÚMOV. [*Takes a chair and sits down beside her*] A young woman has her own affairs, her own interests. Why should she waste her time worrying about her poor relations? But an old woman has only one business in life: the care of her family and relations.

MAMÁYEVA. But why mayn't a young woman also care about her relations?

GLÚMOV. She may, but, somehow, one doesn't expect her to. All she's keen on is fun, amusements, distractions, and here's the boring face of her nephew, continuous demands, requests. . . .

MAMÁYEVA. If I were an old lady what would you have asked me to do for you?

GLÚMOV. If you were, but you aren't! On the contrary, you're a very young woman. You're not trying to catch me out, are you?

MAMÁYEVA. Never mind, never mind, tell me!

GLÚMOV. But I do mind. For instance, I know that you've only to say a word to Gorodulin and I'd get a good job.

MAMÁYEVA. Yes, I do believe that one word of mine would be enough.

GLÚMOV. There you are! But I shan't ask you to do it all the same.

MAMÁYEVA. Why on earth not?

GLÚMOV. Because that would be tantamount to forcing him.

MAMÁYEVA. Do you really think so?

GLÚMOV. I know it would. He's so much your slave!

MAMÁYEVA. You do seem to know a lot. Well, but what about me? Am I his slave?

GLÚMOV. That's your business.

MAMÁYEVA. [*Aside*] He doesn't seem to be jealous. This is strange.

GLÚMOV. He won't dare refuse you anything. Besides, your

request will be a pleasure to him: to press you to ask him would be like bribing him.

MAMÁYEVA. That's absolute nonsense, I assure you. So you don't want me to ask him?

GLÚMOV. Certainly not. Besides, I don't want to be in your debt for anything, for how could I repay you?

MAMÁYEVA. And how would you have repaid an old lady?

GLÚMOV. By always trying to be pleasant to her. I would carry her lap-dog about, I would place the footstool under her feet, I would keep on kissing her hand, I would be the first to pay her the compliments of the season, I would be the first to congratulate her on her birthday. All that is greatly appreciated by old ladies.

MAMÁYEVA. Why, of course.

GLÚMOV. Then if she were really good to me, I could become attached to her. I could even learn to love her.

MAMÁYEVA. But can't you learn to love a young one?

GLÚMOV. I could, but I shouldn't.

MAMÁYEVA. [*Aside*] At last, at last!

GLÚMOV. For that would lead only to unnecessary suffering.

[FOOTMAN *enters.*]

FOOTMAN. Mr. Gorodulin, ma'am.

GLÚMOV. I'll go into the study. I have work to do.

[*Bows himself out very respectfully.*]

MAMÁYEVA. Show him in.

[FOOTMAN *goes out*, GORODÚLIN *comes in.*]

GORODÚLIN. How d'you do?

MAMÁYEVA. [*Reproachfully*] You naughty man, sit down. What whirlwind, what gale has brought you here?

GORODÚLIN. [*Sitting down*] The whirlwind in my head, my dear lady, the gale of passion which is raging in my heart.

MAMÁYEVA. Thank you. It's very nice of you not to have forgotten me, the forsaken one.

GORODÚLIN. Where is he? Where is the wretch who has forsaken you? Show me him, I'm in a particularly fighting mood to-day.

MAMÁYEVA. It's you, my dear sir, it's you who ought to be shot or something.

GORODÚLIN. I wish it were someone else.
MAMÁYEVA. But I've already thought out a punishment for you.
GORODÚLIN. Let me hear it, dear lady. Tell me first what it is to be. You can't execute a man without letting him know how he is to meet his end. If you've decided to smother me in your arms, I shan't ask for a reprieve.
MAMÁYEVA. No, no. It's I who come to you as plaintiff.
GORODÚLIN. You want to change parts with me?
MAMÁYEVA. Can you be the plaintiff? Aren't you almost a judge?
GORODÚLIN. And so I am, and so I am, dear lady. But in the company of ladies I'm always . . .
MAMÁYEVA. Enough of that. I want to talk business with you.
GORODÚLIN. I'm at your service.
MAMÁYEVA. My nephew wants a . . .
GORODÚLIN. What does your dear little nephew desire? A pair of knickerbockers or a darling little coat?
MAMÁYEVA. Don't be such a bore. Listen and don't interrupt me. My nephew isn't a child. He's a very nice young man, handsome, clever, educated.
GORODÚLIN. The better for him and the worse for me.
MAMÁYEVA. He wants a job.
GORODÚLIN. What kind of job do you wish me to find him?
MAMÁYEVA. A good job, of course. He's a man of great ability.
GORODÚLIN. Great ability? My dear lady, I'm sorry to hear that. There are only two posts he could fill then and both are filled already: the one by the Prime Minister of England and the other by the President of the United States.*
MAMÁYEVA. You're so exasperating! I shall quarrel with you in a minute, I warn you, if you go on like this. Tell me have you any job in mind?
GORODÚLIN. For an ordinary mortal, I suppose, one could be found.
MAMÁYEVA. That's fine!

* In the text: "the one by Bismarck and the other by Beist." Beist, Friedrich Ferdinand, a famous Austrian statesman.

GORODÚLIN. [*With feeling*] We're always on the look-out for the right men. Let me have a peep at that wonder of yours and I'll tell you definitely what he's good for and what job I can recommend him for.

MAMÁYEVA. George, come here! [*To* GORODÚLIN] I'll leave you with him. Come and see me afterwards. I'll be waiting for you in the drawing-room. [GLÚMOV *comes in*] Let me introduce you to my nephew, George Glumov. [*To* GLÚMOV] Mr. Gorodulin wants to make your acquaintance. [*Goes out.*]

GORODÚLIN. [*Shaking hands with* GLÚMOV] Are you in the Civil Service?

GLÚMOV. I was, but I have no desire to be a civil servant any more.

GORODÚLIN. Why not?

GLÚMOV. God hasn't bestowed upon me the necessary gifts. A civil servant must possess all kinds of talents which I do not possess.

GORODÚLIN. It seems to me that all you want is brains and a certain amount of elbow-grease.

GLÚMOV. Let's assume I have both, but of what use are they to me? However hard I may work, I shall never be able to rise sufficiently high in the service. To get anywhere without someone to push you, one needs something quite different.

GORODÚLIN. What, for instance?

GLÚMOV. You must be able to stop thinking when ordered to and you must be able to laugh when your superior deems it necessary to crack a joke. At the same time you must do all the thinking and slaving for your superiors and, God help you, if you're not quick enough to assure them, and that with the utmost humility, that you are, as it were, a complete halfwit and that it is their ideas and not yours that you're carrying out. In addition, you must possess a certain aptitude for cringing which, however, must not be carried without a modicum of grace. For instance, you must know how to jump to your feet and stand to attention in a way that will appear both obsequious and not obsequious, servile and at the same time free and easy, as straight as an arrow, but also graceful. When your superior sends you on some errand you must know how to achieve a kind of light-footed flutter, something between a gallop, a march and your usual step. I'm afraid I haven't mentioned even half of what you ought to know before getting anywhere in the Civil Service.

GORODÚLIN. Exquisite! I mean, it's as bad as can be, but you put it very nicely, which is very important. Besides, what you say of the Civil Service may have been true in the past, but to-day things are different.

GLÚMOV. The difference, somehow, is not very apparent. Furthermore, everything in the Civil Service is so much a matter of filling up forms. Papers, papers, papers! Wall after wall, fortress after fortress of papers and forms. But the shells that are fired from these fortresses are nothing but dry-as-dust circulars and regulations.

GORODÚLIN. Exquisite, exquisite! You're a genius!

GLÚMOV. I'm very glad that you approve of my ideas. I wish we had more men like you.

GORODÚLIN. Ideas? Who wants ideas? Who hasn't got ideas? It's your choice of words, your turn of phrase that wrings my approval. Do you know? You could do me a great favour.

GLÚMOV. I'm entirely at your command.

GORODÚLIN. Put it all on paper.

GLÚMOV. With pleasure. What do you want it for, if I may ask?

GORODÚLIN. I'll tell you, I feel I can open my heart to you. Both of us are honourable men and we must be frank with one another. It's this: I have to make a speech at a dinner to-morrow and I've absolutely no time to think.

GLÚMOV. Why, I shall be glad to help you.

GORODÚLIN. [*Pressing his hand*] Thank you. Just do it for me as one friend for another.

GLÚMOV. Don't mention it.—No, I want a job where I can meet my less fortunate fellow-men face to face! Give me the chance of seeing for myself what they want and of satisfying their needs expeditiously and with sympathy!

GORODÚLIN. Bravo, bravo! Don't forget to put that in, too. Am I to understand that what you as a man of sterling honesty would most desire is a job as treasurer of a Government department or of a charitable institution?

GLÚMOV. Just as you like. I don't mind what kind of work I do and I'm quite willing to put everything into my work, but on one condition: I must feel that my work is of real value, that it increases the share of happiness necessary for the well-being of the masses. To pour water through a sieve and to consider that serving your country—I shall never agree to that!

GORODÚLIN. That, too, you might include in my speech to-morrow.

GLÚMOV. Do you know what? I think I'd better write the whole speech for you.

GORODÚLIN. Really? I am so glad. You see, how easy it is for two honourable men to become friends? They have just to exchange a few words and, lo and behold, they're friends! And how well you express yourself. Yes, the country certainly needs men like you. My dear boy, our country needs you badly. [*Consulting his watch*] Look me up to-morrow about noon. [*Shakes hands with* GLÚMOV] Pleased to have met you.

[*Goes into drawing-room.*]
[MAMÁYEV *enters.*]

MAMÁYEV. Ah, here you are, my dear fellow. [*Mysteriously*] Krutitzky came to see me a short while ago about some business. He's a good old stick. He seems to have written something and he badly wants someone to put it straight for him. His style, you know, is very slovenly, it wants polishing up. I mentioned you to him. In our circle we don't consider him a very clever man and, I suppose, what he's written is utter rot, but when you see him just flatter him a little.

GLÚMOV. What are you telling me to do, uncle!

MAMÁYEV. To flatter is wrong, it's true, but to put it on a little, you know, is quite permissible. Praise something here and there. The old man will like it. He can be of use to you. You leave it to us to take him down a peg or two. He won't escape that, anyway. But you ought to pat him on the back: you're still young. I'll take you to him to-morrow. Wait, there's another thing, rather a delicate matter. What exactly are your relations with your aunt, my boy?

GLÚMOV. I've been well brought up, sir. You needn't teach me how to behave to a lady.

MAMÁYEV. No, no, no, my boy, don't be so stupid! Your aunt is still quite young and beautiful. A lot she cares for your good manners! You don't want to make an enemy of her, do you?

GLÚMOV. I don't understand what you're driving at, uncle.

MAMÁYEV. If you don't understand, then listen to me and learn. Thank God you have someone to teach you. Women never forgive a man who does not notice their beauty.

GLÚMOV. Quite so, quite so, sir. Gosh, what a fool I am!

MAMÁYEV. There, there, you see now, don't you? They say blood is thicker than water, but I'm afraid, my boy, that our blood, yours and mine, I mean, has been rather diluted. Still you are a relation of mine, albeit a very distant one. You can therefore allow yourself more latitude with my wife than a mere acquaintance. Sometimes, you may pretend it is out of sheer forgetfulness, it may be a good thing if you kissed her hand twice and, well . . . er . . . with the eyes, you know, something. You know what I mean, don't you?

GLÚMOV. I think I do, but I don't know how to do it, sir.

MAMÁYEV. What an innocent you are, to be sure, my boy. Look, this is what I mean. [*He turns up his eyes in a glad-eye.*]

GLÚMOV. Really, sir, how can you even suggest such a thing, to me!

MAMÁYEV. Why not, my boy, why not? There, be a good boy and practise it before a mirror and get it right. Then again, occasionally, you may just sigh, you know, with a languorous expression on your face. All this flatters their vanity, you know.

GLÚMOV. I'm sorry, sir, but I refuse to do it. No, thank you, sir.

MAMÁYEV. But do try to understand, my boy. I'm doing it for my own peace of mind.

GLÚMOV. I'm afraid, sir, I can't follow you at all.

MAMÁYEV. Your aunt, my boy, is a woman of a sanguine temperament, she's hot-headed, she can be easily carried away by some fop or other, or even, the devil take her, by some labourer, or again even by some jailbird. In these affairs there is no fear of God, you must understand. So that's how things stand, and that's where you come in, my boy. "If you must flirt, madam, here's the man for you, a reliable man and your own flesh and blood." You see it now, don't you? Ha-ha-ha! The lady can have her fling and her husband needn't worry!

GLÚMOV. What a mind you have, uncle, what a mind!

MAMÁYEV. I should say so.

GLÚMOV. There's something else, sir. To make sure that there shouldn't be any gossip, you know what people are, sir, I think that it would, perhaps, be a good thing if you introduced me to Mrs. Turussina. At her house I can openly pay court to her niece and even, to make things quite easy for you, get engaged to her. Then, indeed, the lady could have her fling and her husband need not worry.

MAMÁYEV. Quite right, quite right. That'll make everything perfect!

GLÚMOV. Of course, sir, we shan't mention a word about Turussina to your wife. Not that she will be jealous, but you know how women look at things with different eyes.

MAMÁYEV. I know, I know. Mum's the word!

GLÚMOV. When shall we pay our visit to Turussina, sir?

MAMÁYEV. To-morrow evening. Well, now you know what to do, don't you?

GLÚMOV. What to do? Why, sir, admire your great intellect!

[*Enter* MAMÁYEVA *and* GORODÚLIN.]

GORODÚLIN. [*Whispers to* MAMÁYEVA] In two weeks he'll have the job.

MAMÁYEV. Ah, Gorodulin. I called on you to-day. I wanted to give you my advice about that business at the club.

GORODÚLIN. I'm afraid, I'm in a hurry. [*Shakes hands with* GLÚMOV] *Au revoir.*

MAMÁYEV. Let me share your carriage. I'm going the same way. I have some business at the Senate.

[MAMÁYEV *and* GORODÚLIN *go out.*]

MAMÁYEVA. [*Sitting down in an arm-chair*] Kiss my hand, your business is settled.

GLÚMOVA. I didn't ask you for anything.

MAMÁYEVA. Never mind. I did it off my own bat.

GLÚMOV. [*Kissing her hand*] Thank you. [*Picks up his hat.*]

MAMÁYEVA. Where are you off to?

GLÚMOV. Home! I am so happy. I want to run off and share my happiness with my mother.
MAMÁYEVA. You are happy? I don't believe it.
GLÚMOV. I am as happy as 1 possibly can be.
MAMÁYEVA. Which means that you're not quite happy, that you still desire something, isn't that so?
GLÚMOV. I've got everything that I dare hope for.
MAMÁYEVA. No, no. Tell me straight: have you got all you want?
GLÚMOV. What else can I want? I shall get a job.
MAMÁYEVA. I can't believe it, I can't believe it. Being so young you want to make people believe that you're a materialist, that all you care for is a job and money.
GLÚMOV. Please, please . . .
MAMÁYEVA. . . . that you have no heart, that you never dream of happiness, that you don't cry, that you're not in love with anyone . . .
GLÚMOV. I never said that.
MAMÁYEVA. You said that you'd got all you wanted.
GLÚMOV. I said that I'd got all that I could possibly get, all that I could dare hope for.
MAMÁYEVA. Which means that you dare not hope that your feelings are reciprocated. Why, therefore, waste them, these pure pearls of your heart? Tell me, who is the cruel one?
GLÚMOV. But this is an inquisition!
MAMÁYEVA. Tell me, you bad man, tell me at once. I know, I can see it in your eyes: you're in love! My poor darling, is it really as bad as that?
GLÚMOV. You have no right to question me like this. You know I do not dare conceal anything from you.
MAMÁYEVA. Who are you in love with?
GLÚMOV. Have pity on me!
MAMÁYEVA. Is she worthy of you?
GLÚMOVA. Don't torture me, please.
MANÁYEVA. Is she able to do full justice to your passion, your devoted heart?
GLÚMOV. I shan't tell you. Kill me if you will, but I shan't say a word.
MAMÁYEVA. [*Whispers*] Courage, my friend, courage!

GLÚMOV. You want to know who I am in love with?
MAMÁYEVA. Yes, yes . . .
GLÚMOV. You!
MAMÁYEVA. [*With a soft cry*] Ah-h-h!
GLÚMOV. I am your slave for ever. Punish me for my boldness, but I love you. Force me to keep silence, forbid me to look at you, to stop admiring you, or, what is even worse, make me keep at a polite distance from you, but do not be angry with me! You are yourself to blame. Were you not so beautiful, so gracious to me, I might have kept my passion within the bounds of propriety, however big a price I'd have had to pay for it. But you, an angel so good and beautiful, robbed me, a decent man, of my reason. Yes, I am mad. I thought that heavenly bliss was awaiting me and I did not see the chasm opening up before my feet and ruin staring me in the face. Forgive me, forgive me! [*He falls on his knees before her and bows his head disconsolately.*]
MAMÁYEVA. [*Kissing his bent head*] I forgive you.

[GLUMOV *gets up and, bowing low, goes out.* MAMÁYEVA *follows him with a gaze full of speechless adoration.*]

ACT THREE

[*Richly furnished drawing-room of a country house in Sokolniki, one door in the middle, another at the side.*]
[Mrs. Turússina *and her niece* Mary *enter through middle door.*]

Mary. Do let's go, auntie! Please, let's go!
Turússina. No, my dear, no. Not for anything in the world. I've already ordered the horses to be unharnessed.
Mary. But, really, auntie, we've been planning to go out for days and all we did was to drive out of the gates and then turn back.
Turússina. [*Sitting down*] My dear, I know perfectly well what I'm doing. Why expose oneself needlessly to danger when one can avoid it?
Mary. But why should we of all people be in any danger?
Turússina. What a question to ask, child! Didn't you see it yourself? The woman crossed our path while we were driving through the gates. I wanted to stop at once, but, somehow, though my heart was heavy, I said nothing, and, then, suddenly, this meeting. . . .
Mary. What about it?
Turússina. If the woman had crossed from the left, but she crossed from the right. . . .
Mary. But what does it matter, auntie, whether she crossed from the right or the left?
Turússina. Please, don't talk like that. You know I don't like it. I cannot permit any free-thinking in my house. As it is, I have to put up with enough blasphemy from my guests. I can't ask strangers to curb their tongues, but I forbid you to talk like that. We must take care of ourselves. Of course, to over-indulge ourselves is a sin, but to take care of ourselves is our duty. We mustn't be obstinate! All sorts of accidents happen every day: horses panic and stampede, carriages get smashed up, coachmen get drunk and land everybody in a ditch. Providence keeps constant watch over people. If you've been warned clearly that if you go you'll be exposing yourself

to danger, whose fault is it if you don't listen and break your neck?

MARY. No one told us not to go.

TURÚSSINA. Has one got to be told in so many words? Isn't an inauspicious meeting more eloquent than any words? Besides, if we had to go, if it were a matter of life and death, then, of course, we should have gone, but, God knows, what we wanted to go there for at all! To spend a whole evening in empty talk and gossip, and for that you ask me to overlook a sign from above and expose myself to certain danger. No, my dear, thank you very much. I can see why you are so anxious to go there! You hope for a meeting with Kurchayev, an out-and-out atheist whom I've forbidden my house. That's why you want to drag me out visiting. All you care for is your own pleasure! What do you care if I break a leg or an arm?

MARY. I can't understand why you dislike Kurchayev so much, auntie.

TURÚSSINA. Why should I like the man? He makes fun of the most sacred things in my presence.

MARY. But when, auntie, when?

TURÚSSINA. Always! He's continually making fun of the women pilgrims and God's naturals who come to visit me.

MARY. You said that he showed disrespect for sacred things.

TURÚSSINA. Of course, he did. Once I said to him, "Look at my Martha, she's so wonderfully pious that a distinct halo is beginning to appear all round her face." That's not a halo, he said, her face is merely beginning to shine from too much fat. I shall never forgive him that! That's what free-thought leads to, that's how our youth is losing all respect for sacred things. I very rarely make a mistake about people. There, you see what kind of man he is? I received two letters about his goings on yesterday. You can read them for yourself, if you wish.

MARY. But can you trust anonymous letters?

TURÚSSINA. If it were only one letter, but there were two, and from different people.

[GRIGÓRY *enters and hands* TURÚSSINA *a letter.*]

GRIGÓRY. More pilgrims have arrived, ma'am.

TURÚSSINA. All right, tell cook to give them a meal.

[GRIGÓRY *goes out.* TURÚSSINA *reads letter.*]

Here's another letter. You can tell that it's been written by a respectable woman. [*Reads aloud*] "Dear madam, although I haven't the honour . . ." [*Continues to read to herself*] Now, listen to this. "Your choice of a man like Kurchayev makes me shed tears for the fate of poor Mary . . ." There you are!

MARY. How strange! I don't know what to make of it.

TURÚSSINA. Well, will you still go on arguing with me about it? However, if you still wish to marry him, my dear, you can do so. [*Inhales smelling salts*] I don't want to be called a tyrant. But you realize, of course, that by marrying him you'll greatly displease me and you'll hardly have a right to reproach me should I . . .

MARY. . . . cut me off with a penny?

TURÚSSINA. Not only that, my dear, I should also refuse to give you my blessing!

MARY. Don't be afraid, auntie. I am a Moscow girl. I shan't marry anyone without money and without the blessing of my relatives. I like George Kurchayev very much, but if you're against the match, I shan't marry him and I shan't die of consumption because of it. But do have pity on me, auntie. Thanks to you I have all the money I need. Do let me have a good time.

TURÚSSINA. I quite see what you mean, my dear.

MARY. Find me a husband. Any man will do so long as he is decent. I shall marry him without any protest. I want to cut a fine figure in society, I want to be admired. To live as we are living now is so boring, auntie. I'm bored to tears!

TURÚSSINA. I realize your position, my dear. Vanity is forgivable at your age.

MARY. When I grow older I shall probably live like you, auntie. It's in our family.

TURÚSSINA. May God grant you do, my dear. I wish it with all my heart. This is the only way to live, the real way.

MARY. Yes, auntie, yes. But I want to get married first.

TURÚSSINA. I don't want to conceal my great perplexity from you, my dear. Our modern youth is so spoilt that it is extremely difficult to find a suitable young man. You know the kind of husband I want for you.

MARY. But, auntie, in Moscow it should not be difficult to

find the right man. You can find anything in Moscow, anything you want. You have such a large circle of friends. You could consult one or the other. Krutitzky, Mamayev, Gorodulin will help you to choose the right husband for me, I'm sure of that.

TURÚSSINA. Krutitzky, Gorodulin! But they are only men, Mary. They can easily mislead me or they can be deceived themselves.

MARY. What shall we do?

TURÚSSINA. We must wait for a sign. Without a special sign I shall never be able to make up my mind.

MARY. But where is this sign to come from?

TURÚSSINA. You'll soon find out where it will come from. It may even come to-day.

MARY. Please, don't forbid Kurchayev to visit us. Let him come as before.

TURÚSSINA. But remember, he'll never be your husband!

MARY. I shall rely on your choice entirely, auntie. I am your obedient, your most obedient niece!

TURÚSSINA. [*Kisses her*] You're a darling!

MARY. I shall be rich, I shall have lots of fun. You had your fun, too, auntie, didn't you?

TURÚSSINA. What do you know about that?

MARY. I know, I know you had lots of fun.

TURÚSSINA. You may know something, but you can't and you ought not to know everything, my dear.

MARY. Never mind, you're the most wonderful woman, auntie, and I shall take an example from you. [*Embraces her aunt*] If I sin, I shall repent. I shall go on sinning and I shall go on repenting, just like you, auntie.

TURÚSSINA. What idle talk, Mary. What idle talk!

MARY. [*Crossing her hands*] I'm sorry.

TURÚSSINA. You do talk a lot, don't you? I feel so tired. I must rest a little. Please, leave me.

[*Kisses* MARY *who leaves the room.*]

She's a darling! You can't even be angry with her. I don't think she knows herself what she's talking about. How can she know? She just prattles away like a child. I'll do my best to make her happy. She fully deserves it. How reasonable she is and how dutiful! She touched me to tears by her childish loyalty. I feel so touched, so touched . . . [*She inhales smelling salts.*]

[GRIGÓRY *enters.*]

GRIGÓRY. Mr. Krutitzky, ma'am.

TURÚSSINA. Ask him to come in.

[*Enter* KRUTÍTZKY.]

KRUTÍTZKY. [*Taking hold of her hands*] Is it your nerves again to-day, eh?

TURÚSSINA. My nerves.

KRUTÍTZKY. That's bad. Here, your hands are ice-cold. You . . . er . . . you're a bit too . . .

TURÚSSINA. Too what?

KRUTÍTZKY. Too . . . er . . . you're overdoing things. You oughtn't to, you know.

TURÚSSINA. I've asked you before not to speak to me about that.

KRUTÍTZKY. All right, all right. I shan't.

TURÚSSINA. Sit down, please.

KRUTÍTZKY. Thank you, I'm not tired. I just went out for a walk and, well, I thought to myself, why not pay a visit to a dear old friend, a dear old . . . er . . . ha-ha-ha . . . You remember we were . . .

TURÚSSINA. Please, leave our memories alone. Now that I'm . . .

KRUTÍTZKY. But why, why forget the past? We didn't have such a bad time together, did we? And if there was something which, according to your present way of thinking, was wicked, then you most probably have long ago repented, confessed and obtained absolution. To tell you the truth, I always remember our past with pleasure and I don't at all feel repentant if . . .

TURÚSSINA. [*Imploringly*] Stop, please, stop!

[GRIGÓRY *enters.*]

GRIGÓRY. An unnatural has arrived, ma'am.

KRUTÍTZKY. What's that?

TURÚSSINA. What are you talking about, Grigory? Not an unnatural. A natural! Tell cook to give him a meal.

[GRIGÓRY *goes out.*]

What fools these servants are! They don't know the most common words.

KRUTÍTZKY. I can't say that naturals are very common to-day. You rarely come across them except at your house. But to resume our conversation. You will pardon me, but all I wanted to say was that before, when you lived differently, you were in much better health.

TURÚSSINA. My body may have been in better shape, but not my soul.

KRUTÍTZKY. Well, of course, I don't know anything about that. It's not my business. All I meant was that you looked better. You're still quite young, you know, and you can still live as one should.

TURÚSSINA. But I do live as one should.

KRUTÍTZKY. What I mean is that it is a little early to . . . to be so sanctimonious.

TURÚSSINA. I've asked you . . .

KRUTÍTZKY. I'm sorry. I'm sorry. I shan't mention it again.

TURÚSSINA. You are such a queer man.

[*Enter* GRIGÓRY.]

GRIGÓRY. A very queer man has just arrived, ma'am.

TURÚSSINA. Where has he come from? Have you inquired?

GRIGÓRY. He says he has come from a far-away land.

TURÚSSINA. Admit him and tell cook to feed him with the rest.

GRIGÓRY. But, ma'am, together they might have a . . .

TURÚSSINA. You can go. [GRIGÓRY *goes out.*

KRUTÍTZKY. I think you ought at least to ask to see the passports of those who come from far-away lands.

TURÚSSINA. Whatever for?

KRUTÍTZKY. Because they may cause a lot of trouble. I know of a man who gave refuge to three such travellers.

TURÚSSINA. And? . . .

KRUTÍTZKY. Well, all three of them appeared to be excellent engravers.

TURÚSSINA. What's wrong with that?

KRUTÍTZKY. What's wrong with that? It's a very bad occupation.

TURÚSSINA. Why is engraving such a bad occupation?

KRUTÍTZKY. You see, they were not engraving portraits in their huts...
TURÚSSINA. [*Softly*] Images of saints?
KRUTÍTZKY. No, no. Not images of saints. Paper money!
TURÚSSINA. [*With a cry of dismay*] Really?
KRUTÍTZKY. [*Sitting down*] Exactly. Charity is all very well, but a little circumspection does no harm. You, in particular, must be careful. It's a well-known fact that when a lady devotes herself to a life of charity, all kinds of crooks begin to flock round her. It is easy for you to fall a victim to deceit in this business.
TURÚSSINA. I do good for the sake of good without any distinctions. By the way, I wanted to ask your advice about rather an important matter.
KRUTÍTZKY. What is it? Tell me. You know I shall be only too glad to be of service to you.
TURÚSSINA. Mary, you know, is now of an age when...
KRUTÍTZKY. [*Drawing nearer*] Yes, yes, I know.
TURÚSSINA. Do you know of a man who might suit her? You know the kind of man I want.
KRUTÍTZKY. What kind of man do you want? That's the difficulty. There are plenty of young men about. Wait. I think I have just the one you want.
TURÚSSINA. Really?
KRUTÍTZKY. Yes, yes. A modest fellow, unusually so for his years, clever, a nobleman, quite certain to make an excellent career. Altogether a fine fellow, a very fine fellow. He was recommended to me for a certain job, and I, of course, tested him to see what sort of bird he is. An excellent fellow. He'll go far, you'll see.
TURÚSSINA. But who is he?
KRUTÍTZKY. What's his name? Wait. Let me remember. I think I've got his address. I don't want it any more, I've made a note of it. [*Takes out a piece of paper*] Here it is. [*Reads*] George Glumov. Look at his handwriting. Clear, straight, elegant. You can at once guess his character from his handwriting. Straight, therefore he's an accurate man, round, without any flourishes, well, that means he's not a free-thinker. Take it. It might come in useful.

TURÚSSINA. [*Taking the address*] Thank you.
KRUTÍTZKY. Why thank me? It's only my duty. [*Getting up*] Good-bye. Shall I look in again or are you angry with me?
TURÚSSINA. What are you talking about? I'm always glad to see you.
KRUTÍTZKY. That's better. You mustn't be angry with me for what I said. I meant it just as an expression of . . . of my love. I felt so sorry for you . . .
TURÚSSINA. Do look in.
KRUTÍTZKY. As in the old days, eh? Ha-ha-ha! Well, good-bye.
[*Goes out.*]
TURÚSSINA. An old man and yet how frivolous! How can I trust him? [*Secretes address in pocket*] All the same, I shall have to make inquiries about this Glumov.
[*Enter* GRIGÓRY.]
GRIGÓRY. Mr. Gorodulin, ma'am.
TORÚSSINA. Show him in.
[GRIGÓRY *goes out*, GORODÚLIN *comes in.*]
TURÚSSINA. I'm so glad to see you. Aren't you ashamed of yourself? Where have you been hiding yourself?
GORODÚLIN. Business, business. One day an official dinner, another day a new railway opening ceremony.
TURÚSSINA. I don't quite believe you. You probably find it very boring here. I suppose I must be grateful to you for looking in from time to time. How's our business been getting on?
GORODÚLIN. What business?
TURÚSSINA. So you have already forgotten all about it? Thank you, thank you very much. I was a fool to entrust you with it. You're always immersed in important business, how can you be expected to remember the poor, the unhappy, the afflicted? Is it worth your while to bother yourself about them?
GORODÚLIN. The afflicted? You said the afflicted, didn't you? Well, I can't somehow recall anything about the afflicted. Ah, wait, wait! I seem to remember. You asked me to inquire about some kind of female magician.
TORÚSSINA. Not a magician, a fortune-teller. There's a

great difference between the two. I should never have consulted a magician.

GORODÚLIN. I'm sorry. I'm afraid I know nothing about these things. I can't tell the difference between one and the other, Such subtleties are quite beyond me. However, you probably mean the widow of the registrar Ulita Shmygayeva.

TURÚSSINA. I don't care who her husband was. She is a respectable woman, of high morals and I'm proud to have been one of her friends.

GORODÚLIN. It would appear from the police records that a certain ex-soldier was also one of her friends.

TURÚSSINA. Nonsense! It's all tittle-tattle, slander. She was successful, she was admitted to the best houses, no wonder she was envied and slandered. But I hope she was acquitted. Innocence must triumph in the end.

GORODÚLIN. I'm afraid she wasn't. She'll have to serve a stiff sentence.

TURÚSSINA. [*Half rising*] What? There's justice for you, our much-lauded justice! To send an innocent woman to jail! And for what? Because she's so useful to her fellow-men?

GORODÚLIN. She was tried for fortune-telling.

TURÚSSINA. Don't talk to me about that. The poor woman was sent to jail just as a sop to our fashionable free-thinking age.

GORODÚLIN. She was also found guilty of receiving stolen goods, of keeping a disreputable house and of poisoning a shopkeeper.

TURÚSSINA. Good Heavens! It can't be true!

GORODÚLIN. It's Gospel truth. The wife of the shopkeeper asked her for some potion for her husband, to make him love her more. Well, the potion was made according to all the best recipes, it seems. It only lacked one thing: a medical prescription.

TURÚSSINA. And how's the shopkeeper?

GORODÚLIN. The potion worked all right. The shopkeeper nearly died, but not of love.

TURÚSSINA. I can see you think it all great fun. Lawyers and doctors have no hearts. Wasn't there anyone to take the poor woman's part?

EVEN A WISE MAN STUMBLES

GORODÚLIN. Wasn't there anyone to take her part? Why, she had one of the best lawyers in town to defend her. His eloquence poured forth, went up in clouds, filled the whole courtroom and, finally, died down in a hardly audible murmur. But it was all of no avail: the woman herself confessed everything. The soldier, who was a very good friend of hers, was first to confess, then she, too, confessed.

TURÚSSINA. I didn't expect it. How easy it is to make a mistake! How is one to live in this world!

GORODÚLIN. It isn't so impossible, but when one has only a hazy notion of affairs it is certainly not easy. Now that the study of mental diseases has progressed a little and hallucinations . . .

TORÚSSINA. I've asked you not to talk to me about it!

GORODÚLIN. I'm sorry. I forgot.

TURÚSSINA. What if I do make mistakes about people! Let them deceive me. But to stretch out a helping hand to people, to worry about the unfortunate ones—that's my only inspiration in life!

GORODÚLIN. Inspiration is not so simple a matter. To-day one rarely comes across an inspired man.

[*Enter* GRIGÓRY.]

GRIGÓRY. One of them inspired men has arrived, ma'am.

GORODÚLIN. Really?

TURÚSSINA. Who is he?

GRIGÓRY. I think he must be an Asiatic.

GORODÚLIN. I think so, too.

TURÚSSINA. Why do you think he's an Asiatic?

GRIGÓRY. Well, ma'am, he looks so awe-inspiring. It gives me the creeps to look at him. If he'd come at night, ma'am, I really would have been terrified.

TURÚSSINA. How do you mean, he's awe-inspiring? What nonsense is that?

GRIGÓRY. He has such a wild look about him, ma'am. He's all covered with hair. All you can see of his face is his eyes.

TURÚSSINA. He must be a Greek.

GRIGÓRY. He don't look very much like a Greek, ma'am. He isn't dark enough. He must be one of them Hungarians.

TURÚSSINA. Why a Hungarian? Don't talk such nonsense!

GRIGÓRY. One of them Hungarians, ma'am, who go about selling mousetraps.
TURÚSSINA. All right. Let him in and tell cook to give him food and to ask him if he needs anything else.
GRIGÓRY. If you ask me, ma'am, what he needs is . . .
TURÚSSINA. Never mind. You can go.
GRIGÓRY. Very good, ma'am.   [*Goes out.*]
TURÚSSINA. I should like to ask you something, Mr. Gorodulin.
GORODÚLIN. I'm all attention.
TURÚSSINA. I want to talk to you about Mary. Can you think of anyone?
GORODÚLIN. A husband? My dear lady, please spare me. Why ask me? Do I look like a Moscow matchmaker? My calling is divorce, not marriage. I am against any kind of lock, even wedlock.
TURÚSSINA. But you are married.
GORODÚLIN. Exactly, that's why I hate to lure anyone else into the state of matrimony, be he even a wild tartar.
TURÚSSINA. Joking apart, are you sure you can't think of anyone?
GORODÚLIN. Wait a minute. I met someone the other day who had it writ all over him: *a good husband!* You would expect him to marry an heiress any moment.
TURÚSSINA. Do try to remember who it was, will you?
GORODÚLIN. Wait, wait . . . I have it. Glumov!
TURÚSSINA. George Glumov?
GORODÚLIN. Yes.
TURÚSSINA. Is he a good man?
GORODÚLIN. He seems an honest one. That's all I can tell you.
TURÚSSINA. Krutitzky, too, mentioned him to me.
GORODÚLIN. Well, it seems he's your man. I'm telling you he had it written all over him. It's fate. [*Getting up*] Well, I must be going. Good-bye.   [*He bows and goes out.*]
TURÚSSINA. Who is this Glumov? I don't trust either Krutitzky or Gorodulin, but there must be something in him if people of such divergent views praise him.
                                        [*Rings. Enter* GRIGÓRY.]

EVEN A WISE MAN STUMBLES

Call Miss Mary and tell everybody to come in here, too.

[GRIGÓRY *goes out.*]

What a loss for Moscow that Ivan is no longer alive. How easy and simple life was when he was still with us. I can't sleep for thinking how to marry off my darling. What a sin it would be to make a slip in the choice of a husband for her. If Ivan had been alive, I needn't have worried. I should have gone to him, asked him and everything would have been settled. It's only when a man is dead that you begin to miss him. I wonder whether Manefa could replace him. She, too, possesses quite a lot of supernatural power.

[*Enter* MARY, *the* 1ST POOR RELATION *with a pack of cards, which she carries before her like a book, and the* 2ND POOR RELATION *carrying a lap-dog.*

1ST POOR RELATION *sits down at a table, the* 2ND *on a stool at* TURÚSSINA's *feet.*]

1ST POOR RELATION. Shall I lay out the cards?

TURÚSSINA. Wait a bit. Well, Mary, I spoke to Krutitzky and Gorodulin about you.

MARY. [*Excitedly*] What did they say? Please, tell me. I've agreed to accept your decision and I'm dying to hear it.

TURÚSSINA. Both with one voice recommend a certain man.

MARY. That sounds all right. He must be a nice man. Who is he?

TURÚSSINA. But I don't trust them.

1ST POOR RELATION. Shall I?

TURÚSSINA. All right, try to find out if they were speaking the truth. [*To* MARY] I don't trust them. They can make a mistake.

MARY. But why should they, auntie?

TURÚSSINA. They're men! [*To the* 2ND POOR RELATION] Don't drop the dog!

MARY. Whom can you trust, auntie? An oracle? I'm so afraid.

TURÚSSINA. That is only natural, child. You ought to be afraid. We mustn't, we have no right to lift the veil from the future without fear and trembling. There, behind that veil is happiness and sorrow, there is both your life and your death.

MARY. But who is to lift the veil?

TURÚSSINA. Only those who have the power to do it.
[*Enter* GRIGÓRY.]
GRIGÓRY. Manefa, ma'am.
TURÚSSINA. There she is. She'll do it.
[TURÚSSINA *gets up and goes to meet* MANÉFA, *followed by the rest.* MANÉFA *enters.*]
TURÚSSINA. Come in, Manefa.
MANÉFA. I'm coming, I'm coming.
1ST POOR RELATION. [*With feeling*] Oh, I'm so excited!
TURÚSSINA. [*Angrily*] Shut up!
MANÉFA. [*Sitting down*] Here I am and here I sit like a sack of coals.
2ND POOR RELATION. Oh, oh, oh. What wisdom!
1ST POOR RELATION. At last, at last. Glory be.
MANÉFA. [*Softly*] What are you all glaring at me for?
TURÚSSINA. We're so glad you've done us the honour to come.
1ST POOR RELATION. Such an honour, indeed!
2ND POOR RELATION. We are all honoured!
TURÚSSINA. We're waiting. What do you say, mother Manefa?
MANÉFA. Waiting! Waited in boots and came in clogs!
1ST POOR RELATION. Glory be. Mark her words. Mark them well.
TURÚSSINA. I wanted to ask you . . .
MANÉFA. Don't ask me. I know. He who knows runs, he who knows not lies down. A maid less, a housewife more.
2ND POOR RELATION. So, so, so.
TURÚSSINA. We want to know who the man is? Have you nothing to say to your handmaid Mary? Maybe in a vision or a dream . . .
MANÉFA. I had. I had a vision. Down the mountainsides Yegor slides.
2ND POOR RELATION. Do you hear? Yegor! George!
MARY. [*Whispers to* TURÚSSINA] But Kurchayev's name is also George.
TURÚSSINA. Wait. Who is he?
MANÉFA. How do I know? When you see him, you'll know him.

TURÚSSINA. When shall we see him?
MANÉFA. A welcome guest waits for no call.
1ST POOR RELATION. Mark that! Mark that!
TURÚSSINA. Tell us at any rate how we shall recognize him?
2ND POOR RELATION. First of all we must find out the colour of his hair. That is the first thing one asks. Don't you know that?
TURÚSSINA. All right. Keep quiet, will you? What is the colour of his hair?
MANÉFA. He's bland to some, but to you he is blond.
MARY. Blond? But Kurchayev, too, is blond. Maybe it's he.
TURÚSSINA. But haven't you heard? She saw him in a vision. Who has ever heard of a hussar appearing in a vision? Don't be silly, child.
1ST POOR RELATION. How wonderful! The cards, too, say George.
TURÚSSINA. Don't be silly! How could you find out his name by the cards?
1ST POOR RELATION. Bother! I've made a slip. . . . My tongue . . . I mean, the cards say he's blond.
TURÚSSINA. [*To* MANÉFA] You know everything, but we, poor sinners that we are, are still in the dark. There are many Yegors and many blonds.
MANÉFA. The stranger, he is late, the destined one is at the gate.
TURÚSSINA. [*And the rest*] At the gate?
MANÉFA. Dress up, get ready. The guests are coming.
TURÚSSINA. When?
MANÉFA. Now. Even now. They come bearing gifts.
 [*All turn to the door.* GRIGÓRY *enters.*]
GRIGÓRY. Mr. Mamayev, ma'am.
TURÚSSINA. Alone?
GRIGÓRY. There's a young man with him, a blond one.
1ST POOR RELATION. Help! I'm going to faint!
2ND POOR RELATION. Is it true, or is it all a dream?
TURÚSSINA. Show them in. [*Embracing* MARY] Well, Mary, your prayers have been answered. [*Sits down and inhales smelling salts.*]
MARY. This is all so strange, auntie. I'm all of a tremble.

TURÚSSINA. Go to your room, calm yourself. You may come in later.

[MARY *goes out.*]

MANÉFA. Virtue is its own reward.

TURÚSSINA. [*To the two* POOR RELATIONS] Lead her to the kitchen. Support her. Give her tea, tea!

MANÉFA. He who drinks tea is a drunkard.

TURÚSSINA. All right, give her anything she wants.

[*The two* POOR RELATIONS *take* MANÉFA *under the arms and lead her to the side door. They linger on the threshold.*]

[*Enter* MAMÁYEV *and* GLÚMOV.]

MAMÁYEV. Permit me to introduce to you my nephew, George Glumov.

THE TWO POOR RELATIONS. [*In the doorway*] George! The blond one!

MAMÁYEV. I hope you'll like him.

TURÚSSINA. [*Gets up*] Thank you. I shall love him as my own son!

[GLUMOV *kisses her hand respectfully.*]

ACT FOUR

SCENE ONE

[*Reception-room at* KRUTÍTZKY'S *home. Entrance door, a door to the right, leading to the study, another door to the left leading to the drawing-room. A table and a chair.*]
  [*Enter* GLÚMOV, FOOTMAN *at door, then* KRUTÍTZKY.]

GLÚMOV. Announce me.
FOOTMAN. [*Glancing into the study*] The master will be here presently, sir.
  [KRUTÍTZKY *comes in,* FOOTMAN *goes out.*]
KRUTÍTZKY. [*Nodding*] Ready?
GLÚMOV. Ready, sir. [*Produces manuscript.*]
KRUTÍTZKY. [*Taking manuscript*] Clear, beautiful, excellent. Bravo, bravo! A treatise? Why not a project?
GLÚMOV. A project, sir, is a scheme which introduces some new proposals. In your work, sir, on the other hand, every new proposal is rejected . . . [*with an ingratiating smile*] and quite rightly, too, sir.
KRUTÍTZKY. So you think "treatise" sounds better?
GLÚMOV. Treatise is better, sir.
KRUTÍTZKY. Treatise? Well, I suppose, it will do. "A Treatise on the Harm of Reforms in General." Why in general? Isn't that superfluous?
GLÚMOV. That is the chief idea of your work, sir, that all reforms are harmful in general.
KRUTÍTZKY. Yes, yes. Reforms that go too far; all radical reforms. But I'm not against small changes or improvements. I said nothing against that.
GLÚMOV. But in that case you would hardly call them reforms, sir. They'd be merely improvements or revisions.
KRUTÍTZKY. [*Taps forehead with pencil*] Of course, of course. That was well said. Young man, you've something there. I'm very glad. Do your best. Do your best.
GLÚMOV. Thank you, sir.
KRUTÍTZKY. [*Puts on his glasses*] Now let's see. Let's look into

it a little more closely. I am anxious to know how you begin the explication of the main theme. "Clause 1. Every reform is harmful *per se*. What is the essence of a reform? Every reform includes the following acts: 1. abolition of the old and 2. the replacing of the old by something new. Which of these acts is harmful? Both are equally so. First. By sweeping away the old we make room for the dangerous propensity of the mind to enter upon the causes of the whys and the wherefores of changes and to reach the following conclusions therefrom: what is changed is something which is no longer of any use; a certain institution is abolished, therefore it is no good. But this cannot be permitted since by such action free-thought is born and a challenge is, as it were, thrown out to discuss what must not be discussed." Very clear, very sound.

GLÚMOV. And absolutely right, sir.

KRUTÍTZKY. [*Reads*] "Secondly. By introducing something new we make, as it were, some concession to the so-called spirit of the age, which is nothing but an invention of idle minds." Yes, it couldn't be put more clearly. I hope everyone will be able to grasp it. I want it to have a wide appeal.

GLÚMOV. Only sophistries are expressed in an involved style, sir. Incontrovertible truths . . .

KRUTÍTZKY. So you think these are incontrovertible truths?

GLÚMOV. Absolutely, sir.

KRUTÍTZKY. [*Looking round*] Why don't they bring in another chair?

GLÚMOV. I don't mind standing, sir.

KRUTÍTZKY. Of course, not everyone can be permitted to take a chair. Some people no sooner sit down than they sprawl all over the place. Some shopkeeper with his bill or the tailor . . .

GLÚMOV. Don't mind me, sir. I . . . I should like to ask you to forgive me, sir.

KRUTÍTZKY. What is it, my friend, what is it?

GLÚMOV. I left certain words and phrases in your treatise unaltered.

KRUTÍTZKY. Why?

GLÚMOV. Our modern idiom is much too weak to express the grace of your thoughts.

KRUTÍTZKY. For instance?
GLÚMOV. In clause twenty-five relating to the position of the lower-grade civil servants . . .
KRUTÍTZKY. Well?
GLÚMOV. . . . you have given very strong expression to the fine thought, sir, that it is not necessary to raise the salaries and, generally, improve the position of such lower-grade civil servants, but, on the contrary, it is necessary to raise considerably the salaries of the higher-grade civil servants.
KRUTÍTZKY. Can't remember. [*He turns the pages of the manuscript.*]
GLÚMOV. I know not only that clause, but the whole of your treatise by heart, sir.
KRUTÍTZKY. I believe you, but, quite candidly, I am surprised.
GLÚMOV. My whole life is still ahead of me, sir; I must accumulate wisdom; it is not often that I get such a chance of improving my mind, but, having got it, I must make the most of it. You can't expect me to learn anything of any value from the newspapers, can you, sir?
KRUTÍTZKY. Quite right.
GLÚMOV. A young man can easily go off the rails, sir.
KRUTÍTZKY. Quite true, quite true.
GLÚMOV. It means everything, sir.
KRUTÍTZKY. Well, what about clause twenty-five?
GLÚMOV. Clause twenty-five. "A rise in remuneration in government offices, should such a rise for some reason become necessary, must be introduced with the utmost circumspection, and that only for the higher-grade officials and not for the lower grades. An increase in the remuneration of the higher-grade officials must be made with that end in view that these latter should be able by their external magnificence to uphold the majesty of the government, which is its due. A lower-grade official, however, if he have enough to keep body and soul together and be generally satisfied, is apt to acquire a certain complaisance of manner and a certain self-esteem which are inappropriate to his position, whereas to assure an uninterrupted and rapid dispatch of business a lower-grade official must be timid and always tremulous."

KRUTÍTZKY. That's right. That's quite right.

GLÚMOV. The word "tremulous," sir, is rather apt, I think. I simply can't get it out of my head.

KRUTÍTZKY. [*Reads manuscript, but occasionally, as though by chance, throws a sidelong glance at* GLÚMOV] If you smoke, smoke. You'll find the matches on the mantelpiece.

GLÚMOV. I don't smoke, sir. But, of course, if you'd rather . . .

KRUTÍTZKY. It's not my business. Has your uncle seen your work?

GLÚMOV. Good heavens, no, sir. I should never have dreamt of showing it to him.

KRUTÍTZKY. That's all right. He goes about telling everybody how clever he is, but in reality he is an imbecile.

GLÚMOV. I dare not gainsay you, sir.

KRUTÍTZKY. He only knows how to preach to others, but let him try to write anything himself, then we'll see. His wife, too, is a damn fool.

GLÚMOV. I'm afraid, I don't feel like taking her part, either, sir.

KRUTÍTZKY. What I can't understand is how you can stick them.

GLÚMOV. I have to, sir. I can't afford not to.

KRUTÍTZKY. Aren't you in the Civil Service?

GLÚMOV. I hope soon to enter it, sir. On the recommendation of my aunt, Mr. Gorodulin promised to get me a job.

KRUTÍTZKY. Couldn't she have found somebody better? Some job he'll get you! You'd better be looking round for something safe. All these Gorodulin jobs are shaky, no stability in them, here to-day and gone to-morrow. He is considered to be a dangerous man among us. You'd better make a note of that.

GLÚMOV. Myself I'd rather not get a job in any of the new departments, sir.

KRUTÍTZKY. Yes, yes. I thought so. Very well, but you'd better take the job. It's worse to run about without one. Later on, should you so desire, I could give you letters of recommendation to Petersburg. You can get yourself transferred.

It's much more worth while to serve there. Your past is clean, isn't it?
GLÚMOV. I'm afraid I was rather lazy at school, sir.
KRUTÍTZKY. Well, that doesn't matter. Not much use being a swot, eh? There is nothing else, is there?
GLÚMOV. I feel ashamed to tell you, sir.
KRUTÍTZKY. [*Severely*] What's that? You'd better tell me everything.
GLÚMOV. I'm afraid, sir, I rather let myself go as a young man, all kinds of distractions . . .
KRUTÍTZKY. Go on. Don't be afraid.
GLÚMOV. As a student, sir, I . . . I kept up the old traditions.
KRUTÍTZKY. How do you mean, the old traditions?
GLÚMOV. I mean I behaved differently from the present-day students.
KRUTÍTZKY. How?
GLÚMOV. I sowed my wild oats, sir. I also was involved in certain clashes with the police after curfew hours.
KRUTÍTZKY. Is that all?
GLÚMOV. That's all, sir. God forbid that I should do anything illegal.
KRUTÍTZKY. Well, I can't say that I disapprove of that. On the contrary, when one is young one should smoke and drink. That's nothing to be ashamed of. You're not a girl. All right, my mind is at peace. I don't like to be unappreciative. I don't mind telling you that I liked you from the first glance. I have already put in a good word for you in one place.
GLÚMOV. Yes, Mrs. Turussina told me. I can't find words to thank you, sir.
KRUTÍTZKY. Are you going to marry the girl? She's an heiress, you know.
GLÚMOV. Money means nothing to me, sir. I like the girl, sir.
KRUTÍTZKY. Well, I can't say anything about that. All women look alike to me. Her aunt, I know, is a bit on the pious side.
GLÚMOV. I know, sir, that love is rather at a discount nowadays, but I think it's a great thing.

EVEN A WISE MAN STUMBLES

KRUTÍTZKY. Well, maybe it's wiser not to believe in it. After all, people don't like you any better if you do. But, of course, once you fall in love, you can't mistake the feeling. I remember once, in Bessarabia it was, about forty years ago, I nearly died of love. What are you staring at me for?

GLÚMOV. Really, sir?

KRUTÍTZKY. Yes. It all ended up in a fever. Maybe you'd better not believe in love. Well, I wish you all the best. I'm very glad to hear of your betrothal. Once you become a capitalist, we shall find you an important position. We need such men as you. You will be one of us, won't you? We are badly in need of support now: the youngsters have already begun to submerge us. However, my dear fellow, what do I owe you for your work?

GLÚMOV. Really, sir, don't offend me.

KRUTÍTZKY. Don't you offend me!

GLÚMOV. If you really want to reward me, sir, then you could easily make me very happy.

KRUTÍTZKY. How do you mean? What do you want?

GLÚMOV. Marriage is such a big thing, sir, such an important step in life. . . . Don't refuse me! A blessing from you, sir, from such a patron as you, will always be considered by me as a pledge of . . . To know you, sir, is already a piece of good fortune, but your blessing will imply a certain relationship, even if only a spiritual one, and this even my children . . .

KRUTÍTZKY. Do you want me to act as your father at your wedding or what? I can't understand what you're driving at.

GLÚMOV. Yes, sir. That will make me very happy, sir.

KRUTÍTZKY. With pleasure, with pleasure. Why not? You should have said so at once. That's nothing.

GLÚMOV. May I tell Mrs. Turussina, sir?

KRUTÍTZKY. By all means. Tell her if you want to.

GLÚMOV. You don't need me any more, sir?

KRUTÍTZKY. No.

GLÚMOV. I shall then take my leave of you, sir.

KRUTÍTZKY. Remember, about my scribbling, not a word to anyone. It will soon be published, anonymously of course. One publisher has already approached me. He is, strange to say, quite a gentleman, writes so courteously: do me the honour, sir, and so on and so forth. When you're asked who is the author, pretend that you don't know.

GLÚMOV. Certainly, sir.

[*Bows and goes out.*]

KRUTÍTZKY. Good-bye, my dear fellow. Maybe we do inveigh a bit too much against the young. After all, here's one of them, a clever and understanding fellow. It's true he likes to flatter you a little and, who knows, he's probably a rogue in a small way, but let him get fledged and he'll grow out of it. If he's a born rogue, it's bad, but if he's a rogue only in his manners, then it doesn't signify much. Let him get money and high rank in service and there will remain no trace of it. His father must have been very poor; his mother is a typical scrounger: "Kiss this gentleman's hand, kiss the other gentleman's hand!" No wonder it has left its trace. However, it's better than outright rudeness all the same.

[FOOTMAN *enters.*]

FOOTMAN. Mrs. Mamayeva, sir. The lady is in the drawing-room. I told her madam was out.

MAMÁYEVA. [*Behind the door*] May I come in?

KRUTÍTZKY. Do, do. [*To the* FOOTMAN.] Bring in another chair.

[FOOTMAN *goes out and comes back with chair.* MAMÁYEVA *enters.* FOOTMAN *goes out.*]

MAMÁYEVA. Always busy! Drop your work and try to entertain a young lady. What's the use of sitting in your study all day long? Don't be such an ungallant old man.

KRUTÍTZKY. Ha-ha-ha! It's high time I retired and left beauty to the young.

MAMÁYEVA. [*Sitting down*] To-day the young are worse than the old.

KRUTÍTZKY. Are you complaining about anyone?

MAMÁYEVA. Am I wrong?

KRUTÍTZKY. It's true, it's true. They have no poetry in their souls, no sentiment. I think it's because no more tragedies are performed on our stage. Ozerov should be revived. Then our young would gather these delicate, gossamer sentiments. Yes, tragedies should be performed more often, every other day. Sumarokov, too. I have a plan ready for the improvement of the morals of the young. For the nobility—the tragedies of Ozerov; for the common people the legalization of the sale of home-made liquor. We used to know the tragedies by heart, but now they have grown shy of them: they don't even bother to read them. That's why we knew what chivalry meant, and honesty, too, but to-day all they care about is money. [*Recites*]

> Shall I wait for fate to stop the flow of days
> When sadness adds its sting to a heart suppressed?
> I pause.

Do you remember?
MAMÁYEVA. How can I forget? After all, its' only fifty years ago, or is it more, since that poem was popular. So, of course, I must remember it.
KRUTÍTZKY. I beg your pardon! I always think of you as one of my contemporaries. By the way, I forgot to mention it to you. I am very pleased with your relative. He is a fine young man!
MAMÁYEVA. Yes, isn't he? He's so sweet!
KRUTÍTZKY. Yes, yes. But you're spoiling him.
MAMÁYEVA. How?
KRUTÍTZKY. Permit me, I recollect some more verses. [*Recites*]

> Ye gods! I do not beg your eloquence to prove,
> But grant me now your gift of sentiment and love!

Charming!
MAMÁYEVA. How do we spoil him, pray?
KRUTÍTZKY. How? Why, you're marrying him off, aren't you? What a lovely bride you've found for him . . .
MAMÁYEVA. [*In dismay*] A bride? Surely, you must be mistaken.
KRUTÍTZKY. [*Recites*]

> O mother, dry thy tears' rich flood,
> And you, dear sister, still your burning blood!

MAMÁYEVA. Tell me who is the bride, who is the bride?
KRUTÍTZKY. Dear me, don't you know? Turussina. Why pretend ignorance? Two hundred thousand roubles!

MAMÁYEVA. [*Gets up*] It isn't true, it isn't true, I tell you!
KRUTÍTZKY. [*Recites*]

> At such bad news thy thoughts run wild,
> Suppress thy sighs, my poor, poor child,
> For sorrow dark thy countenance disfigures.

MAMÁYEVA. How you bore me with your poetry!
KRUTÍTZKY. But he does seem to be a fellow whose heart is in the right place. You mustn't think I'm marrying for money, sir, he says to me. He asked me to take the place of his father at the wedding. Do me the honour, sir, he says. Well, why not? I couldn't very well refuse him, could I? I, he says, am not marrying her for her money. No, sir. I like the girl, he says. She's an angel, he says, a real angel. And, you know, he spoke with real feeling. Well, why not? May the Lord grant him both happiness and riches. Apropos, do you remember these lines by Donskoy? [*Recites*]

> When his word a Russian once hath given,
> His honour he hath pledged to Heaven.

MAMÁYEVA. Oh!
KRUTÍTZKY. What's the matter?
MAMÁYEVA. My head aches. I'm feeling ill.
KRUTÍTZKY. Never mind. It'll pass off. [*Recites.*]

> You know our union till death we pledge.

MAMÁYEVA. Enough, enough. Tell your wife that I couldn't wait for her, that I was taken suddenly ill. Ah-h! Good-bye.
KRUTÍTZKY. But are you quite sure you're ill? You look well enough to me. [*Recites*]

> His treason in my rival's presence to unmask,
> To poison his joy now is my task!

MAMÁYEVA. Good-bye, good-bye!
[*Hurries out.*]
KRUTÍTZKY. I wonder what's bitten her. Just like a woman. I'd rather command a division. [*Picks up his manuscript*] I'd better put in a spot of real work. [*Shouts*] I'm not receiving anyone else to-day!...

SCENE TWO

[*Room of Act One.*]

[GLÚMOV *comes out of side-door with diary, then* GLÚMOVA.]

GLÚMOV. Finished at last. The interesting conversation with Krutitzky noted down in full. What a memorial for posterity! How worth while it was to memorize all this nonsense. I possibly overdid my part a little in my talk with him. I am still young and am too easily carried away. It doesn't much matter, though, you won't spoil a pudding by putting a few more plums in it. As for my uncle, he's a real treat! Teaching me to make love to his own wife! But here, too, I went a bit too far. It's like playing with fire: you can't be too careful. However we try to hide my engagement from her, she's bound to find out. She may even contrive to break it off, if not from love, then from jealousy: women are so vindictive. Not every woman knows how to love, but they are all past masters when it comes to jealousy. [GLÚMOVA *enters.*]
Mother, are you off to Mrs. Turussina's?
GLÚMOVA. Yes.
GLÚMOV. [*Consulting his watch, sternly*] You're late, mother. You should be there from the early morning, every day, every day. You should spend all your free time there.
GLÚMOVA. They may get bored with me.
GLÚMOV. It can't be helped. Make friends with the servants, the fortune tellers, the women pilgrims, the poor relations. Don't be too niggardly with your presents for them. On your way there now, you'd better go to town and buy two snuff-boxes, small silver ones. All these poor relations are mad on snuff and they all adore receiving presents.
GLÚMOVA. All right, all right.
GLÚMOV. Above everything keep a sharp look-out on all the entrances and exits so that nobody in any way untrustworthy can slip into the house. To make sure, hob-nob with the servants, for they have a good nose for things. All right, off you go. See what you can do about hurrying up the preparations for the official engagement party.

GLÚMOVA. I'm told it can't be arranged sooner than in about a week.

[Goes out.]

GLÚMOV. Damn it! That is far too long. I'll get sick and tired of waiting. Here I have riches simply falling into my lap. To miss them would be both a damn shame and an unforgivable sin. [*Sits down at desk*] What was it I wanted to add to my diary? Oh, yes. My latest expenses. [*Writes*] Two silver snuff-boxes for the poor relations. [*Hearing noise of a carriage drawing up to the house, goes over to window*] Who's that? Blast it! My aunt! Does she know or doesn't she know? I shall soon see.

[Enter MAMÁYEVA.]

GLÚMOV. How nice of you to come! I'm so happy to see you. It is as though the gods themselves descended from Olympus to gladden my poor hearth.

MAMÁYEVA. Don't excite yourself unduly. I haven't come to see you, I've come to see your mother.

GLÚMOV. [*Mutters to himself*] She doesn't know. [*Aloud*] She went out a minute ago.

MAMÁYEVA. What a pity.

GLÚMOV. [*Offering a chair*] Please, sit down. I'm so glad you've come. Your beauty makes everything in my poor room look so gay.

MAMÁYEVA. [*Accepting the chair*] Yes, we always try to make people happy, but some people make us extremely unhappy.

GLÚMOV. Unhappy! Whoever does that to you is a criminal. Even to displease you in a trifle a man must have a heart of stone.

MAMÁYEVA. A heart of stone? How right you are!

GLÚMOV. My heart is not of stone, therefore . . .

MAMÁYEVA. What do you mean by "therefore"?

GLÚMOV. Therefore I cannot possibly displease you.

MAMÁYEVA. Do you really expect me to believe that?

GLÚMOV. I want you to believe that.

MAMÁYEVA. I'll do my best.

GLÚMOV. [*Mutters to himself*] She doesn't know. [*Aloud*] How can I displease you! I, a passionate, yet timid, young man, who has so long been praying for some real attachment, who has for so long been yearning for sympathy from some dear womanly heart, whose soul has been pining away in loneliness. With a beating heart, with a terrible longing I have been searching for a woman who would permit me to be her slave. I was ready to worship her as a goddess, I was ready to give my life for her, I was ready to lay at her feet all my hopes and dreams. But I was poor, and shabby and of no account, and women would not even look at me. My prayers, my sighs were all in vain. And then you came and my heart began to beat stronger than ever before. But in you I didn't find a cruel, indifferent beauty, you did not spurn me, you took pity on the unhappy sufferer, you warmed my poor heart by reciprocating my affection, and now I am happy, I am infinitely happy! [*Kisses her hand.*]

MAMÁYEVA. You are about to marry, aren't you?

GLÚMOV. What! No . . . yes . . . no!

MAMÁYEVA. You *are* about to marry?

GLÚMOV. It's your husband who wants to marry me off. I never thought of it. I neither want to marry anyone, nor am I inclined to marry anyone.

MAMÁYEVA. How fond my husband must be of you to wish to make you happy against your will.

GLÚMOV. He wants me to marry for money. I can't always remain a poor scribbler. It's time I became a man of independent means, a man of some importance. It's very natural that your husband should be anxious to do me a good turn. The only thing I regret is that he hasn't consulted me about my feelings.

MAMÁYEVA. For money? But you don't care a bit for your fiancée, do you?

GLÚMOV. Of course, I don't. Could I . . .

MAMÁYEVA. So you're not in love with her?

GLÚMOV. How can I be in love with her? Who should I be deceiving: her—or you?

MAMÁYEVA. Maybe both.

GLÚMOV. Why do you torture me with your suspicions? I suppose, I'd better put an end to it.

MAMÁYEVA. To what?

GLÚMOV. Let my uncle be angry with me as much as he

likes, but I'm going to tell him definitely that I shall not marry that girl.

MAMÁYEVA. Really and truly?

GLÚMOV. Really and truly! I shall tell him so to-day.

MAMÁYEVA. That's the best thing you could do. What kind of marriage will it be, if you don't love her?

GLÚMOV. How could you even doubt me? Aren't you ashamed?

MAMÁYEVA. Now that I see how noble you are, I am, I confess, ashamed.

GLÚMOV. [*Passionately*] I belong to you, to you, to you! But don't say anything to anyone, even to my uncle. I'll arrange everything myself, or you might betray yourself.

MAMÁYEVA. Of course, of course.

GLÚMOV. That's what comes of being shy! I was afraid to tell my uncle straight that I don't want to marry, I merely hinted at my unwillingness. I argued with myself, why be in a hurry, let's first see what comes of it all. And now this has come of it. I gave you cause to suspect me in a mean act. [*The doorbell rings*] Who can that be? Somebody would butt in just now! [*Goes to door.*]

MAMÁYEVA. [*Aside*] He's deceiving me. That's quite clear He wants to pacify me so that I shan't interfere with his plans.

GLÚMOV. Please, go to my mother's room. Someone has come to see me.   [MAMÁYEVA *goes out.* GOLÚTVIN *comes in.*]

GLÚMOV. [*Gives* GOLÚTVIN *a penetrating glance*] Well?

GOLÚTVIN. In the first place, old man, that is not the way to welcome a fellow; in the second, I'm tired because I had to walk all the way to your flat. [*Sits down.*]

GLÚMOV. What do you want?

GOLÚTVIN. Nothing much, old man. A trifle of twenty-five roubles, but, of course, if you can let me have more I shan't refuse it.

GLÚMOV. So that's it! You've come begging to me. Who told you that I could afford to give you such a large sum?

GOLÚTVIN. I haven't come to you to beg, but to ask to be paid for work done.

GLÚMOV. For what work?

Golútvin. I trailed you, watched you, took down all the particulars, all the details of your daily life and now I've written your biography with a portrait attached. I have taken particular pains to describe your more recent adventures. So won't you buy it from me, old man, or will you force me to sell it to a newspaper? As you see, my price is not at all too high. I don't over-estimate my powers, you see.

Glúmov. You can't frighten me. Publish it! Who'll care to read it?

Golútvin. But, old man, I'm not asking you for a thousand roubles. I realize I can't do you much harm, but, nevertheless, I can be deucedly unpleasant. A little scandal can't do you much good, old man. So don't you think that, taking everything into consideration, you'd better pay up?

Glúmov. You know what you're doing, don't you? You know what it's called?

Golútvin. I know perfectly, old man. It's called: ability to make the best use of circumstances.

Glúmov. It's called blackmail!

Golútvin. Is it? Well, whatever you choose to call it, I still believe it's more honest than mailing anonymous letters.

Glúmov. What letters? How can you prove it?

Golútvin. Don't get excited, old man. Take my advice and pay up.

Glúmov. Not a penny.

Golútvin. You're about to marry a rich girl, old man. She might, you know, get hold of the story in the paper and she might be curious enough to want to read it. Being a very nice girl, she will most probably not like it. "Ah, what a scoundrel! . . ." she'll say. So be a good boy and pay up. I shall have something to live on and you'll have a weight off your mind. I'm letting you have it dirt cheap, you know.

Glúmov. Why should I pay? You'd be sure to come again and again. I should never be rid of you.

Golútvin. My word of honour, old man! Who do you take me for?

Glúmov. [*Pointing to the door*] Get out!

Golútvin. But remember, this will appear in to-morrow's issue of the paper.

GLÚMOV. Publish it and be damned!
GOLÚTVIN. I'll accept twenty roubles, old man. It's really dirt cheap.
GLÚMOV. You'll get nothing out of me.
GOLÚTVIN. Very well. You haven't any cigarettes?
GLÚMOV. No. Get out!
GOLÚTVIN. I'm not in a hurry, old man. Let me stretch my legs a little.
GLÚMOV. Did Kurchayev send you here?
GOLÚTVIN. No. I've quarrelled with him. He is a damn fool, too, just like you, old man.
GLÚMOV. Very well. That'll do.
GOLÚTVIN. [*Gets up and peeps behind the door*] Who have you got there, old man?
GLÚMOV. What damn cheek! Clear out of here!
GOLÚTVIN. Very interesting . . .
GLÚMOV. I'm telling you, get out!
GOLÚTVIN. [*Leaving*] You are not a man of honour, old man, you don't even know what honour means!

[*Goes out into hall.*]

GLÚMOV. Here's a nice how-d'you-do! Well, let him publish it.

[*Follows after* GOLÚTVIN.]

GOLÚTVIN. [*Behind the door*] One last word . . .

[GLÚMOV *disappears in the hall and closes the door behind him.* MAMÁYEVA *enters.*]

MAMÁYEVA. All gone. Where is he, I wonder. [*Goes up to desk*] What's this? His diary! [*Reads*] Good heavens! What a beast! How awful! And this about his fiancée. Yes, I knew: he was deceiving me. So this is what he really thinks of me! I don't feel well. I'm going to faint. The cad, the mean cad! [*Wipes her tears. After a little reflection*] That's an idea. He'll never suspect me. [*Hides diary in pocket and retreats from desk*] Oh, how I shall humiliate him! How I shall laugh at his humiliation! When everybody has shaken him off, when he is back in the gutter, he'll crawl back to me like a whipped dog.

[GLÚMOV *returns.*]

GLÚMOV. This is the last straw!
MAMÁYEVA. Who was your visitor?

GLÚMOV. Such people should not be allowed into one's house. He has written a libellous article about me and he came to ask me to buy it from him. Give me money, he threatened, or I'll publish it.
MAMÁYEVA. How dreadful! Why, he's a real highwayman. Who is he, by the way?
GLÚMOV. What do you want to know for?
MAMÁYEVA. To keep out of his way, my sweet, if for nothing else.
GLÚMOV. His name is Golutvin.
MAMÁYEVA. Where does he live?
GLÚMOV. One day here, another day there. You can get his address from his paper, but what do you want it for?
MAMÁYEVA. Well, I could employ him if anyone should offend me. What other revenge can a woman have? She can't fight a duel, can she?
GLÚMOV. Are you joking?
MAMÁYEVA. Of course, I am. Have you given him money?
GLÚMOV. A little. He's quite reasonable. Anything's better than a scandal. Why bring unnecessary trouble upon oneself?
MAMÁYEVA. What would happen if someone should pay him more?
GLÚMOV. Who would? I have no enemies.
MAMÁYEVA. I'm glad you're no longer worried. My poor lamb, how he has upset you! Have you quite made up your mind to jilt your fiancée?
GLÚMOV. Absolutely!
MAMÁYEVA. You realize what you're losing?
GLÚMOV. Money. Shall I exchange paradise for money?
MAMÁYEVA. But there is such a lot of it: two hundred thousand!
GLÚMOV. I know.
MAMÁYEVA. Who would do a thing like that?
GLÚMOV. A man who truly loves.
MAMÁYEVA. But such things just don't happen.
GLÚMOV. Here you have proof that they do.
MAMÁYEVA. You're a hero! A real hero! Your name will go down in history. Come, kiss me. [*Kisses him*] Well, good-bye, darling. I shall be expecting you this evening. [*Goes out.*]

GLÚMOV. [*Alone*] Good riddance! It's time I paid a visit to my fiancée. [*Takes his hat and looks at himself in the mirror*] Of course, all this is a storm in a teacup, but when the business is so risky, you're afraid of your own shadow. I have no claims whatever on my fiancée and certainly none on her money. The whole thing is still very much in the air, it's still too much like a castle in Spain. Everything may blow up any minute and vanish without a trace. No wonder I had to be so careful and so circumspect. Well, now at any rate I have nothing more to fear. I've pacified my aunt and I've paid off Golutvin. So far, so good. [*Hums to himself*] So far, so good, so far, so good. I'm getting so absent-minded with all this worry. Where did I put my hat and my gloves? Ah, there they are. [*Goes up to desk*] Now, my wallet in this pocket, my diary in that . . . [*Rummages on desk with one hand without looking, while putting other hand in back pocket*] My handkerchief is here. [*Turns sharply to desk*] What's this? Where is it? [*Opens a drawer*] Where have I put it? What's happened? Damn it, it can't be! I put it here. I saw it only a short time ago. Good God, where is it? It isn't here. It isn't here . . . [*Stands still*] Everything's going to wrack and ruin. Everything. And I'm hurtling down, down into a bottomless pit. Why the devil did I keep a diary? What heroic deed was I recording in it? Nursing a silly, childish spite, that's what I was doing! What a fool, what a fool! If I had to get mixed up in this kind of business, then what induced me to put it all down in writing? Well, I've made a free gift to the public of "The Memoirs of a Cad: An Autobiography by George Glumov." But why pour scorn upon my own head? Leave it to them all to abuse me. Who could have taken it, though? Was it he or was it she? If he's got it, I'll buy it back from him. He'll be too glad to sell it and things could be straightened out. But what if she's got it? Well, I suppose my eloquence may help. A woman's heart is soft. Yes, it's soft all right, but there is nothing in the world more spiteful than a woman whose pride has been hurt. The mere thought of it appals me. A woman will take a terrible revenge on a man. A woman is capable of an infamy that no man would ever think of. Well it's no use crying over spilt milk. Inaction is dangerous. Forward, into the very jaws of the hyena! [*Goes out.*]

ACT FIVE

[*Large terrace of a country house, a garden straight ahead, doors at either side.*]
　　　　　[KURCHÁYEV *and* MARY *come out of the drawing-room.*]

KURCHÁYEV. Everything's happened so quickly!
MARY. I can hardly understand it myself. It's either a very cleverly contrived plot or else . . .
KURCHÁYEV. A miracle, you were going to say?
MARY. I don't know what to say. My head is just going round and round with amazement.
KURCHÁYEV. I've known him a long time and I haven't noticed anything particular about him. He seems quite a good fellow.
MARY. When he first came, he seemed irresistible. Everybody was on his side. All auntie's friends were in raptures about him, her poor relations dreamt about him every night and whenever they laid out a pack of cards, they were sure to find him in it, the fortune-tellers were all pointing at him, the pilgrim women, too, and, last but not least, Manefa, whom auntie considers almost a saint, having never seen him in her life, described what he looked like and foretold to the minute when we should meet him. What could I do against it? My fate is entirely in auntie's hands and she's quite charmed by him.
KURCHÁYEV. So they'll marry you to him, they'll give him all the money, so virtue will be rewarded and vice punished. You don't seem to have any objections and, as for me, all I can do is to retire in silence. If he'd been anyone else, I should have stood my ground, but, confronted by a virtuous man, I'm absolutely helpless. Quite frankly, virtue is not my speciality.
MARY. Sh-sh . . . They're coming.
　　　[*Enter* TURÚSSINA *and* GLÚMOV. TURÚSSINA *sits down in an arm-chair.* GLÚMOV *stops on her left and places his hand on the back of the arm-chair.* KURCHÁYEV *stands a little further off, to the right, in a very respectful attitude.* MARY *is standing at the table and turning over the pages of a book.*]

GLÚMOV. When I felt the call for married life, I considered the question very seriously for a while. To marry for money is against my rules, it is too much like a business deal and not at all like holy matrimony. To marry for love . . . But isn't love a passing, nay, even a carnal impulse? I realized that in the choice of a partner for my whole life, there must be something special, something sanctioned by fate, and that only then would it become a true marriage. I had to find a responsive woman's heart and bind it to mine with unbreakable bonds. I said: "Fate, you find me that heart, I am ready to submit to your choice!" I confess I waited for a miracle! There is much that is miraculous in the world, only we don't want to see it.

TURÚSSINA. I am enirely of your opinion, but not everybody shares it with me. [*Looks in the direction of* KURCHÁYEV, *who bows.*]

GLÚMOV. I waited for a miracle and I lived to see one.

TURÚSSINA. Really? You lived to see one. How marvellous!

GLÚMOV. I went to see a devout woman.

KURCHÁYEV. Not Manefa, by any chance?

GLÚMOV. No, not Manefa, someone else. As soon as I entered, I had not time to say a single word, when she, even without seeing my face—she sat with her back to me—said: "It is not you who are looking for brides, it is they who are looking for you. Go ahead blindfold and you'll find what you're looking for." Where shall I go, I asked, show me the way. "When you enter the first strange house where you've never been before," she said, "there you must seek, there they know you." I was quite astonished at first and couldn't bring myself to believe her. She had told me that in the morning and in the evening of the same day my uncle brought me to your house. Here there was the bride waiting for me and here they knew me.

TURÚSSINA. Yes, the world is full of miracles, but there are only a few chosen ones.

KURCHÁYEV. When my regiment was quartered in the Ukraine, I, too, had a similar experience with a Jew . . .

TURÚSSINA. I think you'd better have a stroll round the garden. [KURCHÁYEV *bows.*]

GLÚMOV. This is quite a clear case of predestination. I even haven't had time to find out from my fiancée what her feelings towards me are. [*To* MARY] Please, forgive me. I was satisfied merely with her consent.

TURÚSSINA. What else do you want?

GLÚMOV. If, perhaps, she doesn't quite like me now, she may like me better later.

KURCHÁYEV. Absolutely.

GLÚMOV. Since the hand of man had nothing to do with this marriage, nothing can go wrong with it.

TURÚSSINA. Excellent rule! You're the man to teach us how to live! [*Enter* GRIGÓRY.]

GRIGÓRY. Mr. Gorodúlin, ma'am.

TURÚSSINA. I'll go in to put something warmer on, it's getting chilly.

[*Goes into the house.*]

MARY. [*To* KURCHÁYEV] Let's go for a walk in the garden.

[*They walk off.*]

[GORODÚLIN *enters.*]

GORODÚLIN. Ah, good evening. How much money are you getting?

GLÚMOV. Two hundred thousand, I believe.

GORODÚLIN. How did you do it?

GLÚMOV. Didn't you recommend me yourself? Mrs. Turussina told me so.

GORODÚLIN. Me? When? Ah, yes, yes. I remember. But how did you manage to get into the old girl's good books? Aren't you an atheist?

GLÚMOV. I don't argue with her.

GORODÚLIN. And when she talks through her hat?

GLÚMOV. It is impossible to cure her, so why try?

GORODÚLIN. Ah, so that's your policy? Very good, very good, indeed. You'll soon be the owner of a fortune. I'll be able to make you a member of my club.

GLÚMOV. [*Softly*] Krutitzky's treatise will soon come out.

GORODÚLIN. Really? Now, if only we could tear it to shreds!

GLÚMOV. It's easily done.

GORODÚLIN. I don't doubt you could do it, but I don't think it's quite safe for you. You are still a young man and it may harm your career. We'll have to keep you in the background. I'll tell you what: you write a critique of the treatise and, so be it, I'll stake my reputation on it and publish it under my own name! It's high time we gave the old brigade a good trouncing.

GLÚMOV. It's high time we did. You've only to consider the kind of stuff they write.

GORODÚLIN. Yes, they must be shown up. I should have done it myself, only I have no time. I'm very glad you've struck oil. Accept my sincere congratulations. We need men like you, we need them badly. There is no lack of men of action, but we have no one who can speak up. The old brigade may launch a surprise attack against us and then Heaven help us. There is quite a number of brainy chaps among the younger generation, but, unfortunately, they're a bit too young. You can't rope them in for a debate, the old ones will not even talk to them. We have, that is, a choir, but we have no soloist to lead it. You'll be our soloist and we shall do our darnedest to keep in tune with you. Where is Mary?

GLÚMOV. In the garden.

GORODÚLIN. I'll go and say something to her.

[*Goes into the garden.*]

GLÚMOV. [*Shouts after him*] I'll join you in a minute! I believe the Mamayevs have arrived. How I got round her! Not only has she given her consent to my marriage, but she's come here herself. That's very sweet of her.

[MAMÁYEVA *enters.*]

MAMÁYEVA. Well, have you found it?

GLÚMOV. No. Golutvin swears his head off that he did not take it. He even bursts into tears. I'd rather starve, he says, than be guilty of such a mean trick.

MAMÁYEVA. Who could have taken it? Perhaps you lost it somewhere?

GLÚMOV. I've no idea.

MAMÁYEVA. I suppose someone will pick it up and throw it away.

GLÚMOV. I hope so.

MAMÁYEVA. But what are you so afraid of? Was there anything in it?

GLÚMOV. Nothing in particular. Soul-stirring avowals, declarations of love, passionate tirades, verses to a pair of sparkling eyes and a head of raven tresses. Everything, in fact, that a man, in a moment of folly, might confide to his diary, but which he'd rather die than show to a stranger.

MAMÁYEVA. So your diary is full of sparkling eyes and raven tresses? In that case you needn't be upset: no one will pay the slightest attention to it. There are hundreds of such diaries about. Why are you here alone? Where's your fiancée?

GLÚMOV. Strolling in the garden with young men. There's proof for you that I'm not marrying for love. I want money, a position in society. I can't go on for ever being a nice young man. I want to become a man of means. You'll see what a fine figure I'll cut, what horses I'll own. No one notices me now, but soon everybody will be saying: "Look, what a strikingly handsome man that is! Where has he dropped from?" As though I had only just arrived from America or something. And everybody will envy you, darling.

MAMÁYEVA. Why me?

GLÚMOV. Because I'm yours.

MAMÁYEVA. Well, yes . . . if you could get the money without the girl, but, as it is, you'll have a young wife.

GLÚMOV. That doesn't matter, I offer my hand to my fiancée, my pocket to the money and my heart to you.

MAMÁYEVA. You're a dangerous man. If I listen to you a little longer, I shall believe you.

GLÚMOV. Wait till you see the thoroughbreds drawing my carriage up to your door!

MAMÁYEVA. I can hardly wait. But now you'd better go to your fiancée. You ought not to leave her. Even if you're not in love with her, you'd better be nice to her just for the sake of appearances and good manners.

GLÚMOV. There, you're sending me to her yourself.

MAMÁYEVA. Go on, go on.

[GLÚMOV *goes*.]

How he triumphs! Wait, my friend, your joy may be short-lived!

[*Enter* KURCHÁYEV.]

Where are you off to?
KURCHÁYEV. Home.
MAMÁYEVA. Home? And so sad? Wait! I understand. [KURCHÁYEV bows] Wait, I tell you. Don't be such a naughty boy! Don't be in such a hurry. I want to talk to you. [KURCHÁYEV bows and stays] Are you in love? [KURCHÁYEV bows and turns to go] Don't you know anything?
KURCHÁYEV. Permit me to leave you.
MAMÁYEVA. I shall go home early and alone, you can accompany me. [KURCHÁYEV bows] What are so you silent for? Be frank with me. I entreat you as your aunt. You're in love, aren't you? But is she in love with you? Answer me! [KURCHÁYEV bows] I'm sure she is. Don't give up. All sorts of unexpected surprises might develop.
KURCHÁYEV. In any case, I could . . .
MAMÁYEVA. But what about Turussina?
KURCHÁYEV. She's putting forward such demands . . .
MAMÁYEVA. What demands?
KURCHÁYEV. I really couldn't expect it. Besides, it cannot be reconciled with the army rules and regulations.
MAMÁYEVA. What cannot be reconciled?
KURCHÁYEV. My education, too, is hardly up to the mark.
MAMÁYEVA. I don't know what you're talking about.
KURCHÁYEV. Mrs. Turussina wants her niece to marry a . . .
MAMÁYEVA. Well?
KURCHÁYEV. How was I to expect that? It hardly ever happens . . .
MAMÁYEVA. What? What?
KURCHÁYEV. I never heard of it.
MAMÁYEVA. Do explain yourself!
KURCHÁYEV. She is looking for a virtuous man.
MAMÁYEVA. Well, what about it?
KURCHÁYEV. I possess no virtues whatever.
MAMÁYEVA. None at all? How awful! Do you mean you have only vices?
KURCHÁYEV. I have no vices, either. I'm just an ordinary man. This search for a virtuous man is very strange. Suppose Glumov had not existed, where would she have found one? In the whole of Moscow there is only Glumov to whom

miracles happen. He is the only man in town who sees visions. Tell me how can such things be expected of everyone?

MAMÁYEVA. Don't give up hope, it may turn out to be better to have had neither virtues nor vices.

[*Enter* MARY *from garden, followed by* TURÚSSINA, MAMÁYEV *and* KRUTÍTZKY.]

MAMÁYEVA. [*To* MARY] Accept my congratulations! You're getting prettier every day. I'm glad to see you looking so happy.

MARY. Mr. Glumov possesses so many good qualities that I'm getting scared. I fear I don't deserve such a husband.

MAMÁYEVA. Where else is one to look for virtue except in your house? Take an example from your aunt. She, I'm sure, will always tell you the right thing to do.

MARY. I am very grateful to her. It's true that it is good to be virtuous, but of all the virtues I only possess one: obedience.

[TURÚSSINA, MAMÁYEV *and* KRUTÍTZKY *enter*.]

MAMÁYEV. [*To* KRUTÍTZKY] I agree with you on principle, but not on the details.

KRUTÍTZKY. Why not on the details?

MAMÁYEV. Why only tragedy and not comedy?

KRUTÍTZKY. Because comedy shows up the mean side of human nature and tragedy its sublime side, and it is the sublime, my dear sir, that we most need.

MAMÁYEV. Yes, yes, but wait a bit. Let's consider it in more detail.

[*They retire to the background.*]

TURÚSSINA. [*To* MAMÁYEVA] It is now the fashion to believe in nothing. People say to me, why do you employ Manefa? she's a cheat! Well, I'd gladly invite these sceptics to see for themselves whether Manefa is a cheat or not. I'm so glad for her, now she's sure to become the rage of Moscow, she's sure to get many clients. Moscow should be grateful to me for having discovered such a woman. I've done a lot for Moscow by my discovery.

MAMÁYEVA. But where is the bridegroom? I can't see him.

TURÚSSINA. Mary, where's George?

MARY. He's in the garden with Gorodulin.

TURÚSSINA. From the recommendations of my friends and for other reasons I expected to meet a model young man, but, having got to know George more intimately, I must confess that he has surpassed all my expectations.

MAMÁYEV. [*Walks up*] Who has surpassed all your expectations?

TURÚSSINA. Your nephew.

MAMÁYEV. I knew you'd be grateful to me for him. I knew what you wanted. I never thought of another fiancée for him. I came straight to you.

KRUTÍTZKY. Yes, Glumov will go far.

MAMÁYEV. With our help, of course.

[*Enter* GRIGÓRY.]

TURÚSSINA. I don't know why such grace has been vouchsafed to me? Is it for my . . . [*To* GRIGÓRY] What do you want? Is it for my acts of kindness? [GRIGÓRY *hands her an envelope*] What is it? [*Opens it*] A newspaper? It can't be for me.

MAMÁYEVA. [*Taking the envelope*] It is for you. Here's your name and address.

TURÚSSINA. It must be a mistake. Who brought it?

GRIGÓRY. The postman, ma'am.

TURÚSSINA. Where is he?

GRIGÓRY. He's gone, ma'am.

MAMÁYEV. Let me have a look at it. I'll explain it to you. [*Takes envelope and produces printed sheet from it*] In the first place, this is a newspaper, or rather not a newspaper, but a page torn out of a newspaper with only one article on it.

TURÚSSINA. Have they sent it to me from the paper?

MAMÁYEV. No, no. Some of your friends must have posted it on to you.

TURÚSSINA. What is it all about?

MAMÁYEV. Now, let's see. The article is headed, "How to make a career."

TURÚSSINA. We're not interested in that. Throw it away.

MAMÁYEV. But why? Let's see. Here's a picture with an inscription: "The Perfect Husband." Hullo! Why, it's our George!

MAMÁYEVA. Give it to me! This is interesting!

[MAMÁYEV *gives paper to his wife.*]

TURÚSSINA. This must be some mean intrigue. He probably has many enemies.

[MAMÁYEV *throws a sidelong glance at* KURCHÁYEV.]

KURCHÁYEV. Are you suspecting me? I'm no good at drawing portraits at all. I can only get your likeness, uncle.

MAMÁYEV. [*Severely*] I know, I know.

MAMÁYEVA. Whoever wrote this article must know George very well: here are the smallest details of his life. They may have been invented, of course.

MAMÁYEV. [*Takes out notebook from the envelope*] Here's something else.

KRUTÍTZKY. That's his handwriting! I know it. It's his! It's his! I'm ready to take an oath on it.

MAMÁYEV. Yes, it's his hand all right, and here is something in another hand: "This diary is enclosed as proof that all the facts in the article are true." Well, what shall we read first, the article or the diary?

KRUTÍTZKY. We'd better have the original.

MAMÁYEV. Let's start with the page which has been turned down. It's a money account. "To Manefa twenty-five roubles, also another twenty-five roubles. . . . What a damn fool she is and yet she's a professional fortune-teller. Wasted hours with her till I got everything into her silly head to my satisfaction. Also sent her: a bottle of rum. Further, another fifteen roubles, given at my house. . . . It's a pity that such fools take up so profitable a business. I should like to know what she picks up at Turussina's. I must ask her later. To the two poor female relations of Turussina for telling fortunes by cards and recounting their dreams in which they see me every night, seven roubles and a quarter and a silver snuff-box each, at ten roubles the two."

TURÚSSINA. [*Inhaling smelling salts*] I'll send them all packing, all of them. To be bad may be a sin, but to be good is just sheer folly! How is one to carry on after that!

MAMÁYEVA. Don't protest so much, you're not the only one to be cheated.

MAMÁYEV. "For three anonymous letters to Turussina, fifteen copecks . . ."

MARY. So that's where those letters came from, auntie.

TURÚSSINA. I see, my dear. You must forgive me. I've made a bad mistake to have taken it upon myself to order your life for you. I can see now that I have neither the strength nor the ability to do it. In future, do as you please, my dear. I shan't interfere with you any more.

MARY. [*Softly*] My choice is already made, auntie.

TURÚSSINA. Very well. At least you won't be disappointed in him because he doesn't promise anything good. [KURCHÁYEV *bows*] But I'll certainly send those poor relations of mine packing.

KRUTÍTZKY. And will you get some others to replace them?

TURÚSSINA. I'm not sure.

MAMÁYEV. Shall I continue?

TURÚSSINA. By all means, it makes no difference to me any more.

MAMÁYEV. "To Mamayev's servant, for having brought his master to my place by deceit, taking advantage of his well-known weakness for flat-hunting—to this great benefactor of mine—three roubles. Very little, indeed." There follows his conversation with me. It's . . . It will hardly interest any of you. "The first visit to Krutitzky. Oh, Muse, let me sing this man of noble mind and his projects. It is impossible to admire thee too much, thou Ancient of Days. Reveal to us, reveal to the whole world how it is that you've lived to the ripe age of sixty and preserved unsullied the mind of a child of six?"

KRUTÍTZKY. Enough of that! It's a lampoon. Who cares for this sort of thing?

[*Enter* GORODÚLIN.]

MAMÁYEV. [*Not noticing* GORODÚLIN] Here's something about Gorodulin. "A certain gentleman had a silly quarrel with Gorodulin about some horses and, in the heat of the argument, he called Gorodulin a Liberal. Gorodulin was so overjoyed that for the next three days he went all over Moscow telling everybody that he was a Liberal. Since then that label has stuck to him." It's probably true.

KRUTÍTZKY. True? You'd better let us hear about yourself. We should like to know if that's true, too?

GORODÚLIN. So you think it's true, do you?

MAMÁYEV. How d'you do? I didn't notice you. Look, how we've all been written up here!
GORODÚLIN. Who is this modern Juvenal?
MAMÁYEV. Why, it's my nephew, Glumov!
TURÚSSINA. [*To* GORODÚLIN] Give this diary back to its author and tell him to leave my house as inconspicuously as possible.

[GLÚMOV *enters*. GORODÚLIN *hands him the diary with a bow*.]

GLÚMOV. [*Accepting diary*] Why inconspicuously? I shan't even attempt either to explain or to justify myself. I want merely to tell you that soon it will be you who will be sorry for having expelled me from your midst.
KRUTÍTZKY. Sir, none but honest men are privileged to be members of our society.
ALL. Hear, hear!
GLÚMOV. [*To* KRUTÍTZKY] And did it occur to you, sir, that I wasn't an honest man? Did you, sir, with your penetrating mind believe that I was dishonest when you asked me to re-write your treatise? For what qualified man would have undertaken such work? Or did you become convinced of my dishonesty when in your study I so cringingly extolled the most absurd of your phrases and humbled myself in the dust before you? No, then you were ready to do anything for me! And if you had not come across this wretched diary, you would have continued to account me an honest man.
KRUTÍTZKY. That may be true, but . . .
GLÚMOV. [*To* MAMÁYEV] And did it occur to you, too, uncle? When? When you instructed me to flatter Krutitzky? Or was it when you taught me to make love to your wife, so that she shouldn't run astray with someone else, when I hoaxed you and played the fool with you, pretending that I didn't even know how to make love to a woman and that my conscience did not permit me to indulge in such deceit? You knew that I was pretending, but you liked it nevertheless, for didn't I present you with such a lovely opportunity to teach me the ways of the world? I am far cleverer than you and you know it, but whenever I pretend to be a half-wit and begin to ask you for all kinds of advice, you are ready to jump out of

your skin with joy, you'd do anything for me then, you'd even take an oath that I am the most honest man in the world.

MAMÁYEV. Why should I bother whether you're honest or not? Don't we belong to the same family?

GLÚMOV. [*To* TURÚSSINA] You, madam, I have really deceived, and I apologize. But I am not sorry for you, but for Mary, because you deserve to be deceived. You pick up some tipsy peasant woman in the street and, trusting her word, obediently choose a husband for your niece. Who does your Manefa know, who can she know? Obviously, she only knows the man who pays her to deceive you. It's a good thing that it was I who got hold of her. She could have forced some convict on you and your niece and you would have married your niece to him.

TURÚSSINA. All I know is that there is no truth in the world. Every day I'm getting more and more convinced of that.

GLÚMOV. And what about you, Mr. Gorodulin?

GORODÚLIN. I say no word against you, I still think you're wonderful. Here, let's shake hands. Everything you said about us, that is to say, about myself, I don't want to speak of the others, is absolutely true.

GLÚMOV. You all need me, gentlemen. You can't live without me. If it's not me, then it will be someone else like me. Or you may even find someone worse than me and, then, you will be saying, "Well, this fellow may be worse than Glumov, but he's not so bad." [*To* KRUTÍTZKY] You, sir, are what is known in the world as a man who believes in the maxim of live and let live, yet, when alone in your study with you, a young man stands meekly to attention and, humbly agreeing with every word you say, keeps on calling you "sir," you seem to like it very much. You would never dream of coming to the assistance of a really honest man, but you would do anything for a man who flatters you, you would fall over yourself to get such a man a good job.

KRUTÍTZKY. I am very much afraid you put a wrong interpretation on our condescension.

GLÚMOV. Pardon me, sir, but I am doing nothing of the

sort. [*To* MAMÁYEV] You, too, can't do without me, uncle. Even your paid servants refuse to listen to your sermons, while I am ready to listen to them for nothing.

MAMÁYEV. That'll do. My dear fellow, if you don't understand how improper it is for you to remain here any longer, then let me explain it to you . . .

GLÚMOV. I understand. [*To* GORODÚLIN] And you, too, need my help . . .

GORODÚLIN. I do, I do.

GLÚMOV. . . . to get some clever phrases for your public speeches . . .

GORODÚLIN. Clever phrases for my public speeches.

GLÚMOV. . . . and to review a book for you.

GORODÚLIN. And to review a book for me.

GLÚMOV. You, auntie, too, need me,

MAMÁYEVA. I don't deny it. I am not accusing you of anything.

KRUTÍTZKY. [*To* MAMÁYEV] You know, I noticed something at once. There was something in . . .

MAMÁYEV. I, too. There was something in his eyes.

GLÚMOV. You didn't notice anything, either of you. You feel hurt because of what I said about you in my diary. I don't know how you got hold of it, but even a wise man occasionally stumbles. I want you to realize, ladies and gentlemen, that while I was in your company I was honest only when I was writing my diary. And no honest man can think of you any differently. You have stirred up my bile. What was it that particularly affronted you in my diary? Have you discovered anything new in it? You say the same thing about each other yourselves, but only behind one another's backs. Had I read out to each of you in turn what I said in my diary about the rest of you, every one would have applauded me. If anyone has a right to be hurt, to be angry, to fly into a passion and scream with indignation, it's me! I don't know who, but one of you, ladies and gentlemen, and you are all such honest people, stole my diary. You wrecked all my plans, you not only robbed me of a fortune, you also robbed me of my reputation. You are now ostracizing me and you think this will be the end of me, you think that I'll bear you no grudge.

No, ladies and gentlemen, I shall pay you back to the last penny! Good-bye.

[*He goes out.*]
[*There is a long pause.*]

KRUTÍTZKY. Whatever you say, ladies and gentlemen, we must admit that he is a man of parts. He has to be punished, no doubt, but I think that after a little while we can restore him to favour.

GORODÚLIN. Certainly.

MAMÁYEV. I quite agree.

MAMÁYEVA. Leave it to me!

CURTAIN

EASY MONEY

A Comedy in Five Acts

(After Shakespeare's "The Taming of the Shrew")

By
ALEXANDER OSTROVSKY

Translated by
DAVID MAGARSHACK

CHARACTERS

Savva Gennaditch Vassilkóv, a provincial business man, aged 35. Speaks with a strong provincial accent, also dresses provincially.

Ivan Petrovich Telyátev (Johnnie), a man about town, aged 40.

Grigóry Borissovich Kuchúmov, aged 60, a very imposing gentleman, a retired civil servant of low rank, has many titled relations on his mother's side and by marriage.

Yegor Dimitrich Glúmov (George).

Nadezhda Antonovna Cheboksárova, an elderly lady of imposing manners.

Lydia Yuryevna Cheboksárova, her daughter, aged 24

Andrey,. Cheboksárov's footman.

Grigóry, Telyátev's footman.

Nicholas, Kuchúmov's footman.

Vassily, Vassilkóv's valet.

Maid.

A boy from the café.

Park strollers.

ACT ONE

(In place of a Prologue)

[*The Sax Gardens, part of the Petrovsky Park in Moscow. To the right of the spectators—gates into the Park, to the left—a café.* STROLLERS *pass over the stage, stop, read the notices on the gates, and walk on.* TELYÁTEV *and* VASSILKÓV *come out of the café.*]

TELYÁTEV. [*Chewing something*] Yes, yes, old fellow, of course . . . [*Aside*] I wish I could shake him off!

VASSILKÓV. What I mean is that, being such a pretty girl, everybody naturally finds her very attractive.

TELYÁTEV. You never said a truer word in your life, old fellow, or a more self-evident one. I must congratulate you on this remarkable discovery. It is, if you don't mind, my saying so, as plain as the nose on your face. [*Takes off hat and bows*] To say that Lydia is beautiful is the same as saying that twice two is four. Hasn't that occurred to you yet?

VASSILKÓV. What I wanted to say was that I liked her very much.

TELYÁTEV. Upon my word, old fellow, that sounds even dafter. Who doesn't like her? Good God, do you think I care a damn whether *you* like her or not? You're quite a stranger here, I suppose?

VASSILKÓV. Yes, I'm not from these parts.

TELYÁTEV. Now, I should have been surprised if you told me that she liked you. That would have been something to write home about! But that you like her is not such a sensation. I know fifteen men, all grown-up and highly presentable, who are head over ears in love with her and there are scores of schoolboys who are in the same boat. They simply swarm round her, crowds of them, with eyes popping out of their heads. Do you know what I should advise you? Just for a change try to get her to like you.

VASSILKÓV. But is it really so very difficult?

TELYÁTEV. Try it, old fellow, try it and see how far you get.

VASSILKÓV. How do I set about it? What qualities must I possess?

TELYÁTEV. Such as neither you nor I have got.

VASSILKÓV. For instance?

TELYÁTEV. To begin with, half a million or thereabouts.

VASSILKÓV. That's nothing.

TELYÁTEV. Nothing? Since when have millions begun to pop out of the ground like mushrooms? Of course, if you are a relation of the Rothschilds, it's a different matter, then we needn't waste any words on it.

VASSILKÓV. Neither the one nor the other, I'm sorry to say, but we live in a time when people with a lot of brains . . .

TELYÁTEV. Ah, there you are, old fellow, with brains and a lot of them, too! This means that you have to have brains in the first place, but brainy chaps are as rare among us as millionaires, and I suppose a damn sight rarer than that. But we'd better quit talking about brains, for if any of my friends should happen to overhear us, they'd laugh their heads off. To hell with brains, then. Who are we to talk of brains, if the good Lord hasn't given us any?

VASSILKÓV. No, sir. I, for one, refuse to renounce my claim to brains so easily. But what else ought a man to possess to make a good impression on her?

TELYÁTEV. The handsome uniform of a Guards officer not below the rank of a colonel at least and the manners of a perfect gentleman, which I'm very much afraid it is quite impossible for you to acquire.

VASSILKÓV. That's very strange. Is there nothing else, no other qualities of mind and heart, by which one could win the affection of that girl?

TELYÁTEV. But how do you expect her to find out these precious qualities of mind and heart of yours? Will you write a book on astronomy and read it to her?

VASSILKÓV. I'm sorry, I'm very sorry indeed that she is so unapproachable.

TELYÁTEV. Why be so very sorry about that?

VASSILKÓV. I'll be quite frank with you. Because I'm engaged in a certain line of business where I simply must have such a wife, I mean, one as beautiful as Lydia and as well bred as she.

TELYÁTEV. There is no must about it, old fellow. You'd better tell me something else: are you very rich or what?
VASSILKÓV. Not yet.
TELYÁTEV. That means that you hope to get rich.
VASSILKÓV. At the present day . . .
TELYÁTEV. Leave the present day out of it.
VASSILKÓV. But why should I? I firmly believe that at the present day it is very easy to get rich.
TELYÁTEV. Well, that depends, old fellow, that depends . . . Tell me, have you anything in the nature of a dead cert at the moment? Don't be afraid, I shan't rob you.
VASSILKÓV. I'm quite sure *you* won't rob me. The only certain source of income I possess is an estate and some woods to the total value of some fifty thousand.
TELYÁTEV. That's not bad, not bad at all. In Moscow with fifty thousand you could easily raise another hundred thousand on credit, which means that you have a sure one hundred and fifty thousand. On so much money you can live a long time very pleasantly.
VASSILKÓV. But you have to pay it back one day, you know.
TELYÁTEV. Why trouble your head about that, old fellow? Why be so over-conscientious? Do you like to have something to worry about? Can't you live without a worry in your head? Let your creditors worry, let them rack their brains how to get their money back. Why should you interfere in somebody else's business? It's our business to borrow, theirs to lend and get their money back.
VASSILKÓV. I'm afraid I don't know anything about that. I've never had anything to do with that kind of financial operation. My business transactions are based on different principles.
TELYÁTEV. You're still young, the time will come when you'll be glad to adopt our principles.
VASSILKÓV. I doubt it. However, I should like you to introduce me to Lydia and her mother. Although I don't seem to stand much of a chance with her, hope springs eternal, you know. Ever since I saw her for the first time about a week ago, I can't get her out of my head. I even found out where they lived and took an apartment in the same house

to make sure that I should see her more often. I admit that for a steady business man of my age it's rather ridiculous to fall in love, but, I'm afraid, I can't do anything about it. Where love is concerned, sir, I am only a boy. Please, introduce me to her, I beg of you.

TELYÁTEV. Why not? It'll be a pleasure, I assure you.

VASSILKÓV. [*Pressing his hand firmly*] Thank you, sir. If I can be of any assistance to you in anything . . .

TELYÁTEV. A bottle of champagne every now and then, old fellow, that's all. I don't take any other bribes. So it's a deal?

VASSILKÓV. Any time you like, sir. [*Grips his hand*] You don't know how grateful I am to you!

TELYÁTEV. Please, please, my hand! Good God, what an iron grip you have!

VASSILKÓV. [*Looking round without releasing his hand*] Isn't it them?

TELYÁTEV. It's them. It's them.

VASSILKÓV. I'll go nearer and have a good look at her. You know, I'm such a sentimental bloke! You probably think me funny . . .

TELYÁTEV. But don't take my hand away with you, old fellow, please, leave me my hand!

VASSILKÓV. I beg your pardon, sir. I hope to find you here again.

TELYÁTEV. To be sure, old fellow.

[VASSILKÓV *hurries off*, GLÚMOV *comes in.*]

GLÚMOV. Who was the funny old boy with you just now?

TELYÁTEV. That's what the good God has sent to plague me with for my sins.

GLÚMOV. What do you get out of it?

TELYÁTEV. Stands me drinks. One bottle of champagne after another.

GLÚMOV. That's not too bad.

TELYÁTEV. I'll lead him on and on and one fine morning I'll probably touch him for a thousand or so.

GLÚMOV. That's even better, if, that is, he really does give you something.

TELYÁTEV. I think he will. You see, he needs me.

GLÚMOV. Cut it out, old man, do me the favour! Who on earth can possibly need you for anything?
TELYÁTEV. You'd better listen to me.
GLÚMOV. All right, I'm listening.
TELYÁTEV. I met him for the first time here in the park about a week ago. I was walking along that path when I suddenly saw a man standing there with his mouth gaping, his eyes wide-open and his hat on the back of his head. I must say, old fellow, I couldn't help wondering what had caught the old boy's fancy. There was no elephant about or any cockfighting. I got nearer and what do you think he was staring at? Have a guess, old fellow.
GLÚMOV. Search me. What kind of a wonder can one see in a public park?
TELYÁTEV. He was staring at sweet Lydia!
GLÚMOV. He certainly knows a good thing when he sees one.
TELYÁTEV. Lydia and her mamma were in their carriage, round them was the usual crowd of young fellows, both of them were talking to someone, I don't know to whom, and there he was, some distance away, simply devouring Lydia with his eyes. As soon as their carriage moved on, he made a rush after it, knocking over half a dozen people in his path, including myself. He apologized, of course, and that's how we got acquainted.
GLÚMOV. Let me congratulate you, old man.
TELYÁTEV. And to-day, just think of it, he saw me talking to Lydia and her mum and he almost took me by the scruff of the neck, fairly dragged me in here and began treating me to champagne, one bottle, then another. We had quite a little celebration. And it was only a few minutes ago that he confessed to me that he was in love with Lydia and wanted to marry her. You see, old fellow, his business—and what his business may be I'm damned if I know—requires that he should marry just such a girl as Lydia and no other. Well, of course, he implored me to introduce him to her.
GLÚMOV. The old idiot! What infernal cheek! Arrives here from Kamchatka or some other such remote hole and makes straight for one of Moscow's loveliest girls. For, his business,

you see, absolutely demands that he should marry her! His business, if you please, demands it! My business demands that I should marry an heiress, but I'm damned if I can get one to marry me. But he . . . What kind of a bird does he think he is? What is his business, by the way?

TELYÁTEV. Allah alone knows that, old fellow.

GLÚMOV. Tell me what his speech and manners are like and I'll tell you at once what his business is.

TELYÁTEV. I bet you anything, you won't. He is a man of good birth, but speaks like a Volga boatman.

GLÚMOV. He's the owner of a steamship line, he runs his steamers on the Volga.

TELYÁTEV. When he settled the bill for the drinks, he took out a wallet, you'll hardly believe me, old fellow, so big [*shows with his his hands how big*], about a foot at least. And you should have seen what was in that wallet! All sorts of shares, balance sheets in foreign languages, greasy letters written on greyish paper by a peasant's hand.

GLÚMOV. Is he rich?

TELYÁTEV. Hardly, old fellow, hardly rich. He says he owns a small estate and some woods worth altogether fifty thousand.

GLÚMOV. Hm . . . Nothing sensational. Sorry, but he is not the managing director of a steamship line after all.

TELYÁTEV. He is not rich, or else he's damned stingy. As soon as he'd paid for the drinks, he entered it in a note-book!

GLÚMOV. Is he a clerk by any chance? What's his character like? What kind of man is he?

TELYÁTEV. A very ingenuous chap, as coy as a boarding-school girl.

GLÚMOV. Ingenuous? He isn't a cardsharper, is he?

TELYÁTEV. Can't say, old fellow, impossible to tell. But he drinks like a fish: empties one glass after another, unflustered and unhurried, as if it were ginger pop. We had a bottle each and his face didn't even colour or his voice crack.

GLÚMOV. Must be a native of Siberia. Yes, quite certainly a native of Siberia.

TELYÁTEV. Smokes expensive cigars, speaks excellent French, though with a slight accent.

GLÚMOV. I've got it! He is a representative of some London firm. No doubt about it!
TELYÁTEV. Have it your own way, old fellow. I give it up.
GLÚMOV. Well, whoever he is, let's have some fun with him. We haven't had a good laugh for a long time and we all seem to be going about like poodles with our tongues hanging out.
TELYÁTEV. The joke may be on us, you know.
GLÚMOV. Not at all. We're going to be the villains in this melodrama, at least I am. This is what we'll do: you'll introduce the old boy to Lydia and I'll tell her mother that he owns goldmines. We'll have good sport watching her spread out the net for him.
TELYÁTEV. But when they find out that it's all a practical joke and that all he owns is some silly little estate in some God-forsaken hole . . .
GLÚMOV. What do we care? We'll say that he told us about his goldmines himself, that he boasted to us about them.
TELYÁTEV. But, really, old fellow, it seems a poor kind of a joke to me!
GLÚMOV. Are you sorry for him or what? Don't be such an ass. We'll say he doesn't gather gold ingots in his mines, but only blackberries in his woods.

[VASSILKÓV *comes up.*]

TELYÁTEV. Well, old fellow, have you gazed your fill on your beauty?
VASSILKÓV. To my entire satisfaction!
TELYÁTEV. Let me introduce to you a pal of mine, George Glumov—Savva Vassilkov.
VASSILKÓV. [*Clasps* GLÚMOV's *hand in his iron grip*] How do you do? Very pleased to meet you, sir.
GLÚMOV. [*Disengaging his hand and shaking it*] But I am not pleased at all to have my hand crushed, old man.
VASSILKÓV. I'm sorry, it's a bad provincial habit of mine.
GLÚMOV. Is your name really Savva, sir? Is it the same as Sabbatai?
VASSILKÓV. [*Very courteously*] No, sir. It's quite a different name.
GLÚMOV. Is it the same as Sebastian?

Vassilkóv. No, sir. Sebastian is really a Greek name, meaning, worthy of honour, but Savva is an Arab name.

Telyátev. Do you know Greek, old fellow?

Vassilkóv. A little.

Telyátev. And Tartar?

Vassilkóv. I can follow a conversation in Tartar if spoken in the Kazan dialect, but in the Crimea I could hardly make myself understood.

Glúmov. [*Aside*] Damn it, can't make him out at all.

Telyátev. Is it long since you left the Crimea, old fellow?

Vassilkóv. Ten days or so. I stopped there on my way back from England.

Glúmov. [*Aside*] The damn liar!

Telyátev. Do you usually go to the Crimea via England?

Vassilkóv. No, I was in England and I came back via the Suez Canal. I was interested in the construction works and the different engineering plants in the Canal zone.

Glúmov. [*Aside*] Maybe he isn't such a liar, after all. [*To Vassilkóv*] We've just been talking of matches, sir. I don't mean those you burn your fingers on, but those which, according to popular belief, are made in heaven.

Vassilkóv. I heartily approve of the subject, sir.

Glúmov. I'd like to marry Lydia Cheboksarova myself, old man.

Vassilkóv. Many folks would like to do the same, I daresay, she's such a picture!

Glúmov. But the many are fools, old man. They hardly know themselves why they want to marry her. They admire her beauty and they want to have it for their own exclusive enjoyment, they want to put it away like frozen capital. No, sir, beauty is not frozen capital. It ought to yield interest. Only a fool can marry Lydia without some ulterior motive. The man who should marry her ought to be either a cardsharper or one who is out to make a brilliant career for himself. The cardsharper could use her to attract custom, inexperienced youths with money to waste, and the man who wants to get on in the Civil Service could use her as a bait for his superiors and as a means to quick promotion.

Vassilkóv. I don't agree with you, sir.

GLÚMOV. That's the only sensible view to take, old man. It's the modern view on life, completely up-to-date.
VASSILKÓV. I still don't agree.
GLÚMOV. All this mawkish talk about virtue being its own reward is damn silly. And why, sir? Because it's so unpractical. Please, don't forget that to-day we live in a practical age.
VASSILKÓV. No, sir. I should very much like to contest your point of view.
GLÚMOV. By all means, old man, if you must.
VASSILKÓV. Honesty is even now a paying proposition, sir. In a practical age it is not only better, but also more profitable to be honest. I'm afraid you don't quite know what a practical age means or you seem rather apt to run away with the idea that dishonesty and deceit is good business. Quite the contrary is the truth, sir. In an age of romance and sentiment deceit has a much better chance of succeeding and is much more easily hidden. To stoop to conquer an innocent maiden with her head full of romantic ideas, to deceive a poet whose eyes are in a fine frenzy rolling, to impose on an incurable dreamer or to play tricks on your superior in the Civil Service who is steeped in elegiac poetry, is much easier than to get the better of a hard-headed, practical business man. No, sir, in the present age honesty is definitely the best policy.
TELYÁTEV. Lydia and her mamma are coming this way.
VASSILKÓV. [*Catches hold of* TELYÁTEV's *hand*] Introduce me, I implore you!
TELYÁTEV. Ouch! [*Snatching his hand away*] With the greatest of pleasure, old fellow.

[MRS. CHEBOKSÁROVA *and* LYDIA *come up.*]

TELYÁTEV. [*To* MRS. CHEBOKSÁROVA) May I introduce you to a millionaire?
MRS. CHEBOKSÁROVA. I daresay you'll overcharge me even for pulling my leg, you naughty man.
TELYÁTEV. Not at all, my dear lady, I assure you. No interest on the transaction whatever.
MRS. CHEBOKSÁROVA. In that case, do! Only you're such a shameless liar that I don't believe a word you say.
TELYÁTEV. Really, my dear lady, you make me blush. Savva Vassilkov!

Mrs. Cheboksárova. Wait, wait! What an extraordinary name!

Telyátev. Never mind the name. All millionaires have such names. [Vassilkóv *comes up*] Let me introduce you to my friend, Mr. Savva Vassilkov.

Mrs. Cheboksárova. I'm so pleased to meet you.

Vassilkóv. Me too, ma'am. I'm afraid I don't know anybody in Moscow.

Telyátev. He's a stout fellow. He speaks Greek. [*Walks up to* Lydia.]

Mrs. Cheboksárova. From your name I should say you were born in Greece.

Vassilkóv. No, ma'am. I am a native of Russia. I was born near the Volga.

Mrs. Cheboksárova. Where do you live?

Vassilkóv. In the country, ma'am, but most of the time I'm travelling about.

Mrs. Cheboksárova. [*To* Glúmov] Be a darling, George, find me my footman.

[Glúmov *comes up*.]

Vassilkóv. Allow me, ma'am. I'll get him for you immediately. What's his name?

Mrs. Cheboksárova. Andrey.

Vassilkóv. I shan't be a minute, ma'am.

Mrs. Cheboksárova. Thank you so much. Get my shawl from him, will you? I'm beginning to feel chilly.

[*Speaks softly to* Glúmov.]

Telyátev. [*To* Lydia] I am always well armed against chills.

Lydia. A pity! You are such a nice man and I could easily fall in love with you, were you not such a disgusting rake.

Telyátev. A rake! Well, perhaps you're right. I'm not particularly fond of the blameless life. Virtuous men, as a rule, are very jealous, and no one can accuse me of jealousy. Shall I prove it to you?

Lydia. Do.

Telyátev. With pleasure. I'm going to introduce you to a rival of mine who is sure to take my place in your heart.

Lydia. That may not be as difficult as you think.

[VASSILKÓV, *carrying shawl, almost runs up to* MRS. CHEBOKSÁROVA, *followed by* ANDREY.]
VASSILKÓV. Here he is! I found him!
[*Gives shawl to* MRS. CHEBOKSÁROVA.]
MRS. CHEBOKSÁROVA. You gave me such a fright! [*Puts on shawl*] Thank you. Andrey, see that our carriage waits for us outside the theatre.
ANDREY. Very good, ma'am.
[*Goes out.*]
TELYÁTEV. [*To* VASSILKÓV] My dear Savva . . .
LYDIA. What a name! Is he a foreigner?
TELYÁTEV. He's a native of Magpie Mountain.
LYDIA. Where's that? I never heard of it. I'm sure there's no such place on the map.
TELYÁTEV. It's only been discovered recently. [VASSILKÓV *comes up*] Let me introduce you to my friend, Savva Vassilkov. [LYDIA *bows*] He was in London, Constantinople, Never-never-land and Kazan. He tells me that he's seen many beautiful girls, but that he's never met such a beautiful creature as you, dear Lydia.
VASSILKÓV. [*Blushing to the roots of his hair*] How do you do?
LYDIA. Do you know Mrs. Churil-Plenkov in Kazan?
VASSILKÓV. [*Stammers*] Very well, indeed.
LYDIA. Is it true that she has separated from her husband?
VASSILKÓV. [*Unable to overcome his shyness, with unexpected explosive emphasis*] God forbid!
LYDIA. [*Looking curiously at him*] Do you happen to know Podvorotnikov?
VASSILKÓV. [*Quickly, with the same explosive energy*] He's one of my best pals, ma'am!
[LYDIA *exchanges glances with* TELYÁTEV. *A short, awkward silence.* VASSILKÓV *effaces himself, completely covered with confusion.*]
LYDIA. What a funny man!
TELYÁTEV. He's a bit odd. He was a prisoner of war in Central Asia for a very long time, poor fellow.
[*They speak apart.*]
GLÚMOV. [*To* MRS. CHEBOKSÁROVA] He owns goldmines,

the richest in the world. I understand that every hundredweight of sand yields him over ten pounds of pure gold.
Mrs. Cheboksárova. [*Looking at* Vassilkóv] Really?
Glúmov. He says so himself. That's why he is such a wild looking man. He spends most of his time in the wilderness with the natives.
Mrs. Cheboksárova. [*Looks fondly at* Vassilkóv] You don't say so? I should never have guessed it, to look at him.
Glúmov. How are you to guess a gold prospector from his looks? Do you expect him to wear an overcoat made of gold? Isn't it enough that his pockets are lined with gold? You should see the tips he gives to the waiters!
Mrs. Cheboksárova. What a pity he's throwing his money about like that!
Glúmov. Who should he be saving it up for? He hasn't a soul in the whole world. What he wants is a good wife and, particularly, a clever mother-in-law.
Mrs. Cheboksárova. [*Looks more fondly at* Vassilkóv] He's quite a handsome man!
Glúmov. Yes, among the aborigines he passes for an Apollo.
Mrs. Cheboksárova. [*To* Lydia] Let's take our last stroll round the gardens, my dear. Gentlemen, I've been ordered by my doctor to take a stroll in the park every evening. Who wants to join us?
Vassilkóv. I should like to very much, ma'am, if you don't mind.
Mrs. Cheboksárova. [*Smiling pleasantly*] Not at all. I should be delighted.
[Mrs. Cheboksárova, Lydia *and* Vassilkóv *walk off.*]
Glúmov. Well, the hunt's up.
Telyátev. Did you spin the jolly old yarn, old fellow?
Glúmov. Catch me missing such a chance!
Telyátev. So that's why she was looking so sweetly at him!
Glúmov. Let mamma and her darling daughter run after him and let him die of love! We shall work them into a state of absolute frenzy with each other and then knock the ground from under their feet.
Telyátev. Only don't make a slip, old fellow. I shouldn't be in the least surprised if he did marry fair Lydia and **carry**

her off to Magpie Mountain. He simply gives me the jim-jams, old fellow, it's like being crushed by some jolly old avalanche.

[KUCHÚMOV *comes up.*]

KUCHÚMOV. [*In the distance, singing to himself*] Ma in Ispania, ma in Ispania . . . mille e tre . . .*
[*Walks up haughtily, holding his head high.*]

TELYÁTEV. How d'ye do, Prince?

KUCHÚMOV. How are you, my dear old chap? What a beefsteak I had to-day, gentlemen! Mmmm . . . it simply melted in the mouth. *Mille e tre* . . .

GLÚMOV. At the Club or at a tea-shop?

KUCHÚMOV. Don't talk tommy rot! A rich business man gave a special dinner in my honour. I was very useful to him, let me tell you, and he wants me to pull some more wires for him. I promised to do my best, of course. It's a mere bagatelle for me, you know!

GLÚMOV. Promises are two a penny.

KUCHÚMOV. What a scorching tongue you have! [*Shakes a finger at him*] You'd better be careful or we'll make it too hot for you in Moscow. I've only to say the word . . .

GLÚMOV. Why don't you? I might with luck find myself among intelligent people for a change.

KUCHÚMOV. All right, all right! [*Waving him away*] One can't say a word to you.

TELYÁTEV. If you can't get the better of a fellow, you'd better not start on him, that's *my* rule.

KUCHÚMOV. *Mille e tre* . . . Yes, yes, of course . . . I forgot to tell you. Listen to this, gentlemen. I had a bit of good luck yesterday. I won eleven thousand off a chap.

TELYÁTEV. Did you or did someone else win it, old fellow?

GLÚMOV. [*Excitedly*] Where and when, tell me quickly.

KUCHÚMOV. At the Club.

TELYÁTEV. And did you get the money?

KUCHÚMOV. I got it all right.

TELYÁTEV. Spill the jolly old beans, old fellow.

GLÚMOV. It's a miracle, if true.

KUCHÚMOV. [*Angrily*] No miracle at all! Do you think me

* From Leporello's aria in Mozart's *Don Juan.*

incapable of winning such a packet? I called at the Club yesterday, walked through the rooms a few times, glanced at the menu, ordered some oysters . . .

GLÚMOV. Oysters this month?

KUCHÚMOV. Did I say oysters? I meant sturgeon, of course. Well, a chappie walks up to me . . .

TELYÁTEV. A stranger?

KUCHÚMOV. A complete stranger, didn't know him from Adam. Says to me, would Your Highness like a game of baccarat? Why not, said I, why not? I had plenty of cash on me, why not take a risk, I thought to myself, all I could lose was only a thousand or so. Well, we sat down to it, started with low stakes at first, one rouble, and, gentlemen, I was in luck! What they call, a fool's luck. He kept on asking for new packs of cards, but it didn't help him any, he had to give it up in the end as a bad job. We cast up the accounts, twelve thousand and five hundred! He took out the money . . .

GLÚMOV. But you just said eleven thousand!

KUCHÚMOV. Did I? Well, you see, I have such an atrocious memory. I suppose it must have been somewhere between the two figures.

TELYÁTEV. Who can afford to lose twelve thousand at one go, old fellow? Such people are worth cultivating.

KUCHÚMOV. They tell me he's only just arrived in Moscow.

GLÚMOV. But I was at the Club yesterday and didn't hear a thing.

KUCHÚMOV. I arrived very early. There was hardly a soul there and the whole thing only took about half an hour.

GLÚMOV. You owe us a dinner to-day.

TELYÁTEV. Vassilkov has invited us to dinner. You'd better stand us a few glasses of brandy, Prince. It's getting chilly and I'd like to get something warm inside me.

KUCHÚMOV. But I can't trust you. Even a couple of glasses will run me into some money and you'll drink up the whole bottle.

TELYÁTEV. Not at all, old fellow! Just a glass or two, I assure you.

KUCHÚMOV. If that's all you want, I don't mind. You'd better have dinner at my place next Sunday. I've some fresh sturgeon, got it alive from Nizhny, a brace of woodcocks, and a Burgundy you've never had the like . . .

TELYÁTEV. [*Takes him by the arm*] Come on, come on, old fellow. My teeth are beginning to chatter. If I'm not careful I'll catch a chill. [*They all go out.*]

[MRS. CHEBOKSÁROVA, LYDIA, VASSILKÓV *and* ANDREY *come up*]

MRS. CHEBOKSÁROVA. [*To* ANDREY] Fetch the carriage, please.

ANDREY. Verry good, ma'am.

[*Goes out and returns presently.*]

MRS. CHEBOKSÁROVA. [*To* VASSILKÓV] Thank you very much for your company. We must go home now. Do come to see us.

VASSILKÓV. When will it be convenient for me to call, ma'am?

MRS. CHEBOKSÁROVA. Any time you like. We are at home every day between two and four in the afternoon, but why not come to dinner, without any ceremony? In the evenings we usually go out for a drive.

VASSILKÓV. I shall consider it a great privilege to call on you at the earliest opportunity, ma'am. [*To* LYDIA] I'm a plain, outspoken business man, Miss Lydia! Permit me to express my admiration for your incomparable beauty!

LYDIA. Thank you, sir.

[*Moves away and, seeing that her mother is still talking to* VASSILKÓV, *signals to her impatiently.*]

MRS. CHEBOKSÁROVA. So we'll be expecting you, Mr. Vassilkov.

VASSILKÓV. I shall not disappoint you, ma'am. If I may, I shall avail myself of your kind invitation to-morrow. I don't live far from you.

MRS. CHEBOKSÁROVA. Indeed?

VASSILKÓV. In the same house, ma'am, only in a different wing.

[*On leaving*, MRS. CHEBOKSÁROVA *turns round and looks at* VASSILKÓV *a few times*. VASSILKÓV, *hat in hand, remains rooted to the spot for a long time, staring after them.*]

VASSILKÓV. How nice she is to me! It's wonderful! She's

either a very goodnatured woman or a very perspicacious one, to have seen through my uncouth exterior and discovered how essentially good I am at heart. But how easily I get bowled over by a pretty face! That's what comes of devoting all my leisure hours to pure and applied mathematics. Dry figures dry up your heart and at the first chance it turns against you and makes an ass of the mathematician. This is how my heart has revenged itself on me. I've fallen in love suddenly, like a boy of sixteen, and am about to make a damned ass of myself. It's a good thing I'm so sure of myself where money is concerned and, however madly I may be in love with a girl, I shall never spend beyond my income. This respect for my bank account has saved my bacon more than once. [*Falls into a reverie*] Lydia! Lydia! What have you done to me! My heart misses a beat every time I think of you. But what if you should have no heart, what if all you should care for is money! With no experience of women I am an easy prey for an unscrupulous and designing girl. She can make me her plaything, her helpless slave. What a blessing it is that I have such a keen sense of business and a holy dread of living beyond my means.

[KUCHÚMOV, TELYÁTEV *and* GLÚMOV *come up.*]

TELYÁTEV. Well, how do you feel now, old fellow? Better? Accept my congratulations!

VASSILKÓV. I don't know how to thank you, sir. But depend on it, I don't easily forget a kindness.

TELYÁTEV. If you should happen to forget it, I shall jolly well remind you of it. You owe me a bottle of bubbly, old fellow. Let's have dinner and you can pay your debt. [*To* KUCHÚMOV] Let me introduce you to our new friend, Prince. Savva Vassilkov!

KUCHÚMOV. How do you do? Are you a newcomer to Moscow?

VASSILKÓV. Yes, Your Highness.

TELYÁTEV. He's no Highness, old fellow. Just Grisha Kuchumov. We call him Prince because we're so fond of him.

KUCHÚMOV. Yes, sir, our society is very exclusive. It's very difficult for a stranger to get into it. You have to possess a lot of . . . er . . .

TELYÁTEV. Don't talk such utter rot, old fellow.

GLÚMOV. If our society had really been so exclusive, you and I would never have got into it.

TELYÁTEV. What about it, gentlemen? Let's have a drink straight from the wood right here!

VASSILKÓV. If you desire it, gentlemen. Waiter, a bottle of champagne!

GLÚMOV. And four glasses!

KUCHÚMOV. Yes, I'll do you the honour of joining you in a glass.

GLÚMOV. And from here straight to the Club for a game of cards. [*To* KUCHÚMOV] I'd like to see some of your twleve thousand!

KUCHÚMOV. Be careful not to add to them yourself.

TELYÁTEV. [*To his* FOOTMAN, *standing at the gates of the park*] Grigory! Help me on with my coat, my dear fellow, will you? Do you know where to find my carriage?

GRIGÓRY. Yes, sir. It's right here near the gates, sir.

KUCHÚMOV. [*To his* FOOTMAN] Nicholas! [NICHOLAS *comes up*] Don't stand there gaping at me, man! Stand by the gates and help me into the carriage.

[BOY *from café brings out champagne and glasses.*]

VASSILKÓV. Help yourselves, gentlemen. Please, do me the honour.

[*All lift their glasses.*]

TELYÁTEV. [*To* VASSILKÓV] Good luck, old fellow. I don't think you'll get her, but I wish you good hunting.

GLÚMOV. Of course, he won't get her. He'll come the hell of a cropper.

KUCHÚMOV. What are you talking about?

GLÚMOV. He wants to marry Lydia.

KUCHÚMOV. Wants what? I shan't allow it!

GLÚMOV. He won't ask your permission.

VASSILKÓV. Gentlemen, I bet you three thousand that I shall marry Lydia.

KUCHÚMOV. I never bet.

GLÚMOV. I'd gladly take you on, but I haven't a bean in the world.

TELYÁTEV. And I, old fellow, am afraid to lose.

VASSILKÓV. Gentlemen, you've got the wind up! Then why laugh at me? What about it? It's my last offer. Here's the three thousand. [*Takes out the money, but all shake their heads*] The wine has loosened my tongue. I am in love with Lydia, gentlemen, and I'm going to marry her, come what may! I'm not in the habit of wasting words. You'll see, it will be all as I say. Now, let's to dinner!

ACT TWO

[*A richly furnished room with oil paintings, carpets, curtains. A door at either side and one in the middle.*
VASSILKÓV *is pacing the room,* TELYÁTEV *enters from door to left.*]

TELYÁTEV. I thought you'd left a long time ago. Why don't you go and join the ladies? Is your courage giving out, old fellow?

VASSILKÓV. One of my chief troubles is that I don't know how to carry on a conversation.

TELYÁTEV. What's there to know? The only thing you must remember is never, especially after dinner, start any discussion on a scientific subject. Keep the ball rolling by saying any darned silly thing that comes into your head so long as it is bright, witty and slightly scandalous, but all you talk about is trigonal pyramids and cubic feet.

VASSILKÓV. I've just been thinking out a very jolly story which I'm sure will raise a laugh.

TELYÁTEV. Marvellous, old fellow. Go right in and tell it to them or you'll forget it.

VASSILKÓV. And where are you off to in such a hurry?

TELYÁTEV. Lydia has expressed a wish for some flowers, and I'm going to a florist's to get them for her.

VASSILKÓV. So you are my most dangerous rival, after all!

TELYÁTEV. Don't give it a thought, old fellow. A man who has for the past twenty years never missed a single ballet is no damn good as a husband. Don't be afraid of me, buck up and go tell them your story!

[VASSILKÓV *goes out through door to left;* GLÚMOV *enters by same door.*]

GLÚMOV. Is *he* still here? What a pertinacious ass! It's high time he was sent packing. He's been given plenty of rope, why doesn't he hang himself? We've had enough fun with him here. What a pity we did not accept his bet.

TELYÁTEV. Even now I should think twice before taking it on.

GLÚMOV. I admit he fleeced us all right that night at the

Club. But what do you think about Kuchumov? What a beauty! Boasts that he's won twelve thousand the day before and can't cough up even six hundred. Meets a man for the first time and already owes him money . . . Where are you off to?
TELYÁTEV. To Petrovka.
GLÚMOV. I'll come with you.
[*They go out.* KUCHÚMOV *and* MRS. CHEBOKSÁROVA *come in.*]
KUCHÚMOV. [*Hums*] *Muta d'accento e de pensier.**
MRS. CHEBOKSÁROVA. For some time now I've been getting nothing but bad news.
KUCHÚMOV. Humm . . . Yes . . . It's very unpleasant! . . . *e de pensier.*
MRS. CHEBOKSÁROVA. Not a day passes without a piece of really terrible news.
KUCHÚMOV. What is he doing there, your husband, I mean? How could he permit things to . . . to come to such a pass? I can't make him out at all. Seems to be one of us, a man of intelligence.
MRS. CHEBOKSÁROVA. But what can he do? You read his letter: bad harvest, drought, all the timber burnt in the sawmill which has been running at an ever mounting loss for years. He writes that he must have thirty thousand immediately or he'll have to sell the estate, which is already in the receiver's hands and is to be sold by public auction.
KUCHÚMOV. What is he worrying about, the imbecile? Hasn't he plenty of friends? Take me, for instance. Tell him to write to me personally. *Muta d'accento . . .*
MRS. CHEBOKSÁROVA. Ah, my dear Grigory, I always knew that you would not let us down!
KUCHÚMOV. What nonsense, my dear. . . . As an old friend of the family I'm always ready to oblige. . . . It's of no account to me. . . .
MRS. CHEBOKSÁROVA. My dear Grigory . . . Heaven help me . . . I must be frank with you, let the others still think we're rich. I have a daughter, she's twenty-four. . . . Think of it, my dear friend!
KUCHÚMOV. Of course, of course . . .

* From the Duke's aria in Verdi's *Rigoletto: Muta d'accenti e di pensieri.*

Mrs. Cheboksárova. We have no one to support us. At present we still get things on credit, but even that's only a drop in the ocean. Winter will soon be upon us: theatres, balls, concerts. Only a mother knows how much money all that eats up. Lydia is only interested in getting everything she wants. She has no idea of the value of money and she doesn't care how much she spends. When she goes shopping, she'll ransack the shops, order everything to be sent home without asking the price of anything and leave me to pay the bills.

Kuchúmov. And what about finding a suitable husband for her?

Mrs. Cheboksárova. It's so difficult to please her.

Kuchúmov. When I was young, such a girl would have been abducted long ago. Even to-day, if only I were a widower . . .

Mrs. Cheboksárova. You're always joking, but what is a mother to do? After so many happy and untroubled years, suddenly such a blow . . . Last winter I took her out everywhere, spared nothing for her, spent everything to the last penny, even the money that was specially put aside for her trousseau, and all for nothing. And now I have been waiting and waiting for money from my husband and instead I get this dreadful letter. I really don't know how we're going to live. How am I to break the news to Lydia? It will kill her.

Kuchúmov. But, of course, if you want anything, then please don't be ashamed to . . . er . . . I mean, let me be a father to Lydia while your husband is away. I've known her since childhood and, believe me, I love her more than a daughter . . . I love her . . . yes.

Mrs. Cheboksárova. I don't know how much you love her, but there is no sacrifice too great that I would not make for her.

Kuchúmov. It's the same with me, it's the same with me, my dear lady. By the way, what's this Vassilkov doing at your house? You ought to be more careful about people.

Mrs. Cheboksárova. Why shouldn't he be here?

Kuchúmov. I don't like him. Who is he? Where did he come from? No one knows.

Mrs. Cheboksárova. I don't know, either. All I know is that he's a gentleman and his manners are unobjectionable.

Kuchúmov. What does that matter?

Mrs. Cheboksárova. He speaks excellent French.

Kuchúmov. Yes, yes, but that doesn't mean a thing, either.

Mrs. Cheboksárova. People say that he's engaged in some business of importance.

Kuchúmov. Is that all you know about him? Not very much, my dear lady, not very much.

Mrs. Cheboksárova. I don't think he's a fool.

Kuchúmov. Let me be the judge of that, ma'am. How did he get here at all?

Mrs. Cheboksárova. I don't really remember. Somebody introduced him. Telyatev, I think. All sorts of people come to see us.

Kuchúmov. Is he thinking of marrying Lydia or what?

Mrs. Cheboksárova. I don't know. He may.

Kuchúmov. Is he a man of property?

Mrs. Cheboksárova. To tell you the truth I'm so little interested in him that it never occurred to me to find out.

Kuchúmov. He talks too much: "at the present day, at the present day..."

Mrs. Cheboksárova. Everybody seems to talk like that nowadays.

Kuchúmov. But he should realize that one gets bored with that kind of talk. If you must talk, go where people want to listen to you. But is the present day so much better than the past? Where are the palaces of our princes and our counts? Who owns them to-day? The Petrovs and the Ivanovs. What's happened to our brass bands, I ask you? In the past there would be brass bands playing by the ponds at sunset and later there would be a display of fireworks and even ambassadors would come to watch.... That was the time of Russia's glory. But now... these newcomers... such gentry should be sent about their business.

Mrs. Cheboksárova. But why? On the contrary, I want to be very nice to him. In our present position anybody might come in useful.

Kuchúmov. You'd hardly find *him* of any earthly use. You'd better put your trust in us old men. Of course, I can't

marry Lydia. I have a wife, alas, alack! But, you know, old
men are liable to have all sorts of fancies. If an old man wants
something badly, nothing is too expensive for him, he'd gladly
give all he has. I have no children. You could do anything
you like with me. I could become Lydia's father by adoption
or . . . just her good friend. An old man would gladly give
everything for . . . er . . . a caress. I can't take all my hundreds
of thousands to the grave with me, can I? Well, good-bye. I
must be off to my club.

MRS. CHEBOKSÁROVA. Will you come to see us again soon?
[She sees him off to the door.]

KUCHÚMOV. Yes, of course. I lost a bet to your daughter
and I must buy her a box of chocolates. You see, that's the
sort of man I am. Hotblooded, like some scalliwag of twenty,
by gad!

[Goes out.]

MRS. CHEBOKSÁROVA. It isn't a box of chocolates we want.

[MRS. CHEBOKSÁROVA *remains standing at the door, lost in
thought.* VASSILKÓV *comes in and picks up his hat.*]

MRS. CHEBOKSÁROVA. Are you going already?

VASSILKÓV. It's time I went home.

MRS. CHEBOKSÁROVA. Why are you in such a hurry? [*Sits
down on couch.*]

VASSILKÓV. Can I do anything for you?

MRS. CHEBOKSÁROVA. Take a seat, please. [VASSILKÓV *sits
down*] I should like to have a talk with you. We have known
each other for some time, but I don't seem to know anything
about you. We've hardly exchanged more than a few words.
I suppose the company of old women bores you.

VASSILKÓV. Not at all, ma'am. What would you like to
know about me?

MRS. CHEBOKSÁROVA. I should like at least to know enough
to be able to answer any questions I'm asked about you. We
have so many visitors and no one seems to know you.

VASSILKÓV. I am so little known here because I spent all
my time in the provinces.

MRS. CHEBOKSÁROVA. Where were you educated?

VASSILKÓV. At a provincial high school, but I specialized in
my particular line without any help.

Mrs. Cheboksárova. That's very nice. Are your parents still living?

Vassilkóv. Only my mother who has lived in the country all her life.

Mrs. Cheboksárova. Then you're almost alone in the world. Are you a civil servant?

Vassilkóv. No, I'm engaged in private business undertakings mostly with small people, builders, contractors, foremen . . .

Mrs. Cheboksárova. Ah, that's very nice. Yes, yes. I remember now. It's rather the rage at present, I believe . . . even some very rich people . . . to get closer to the poorer classes. When engaged in this business of yours you, of course, wear a red silk—or is it velvet?—caftan. Last year I saw a millionaire in a train and—would you believe it?—he wore a simple . . . What do you call it?

Vassilkóv. Sheepskin?

Mrs. Cheboksárova. Yes, sheepskin and a beaver hat!

Vassilkóv. No, I don't wear any fancy dress.

Mrs. Cheboksárova. But you must have a big fortune to spend your time like that?

Vassilkóv. To begin with, my business in itself is rather profitable . . .

Mrs. Cheboksárova. You mean, it's so picturesque, don't you? They sing songs, dance in a ring and, I suppose, you probably have your own private oarsmen to take you out boating on the Volga.

Vassilkóv. I'm afraid I've never come across anything like that, ma'am, but you're quite right, without some capital it is impossible to start my kind of business.

Mrs. Cheboksárova. Of course not. I thought so. One can guess at once that you are a man of means. [*Pause*] Why are you always having arguments with Lydia? It rouses her temper. She's a girl of character.

Vassilkóv. That she is a girl of character is very good. I admire people of mettle. In a woman it is a mark of particular distinction. But it is a pity Miss Lydia has no notion of things which everybody nowadays knows about.

Mrs. Cheboksárova. But why should she, my dear Savva,

have any notion of things which are known to everybody? She's had a higher education. We have a large French library. Ask her something about mythology, please, do! You know, she is so well read in French literature! She knows lots of things which girls of her age haven't a notion of. The cleverest man about town couldn't say anything that would in the least surprise or embarrass her.

VASSILKÓV. Such an education is merely of a self-defensive kind, ma'am. It is useful in a way, but not in our present age. Of course, I have no right to lecture anyone, but I shouldn't have tried to convince Miss Lydia if I hadn't . . .

MRS. CHEBOKSÁROVA. If you hadn't what?

VASSILKÓV. If I hadn't thought that I might be of some help to her. If she'd only change her present ideas, she'd get quite a different view about life and people. She'd be more likely to value a man's inner qualities.

MRS. CHEBOKSÁROVA. Yes . . . inner qualities. . . . You're quite right.

VASSILKÓV. Then I could hope to deserve her friendship. But, as it is, I cannot be amusing and I do not want to appear ridiculous.

MRS. CHEBOKSÁROVA. Of course not. She's still very young, you know, she'll change her views a hundred times. I must confess *I* love to hear you talk and I often repeat the things you say to my daughter when we are alone.

VASSILKÓV. Thank you. To tell you the truth, I was beginning to think that the best thing to do would be to give up trying to change Miss Lydia. I don't like to go on making a fool of myself.

MRS. CHEBOKSÁROVA. Now this is really unworthy of you.

VASSILKÓV. I don't see why I should humiliate myself; after all, it isn't I who need her, it's she who needs me.

MRS. CHEBOKSÁROVA. Young man, please, regard me as your ally, one who is ready to give you all the support you want. [*Mysteriously*] All the support; mind you, because I am convinced that you are not only an honest, but also an honourabe man.   [LYDIA *comes in and stops at the door.*]

VASSILKÓV. [*Gets up and kisses* MRS. CHEBOKSÁROVA'S *hand*] Good-bye, ma'am.

Mrs. Cheboksárova. Good-bye, my dear boy.

[Vassilkóv *bows to* Lydia *and goes out.*]

Lydia. What were you talking to him about, mother? Tell me, please. He's a horrid man. He's mad!

Mrs. Cheboksárova. My dear, I know what I'm doing. Our present position doesn't permit us to be very choosy.

Lydia. What position? What's wrong with our position? I'm not going to put up with him any longer whatever our position may be. He doesn't know our life, our interests. He doesn't belong!

Mrs. Cheboksárova. But, my dear, he very often talks very sensibly.

Lydia. But who gave him the right to lecture people? What kind of a preacher does he think he is? You must admit, mother, that a drawing room is not a lecture hall, or a technological institute, or an engineering laboratory.

Mrs. Cheboksárova. You are so merciless to him, Lydia.

Lydia. But, mother, I'm sick of listening to him! He always talks of economic laws! Who cares about economic laws? The only laws for you and me, mother, are the laws of the world of fashion. If everybody wears a certain style of dress, then I, too, shall wear such a dress. I'd rather die than wear anything else. We have no time to think of any laws, all we have time for is to go to a shop and buy. No, mother, he is crazy!

Mrs. Cheboksárova. But I think, my dear, that he is simply trying to be original. There are many men like that. He's not particularly well educated, you know, perhaps not even clever, and certainly not witty, but he has to talk to be noticed at all. So he's trying to be original. But he probably thinks and behaves like any other decent man.

Lydia. You may be right, mother, but I am nevertheless sick of the sight of him!

Mrs. Cheboksárova. He's a man of means, darling. One has to have patience with such people. Don't we put up with the rest of them? Half of the men who come to see you are frightful boasters and shameless liars.

Lydia. What do I care whether they are liars or not? The important thing is that they are amusing and he is a bore. That's what I shall never forgive him.

Mrs. Cheboksárova. There is another reason, darling, why we should be so patient with him and I would ask you . . .

Lydia. What other reason? Tell me what that other reason is, mother.

Mrs. Cheboksárova. I know you're a sensible girl and I hope you'll be brave enough to listen to me calmly.

Lydia. [*Frightened*] What is it, mother? What is it?

Mrs. Cheboksárova. I got a letter from your father . . .

Lydia. What's the matter with him? Is he ill? Is he dying?

Mrs. Cheboksárova. No.

Lydia. What do you mean? I don't understand you, mother.

Mrs. Cheboksárova. I wrote to your father to ask him to send us money. We owe such a lot to all sorts of people and we want a lot more for the winter season. I got his reply to-day . . .

Lydia. What does he say?

Mrs. Cheboksárova. [*Inhaling smelling salts*] He says that he has no money, that he wants thirty thousand himself, or our estate will be sold by auction, and the estate is our last hope.

Lydia. That's a great pity, mother, but you will agree that you needn't have told me anything about it, that you should have spared me this news, that you had no business to tell me that we were ruined.

Mrs. Cheboksárova. But you were bound to learn of it sooner or later, dear.

Lydia. But why, mother? Why should I have had to hear of it at all? [*Almost in tears*] You'll have to find some way of getting us out of this mess, you must get some money in one way or another, for we can't leave Moscow and go to the country, can we? And we can't live in Moscow like paupers. Somehow or other, you simply must arrange everything so that our life goes on as before. I must get married this winter. I must find a rich husband. You are a mother. You ought to know how important that is. Can't you think of something, haven't you already thought of something to make it possible for us to live through the winter without degrading ourselves?

It is your business to think of some way out, it is your duty, mother! Why should you tell me something which I oughtn't to know? You rob me of my peace of mind, you deprive me of my poise which is the best ornament a girl can have, you make me look harassed and ugly. If you must worry, mother, you should worry by yourself, if you must weep you should weep in your room where I can't see you. Would you feel less miserable, if I wept with you. Please, tell me, mother, would you really be happier, if I were unhappy?

Mrs. Cheboksárova. Of course not, child. Of course, I shouldn't be happier if you were unhappy.

Lydia. Very well, then, mother, why should I be unhappy at all, why should I cry, why should I be robbed of my peace of mind and my poise? People age from worry. Worry brings wrinkles to one's face. I already feel that I've grown older by ten years. I've never known the meaning of want and I don't intend to know it. All I know is that I like to go shopping: I know the best underwear, silks, carpets, furs, furniture. I know that when I want something I go to the best shop in town, get it and pay for it, if I have any money, or tell the shop-assistants to send it, if I haven't any. But I never knew and I don't consider it necessary to know where money comes from or how much money I need for the winter or for the whole year. I never knew whether an article was dear or cheap and I always thought that bargain-hunting was mean and degrading. I hate the very thought of it, it makes me feel so cheap. I remember that once, on returning from a shop, the thought occurred to me: haven't I paid rather a lot for my dress? There was nobody with me at the time, I was in the carriage by myself, and yet I felt so ashamed that I blushed crimson and hardly knew where to hide myself. I recalled seeing an old woman in the shop, a horrible, fat old woman, who was bargaining for a piece of cloth. She'd hold it in her hand, then put it down, then pick it up again: she couldn't bring herself to pay such a lot of money for it and yet she was afraid to let it out of her hands. She was all the time whispering to two other ugly old women, while the shop-assistants were smirking behind her back. Please, mother, why do you torture me like that?

MRS. CHEBOKSÁROVA. I realize, darling, that I ought not perhaps to have told you of our position, but what else could I do? If we are to stay in Moscow, we shall have to cut down our expenses, we shall have to sell our silver, some at least of our pictures, and our jewellery.

LYDIA. No, no, mother! We can't do that! The whole of Moscow will learn that we're bankrupt, they'll come to us with sour faces, feigning sympathy, they'll heap stupid advice on us, they'll shake their heads, they'll make all kinds of commiserating noises in their throats, and everything they do will be so artificial and insincere, so insulting! I tell you, mother, they will not even take pains to disguise their glee. [*Covers face with hands*] No! No!

MRS. CHEBOKSÁROVA. But what are we to do, dear?

LYDIA. What are we to do? We mustn't demean ourselves Let's do up our apartment again, let's buy a new carriage, let's get new liveries for the servants, and the dearer the better.

MRS. CHEBOKSÁROVA. But how are we to pay for it all?

LYDIA. He will pay for everything.

MRS. CHEBOKSÁROVA. Who?

LYDIA. My husband.

MRS. CHEBOKSÁROVA. But who is your husband? Who is he?

LYDIA. I don't know. Anyone will do.

MRS. CHEBOKSÁROVA. Has anyone proposed to you?

LYDIA. No one has proposed to me, mother, no one dared propose to me. All the men who wanted to marry me got nothing but icy contempt from me. For I was myself looking for a handsome man with a big fortune, but all I want now is a man with a fortune, and there are many such men.

MRS. CHEBOKSÁROVA. I hope you're not disappointed in your expectations, dear.

LYDIA. Has beauty lost its price? No, mother, you needn't worry. There are not so many beautiful girls about, but there are thousands of rich fools.

[*Enter* ANDREY.]

ANDREY. Mr. Telyatev, ma'am.

LYDIA. Here's the first one.

MRS. CHEBOKSÁROVA. [*To* ANDREY] Show him in, please.

[ANDREY *goes out.*]

LYDIA. Leave us alone, mother. Don't interfere with us at all. He'll pay for everything.

MRS. CHEBOKSÁROVA. But if . . . ?

LYDIA. But if? Well, didn't you tell me yourself that Vassilkov has a big fortune? You'll have to send for him. He owns goldmines, he is a fool—the gold will be ours.

MRS. CHEBOKSÁROVA. I'd better send for him now. I'd like to speak to him first. He'll have to be prepared.

[*Goes out.*]
[*Enter* TELYÁTEV *with a bouquet.*]

LYDIA. How quick you are and how you spoil me! Tell me why do you go to such trouble to please me?

TELYÁTEV. Does this surprise you, old girl? When didn't I carry out your commands?

LYDIA. But why do you spoil me so?

TELYÁTEV. Well, you see, old girl, I'm made that way. It's my business to be nice to pretty girls. I have nothing else to do.

LYDIA. Then it's just a way of amusing yourself, is it? But, my dear man, don't you realize that you might turn my head by your attentions?

TELYÁTEV. I plead guilty to that crime.

LYDIA. It is either no crime at all or a very great crime. It depends on whether your actions are sincere or not.

TELYÁTEV. Of course, they are sincere!

LYDIA. But your constant efforts to please me, your neverending flattery, don't you think that all this is really a kind of bait with which you hope to catch me? You make me believe that you're so devoted to me that I can hardly remain indifferent to such devotion.

TELYÁTEV. Oh, I say, old girl, all the better, you know, all the better! You don't expect me to like your indifference, do you? It's about time my feelings found an echo in your heart, old girl.

LYDIA. It's easy for you to talk like that, for your feelings are nothing but neatly turned phrases. You've had so much experience in your life that you remain complete master of every situation. But just think of an inexperienced young girl like myself whose feelings for a man awaken for the first time in her life! Don't you agree that her position is extremely difficult, if not dangerous?

TELYÁTEV. Quite possible, old girl. I can't tell you anything about it, I've never been a girl myself.

LYDIA. Once a young girl is foolish enough to betray her true feelings for a man, she runs the risk of either becoming his plaything or making herself ridiculous, neither of which is pleasant. Don't you agree?

TELYÁTEV. You're quite right, old girl, quite right.

LYDIA. So, pray, if you don't mean anything, don't try to turn my head. Be sincere with me, I implore you. Don't tell me anything you don't mean. Don't make love to me if you don't like me!

TELYÁTEV. But who put that horrible idea into your head, old girl? Good heavens! I always say what I mean.

LYDIA. Really?

TELYÁTEV. Of course. As a matter of fact, I say even less to you than I really and truly feel.

LYDIA. But why don't you?

TELYÁTEV. I daren't, old girl. I'm afraid you might give me the cold shoulder, you know. Do you want me to try?

LYDIA. Yes, do!

TELYÁTEV. I can hardly believe it, old girl. Is it a dream, or what? What a lucky day for me! What date is it?

LYDIA. Why is it such a lucky day for you?

TELYÁTEV. But, really, old girl, how could I expect this from you? You're nice to me, you condescend to come down from your unscaleable heights, you actually do not disdain to come down to earth for me! Before, you were always like the goddess Diana, contemning the low tribe of men, with the moon in your hair and a quiver at your side. But now you've become a simple, friendly, even artless shepherdess, one of those they put into the ballet, who dance so charmingly, with their aprons fluttering . . .

[*He imitates a ballerina dancing a shepherdess.*]

LYDIA. Does this really make you happy?

TELYÁTEV. What do you think I am, old girl, a jolly old bronze horseman?*

LYDIA. How easy it is to make you happy! I'm very glad I am able to make you so happy.

TELYÁTEV. You are glad to make me happy? My dear girl, are you really the Lydia I knew or some other heavenly creature?

LYDIA. Why are you so surprised? Don't you deserve happiness?

TELYÁTEV. I don't know if I deserve it, but I do know that I'm about to go raving mad with happiness.

LYDIA. Do go raving mad!

TELYÁTEV. I'm liable to do all sorts of foolish things, old girl.

LYDIA. Do do all sorts of foolish things!

TELYÁTEV. You're either making fun of me, which is not fair, you know, or else . . .

LYDIA. Go on, finish the sentence!

TELYÁTEV. Or else you're in love with me!

LYDIA. Unhappily, I am.

TELYÁTEV. But why unhappily, old girl? What's there to be unhappy about? It's happiness, heavenly bliss. Darling, you couldn't have done anything better!

[*He embraces her lightly.*]

LYDIA. Johnnie, are you mine?

TELYÁTEV. I am yours, darling, I am your slave for ever!

LYDIA. [*Raising her eyes at him*] Really and truly?

TELYÁTEV. Yes, darling, for ever, for my whole life and even longer, if that's possible.

LYDIA. Oh, I'm so happy, Johnnie!

TELYÁTEV. It's I who am so happy, old girl.

[*Kisses her.*]

LYDIA. Oh, God, how wonderful! Mummy!

TELYÁTEV. Why mummy, old girl? What's mummy got to do with it? Three is a jolly old crowd, you know.

LYDIA. I know, Johnnie. We don't want her really, but I'm so happy.

* In the text " 'The Bronze Horseman' or the 'Stone Guest,' " a poem and a play by Alexander Pushkin.

TELYÁTEV. All the better, darling.

LYDIA. I am so happy, Johnnie, that I simply must share my happiness with her.

TELYÁTEV. I'm against sharing anything with anyone! There'll be more left for the two of us, old girl.

LYDIA. Yes, you're quite right, darling, we mustn't share our happiness with anyone, for there's so little happiness in the world as it is. But all the same, Johnnie, we'll have to tell her.

TELYÁTEV. I don't quite get you, old girl. What have we to tell her?

LYDIA. That we love each other, Johnnie, and that we want to be inseparable for the rest of our lives.

TELYÁTEV. So that's it, old girl? The jolly old marriage lines, wedding bells and confetti? Pardon me, but I really didn't bargain for that!

LYDIA. What do you mean, Johnnie? What didn't you bargain for? Tell me.

TELYÁTEV. I am ready to be your lover, your slave, everything, in fact, but if it's wedding bells you want, then I'm very sorry and all that, you know.

LYDIA. How dared you make love to me?

TELYÁTEV. I dared do nothing of the sort, old girl. The only thing I did was not to prevent you from loving me. I should never dream of preventing anyone from loving me, old girl.

LYDIA. You are not worthy of my love, sir!

TELYÁTEV. Quite true, old girl, quite true. I am not worthy of your love, but is one only to fall in love with a girl whom one is worthy to love? What kind of a jolly old ass would I have been to refuse your love and read you a moral lesson instead! Pardon me, old girl, but if you want someone to teach you morals, you'd better turn to someone else. I am not a moralist, either by inclination or on principle. In my opinion, old girl, the less morals a woman has, the better it is for everybody all round.

LYDIA. You are a monster!

TELYÁTEV. You're absolutely right, old girl. You ought therefore to be jolly grateful to me for having refused to marry you.

Lydia. I hate you!
[*Goes out.*]
Telyátev. Gosh, that was a narrow squeak! A jolly lucky thing I got out of it unscathed. I'm afraid I shall have to stop fooling round. If I'm not damn careful some young lady will make a fool of me and, before I realize it, I'm a husband! Flesh is weak, one must run from sin as from the devil. [*Goes to the door. Enter* Vassilkóv] Good luck, old fellow!
[*Goes out.*]
[*Enter* Mrs. Cheboksárova.]
Mrs. Cheboksárova. I'm so glad to see you again, so glad. Your company has become absolutely indispensable to me. Please, sit down beside me.
Vassilkóv. You sent for me, ma'am?
Mrs. Cheboksárova. I'm so sorry if I have troubled you. I want advice badly. I'm such a helpless creature. I know only one serious man and that's you.
Vassilkóv. Thank you. What can I do for you?
Mrs. Cheboksárova. I had a talk with Lydia. We want to change our mode of life, we are tired of all this constant hullabaloo. We've decided to receive no one but you. We're very rich, of course, but even a lot of money doesn't justify a life of senseless pleasure.
Vassilkóv. I quite agree.
Mrs. Cheboksárova. Lydia wants to finish her education and she can't do that without a guide. We decided to turn to you.
Vassilkóv. I should be very pleased to be of service to you, but what could I teach Lydia? Spherical trigonometry?
Mrs. Cheboksárova. Yes, yes, why not? You must admit that to teach a young girl is quite a pleasant occupation.
Vassilkóv. Quite. But what does Lydia want to know spherical trigonometry for?
Mrs. Cheboksárova. She's a very queer girl, but she has a heart of gold. She is a very good girl really. [*Mysteriously*] You know she really hates the sight of those empty-headed young men.
Vassilkóv. That's news to me, ma'am.
Mrs. Cheboksárova. As for me, I have hated the sight of

them for a long time. You are so different. Any mother could entrust her daughter to you without any fear. Forgive me, my dear Savva, for my frankness, but I should be so happy if Lydia learnt to like you.

Vassilkóv. Thank you.

Mrs. Cheboksárova. If I could, I should force her to like you, only to see her happy.

Vassilkóv. Is there no other way than using force?

Mrs. Cheboksárova. I don't know. You'd better try to find out for yourself. You are in love with my daughter, aren't you? Wait, let me look into your eyes. Don't say anything, I can see for myself. But why are you so shy? Shall I speak to her for you? Or else you'll start your arguments again and end up, God forbid, by quarrelling.

Vassilkóv. No, let me talk to her myself, but I shall have to prepare myself, think things over first.

Mrs. Cheboksárova. What's there to think over or to prepare yourself for? [*Enter* Lydia.]

Mrs. Cheboksárova. Darling, Savva has asked me for your hand. I'd be happy if you accepted him, but I don't want to force you to do anything against your own will.

Lydia. In a matter of such importance, mother, I must obviously decide for myself. Had I been in love, I should have listened to the promptings of my heart rather than to you, but I'm absolutely indifferent to any of my admirers. You know, mother, that I have refused many men who've asked for my hand, but I feel that it's high time I got married and I'm ready to do whatever you want.

Vassilkóv. Which means that you don't love me?

Lydia. No, I don't love you. Why should I deceive you? We can talk it over later. Mother, you've undertaken to arrange my life for me. Remember, I shall hold you responsible for my future happiness.

Mrs. Cheboksárova. My dear Savva, she has accepted you!

Vassilkóv. I am very sorry.

Lydia. Sorry? Why? Because I don't love you?

Vassilkóv. No, that I was in such a hurry.

Lydia. You can still refuse to marry me, but you can't

love me very much if you do it so lightheartedly. Don't be angry with me, rather be grateful to me for being so frank with you. I could easily have pretended to be in love with you—pretence costs nothing—but I don't want to. All brides say that they are terribly in love with their husbands, but don't believe them: real love comes later. Don't be vain, take me for your wife. Why should I love you? You aren't handsome, you have such a funny name, and even your surname is so common. All this may not amount to much, but it takes time to get used even to small things. Why should you be angry with me? Because you are in love with me? Thank you very much, but try to win my love and we shall be happy together.

Vassilkóv. I don't want sacrifices from anyone.

Lydia. It seems to me you don't know what you want.

Vassilkóv. Not at all. I know perfectly well what I want. I could marry a girl who did not love me. You are quite right, love may come with time. But I want that you should respect me, for without respect marriage is impossible.

Lydia. That's understood. I shouldn't have agreed to marry you if I didn't respect you.

Vassilkóv. You were frank with me and I'll be frank with you. You told me that you didn't love me and I tell you that I fell in love with you perhaps long before you deserved it. You, too, must be worthy of my love. Otherwise, I'm afraid, it might easily turn to hate.

Lydia. Really!

Vassilkóv. You can refuse to marry me. There is still time.

Lydia. Why should I? [*Laughs*] Let's play a comedy with each other, try to be worthy of each other's love.

Vassilkóv. I don't want to play a comedy. I want our future to be bright and happy.

Lydia. Not at all, you want nothing but a comedy. You propose to me, I accept you. What else do you want? You say you love me, you should therefore be infinitely happy, and not start an argument about my duties to you. We ought each to know our own duties. Only the poor, who have nothing to live on, argue about how to live.

Mrs. Cheboksárova. I can see, my dears, that you really are in love with each other and that your arguments are, so to speak, only literary.

Vassilkóv. Allow me as your fiancé to present you with these. [*He gives her a box with ear-rings and a brooch*] I bought them to-day by chance and, it seems, they have come in very useful.

Mrs. Cheboksárova. [*Gasps*] But they must have cost a fortune!

Vassilkóv. Only three thousand, ma'am.

Lydia. It seems to me there's quite a good chance that I might fall in love with you!

[*She extends her hand to* Vassilkóv *who kisses it politely.*]

ACT THREE

[*Same drawing room as in Act Two, only more richly furnished. To the right of the spectators—a door to* VASSILKÓV'S *study, to the left—a door to* LYDIA'S *room, in the middle—entrance door.* VASSILKÓV *comes out of his study with brief-case and newspapers. He glances quickly through the newspapers and rings. Enter* VASSILY.]

VASSILKÓV. The Kazan estate of the Cheboksarovs with its saw-mill and forest is to be sold in a few days. What a pity! The saw-mill ought to be very profitable and there's plenty of good timber in the forest. Go to Yermolayev and tell him to meet me at the Stock Exchange in about an hour. Let him wait for me there. I'm going to authorize him to buy the estate in my name. Tell him that he should in any case make all the necessary arrangements for leaving immediately for Kazan.

VASSILY. Very good, sir.

VASSILKÓV. I wish you'd dress yourself more decently, Vassily.

VASSILY. It don't make no difference to me, sir. In them boots, jacket and velvet cap I looks exac'ly like the English factory 'ands I seen when I was with you in England. I likes that very much, sir. No one can't mistake *me* for no bloomin' butler.

VASSILKÓV. Very well. It's your business, Vassily, please yourself.

VASSILY. Thank you, sir. [*Goes out.*]

[VASSILKÓV *takes out a bill and checks it carefully.* MRS. CHEBOKSÁROVA *comes out of* LYDIA'S *room.*]

MRS. CHEBOKSÁROVA. You're a real bear, Savva. Only just got married and already you don't seem to care for anything but your business.

VASSILKÓV. One thing doesn't interfere with another, mumsie.

MRS. CHEBOKSÁROVA. What do you mean, mumsie?

VASSILKÓV. I like the word. It's a nice pet name and a very apt one, too.

Mrs. Cheboksárova. Oh, all right. [*Comes up to him*] Are you happy, Savva? Tell me, are you really happy, my son? [*Takes him lovingly by the ear.*]

Vassilkóv. [*Kissing her hand*] Yes, I am happy. I am completely happy. I can frankly say now that I have had a few days of real happiness in my life. Do you know, mumsie . . .

Mrs. Cheboksárova. Again mumsie!

Vassilkóv. I am sorry.

Mrs. Cheboksárova. I knew Lydia would make you happy. I should never have let my darling marry you otherwise.

Vassilkóv. I should have been happier if . . . if . . .

Mrs. Cheboksárova. If what? [*Sits down*] Aren't you satisfied, you ungrateful wretch?

Vassilkóv. I should have been absolutely satisfied if my ideal of life were an interminable succession of visits all over Moscow varied with a concert or a theatre in the evening. I should be perfectly satisfied if I were not ashamed of such a life and if I could afford it.

Mrs. Cheboksárova. But if all decent people live like that there is nothing to be ashamed of. Besides, it doesn't really cost such an awful lot.

Vassilkóv. Doesn't it? According to my reckoning I've already spent a small fortune. I don't know and I don't want to know how much Lydia is spending herself. What she does with her money is not my business.

Mrs. Cheboksárova. And quite right, too.

Vassilkóv. She has her money and I have mine. But I'm beginning to be worried how much more it's going to cost me this year.

Mrs. Cheboksárova. What nonsense, dear! Just go on living as you do. Such expenses will hardly embarrass you.

Vassilkóv. Hardly embarrass me? But only six months of such a life will cost me about twenty-five thousand.

Mrs. Cheboksárova. Is that such a lot? Are you really so mean? You look so sorry for yourself, I can hardly believe my eyes.

Vassilkóv. It doesn't matter at all whether I look sorry for myself or not. What matters is where am I to get all that money?

Mrs. Cheboksárova. That's not my business. You ought to know all about that.

Vassilkóv. To live on such a scale I must be worth a million at least.

Mrs. Cheboksárova. We shouldn't mind if you were worth two.

Vassilkóv. But I'm not worth two or even one. I've just a moderate income.

Mrs. Cheboksárova. I hope at any rate that you're worth half a million. Even that isn't so bad.

Vassilkóv. You know perfectly well that all I have is my estate, a little ready money and what my business brings me in. I cannot afford to spend more than seven or eight thousand a year.

Mrs. Cheboksárova. But what about your goldmines?

Vassilkóv. Which goldmines? What are you talking about?

Mrs. Cheboksárova. Your goldmines.

Vassilkóv. I have no goldmines. I haven't even a coppermine.

Mrs. Cheboksárova. [*Gets up*] Then why have you played such a cruel joke on us?

Vassilkóv. I played no joke on you.

Mrs. Cheboksárova. But you assured us you had a fortune.

Vassilkóv. But I have and not such a small one at that.

Mrs. Cheboksárova. Don't talk such nonsense! You don't seem to know what you're talking about. You don't understand the simplest things which even children understand.

Vassilkóv. What do you mean? How is my fortune not a fortune? What is it then in your opinion?

Mrs. Cheboksárova. What is it? I'll tell you. It's penury, poverty, that's what it is. What you are pleased to call a fortune may satisfy the needs of a bachelor: it may suffice him for glove money. But how do you expect to keep my poor darling on it?

Vassilkóv. I intend to make her happy and I'll do my utmost to make her happy.

Mrs. Cheboksárova. Without a real fortune? This is ridiculous!

VASSILKÓV. I have enough, I'm telling you, and I'm doing my best to get more.

MRS. CHEBOKSÁROVA. How much is enough? She wants a really big fortune to make her happy and it's impossible to get a big fortune with your kind of business. You have to have special Government concessions for that, railway concessions and so on. And these you will never be able to get. One can also obtain a big fortune by inheritance or, if one is very lucky, by winning it at cards.

VASSILKÓV. You forgot to mention something else: you can also get a big fortune by robbing a bank. Would you like me to do that?

MRS. CHEBOKSÁROVA. Do you really think so? How little you know me! I can see I'll have to do something myself to convince you of the error of your ways.

VASSILKÓV. Which errors? Let me give you a good tip: mind your own business!

[*Takes his hat.*]

MRS. CHEBOKSÁROVA. Are you going out?

VASSILKÓV. Yes. Good-bye.

[*Goes out.*]

MRS. CHEBOKSÁROVA. What a worry this son-in-law of mine is! Still, who else would have married Lydia if they'd known that she hasn't a penny in the world? I'll have to do my best for him. What else is there to do?

[*Enter* ANDREY.]

ANDREY. Mr. Kuchumov, ma'am.

MRS. CHEBOKSÁROVA. Just in time! [*To* ANDREY] Show him in. [ANDREY *goes out*] I'll tackle him at once.

[*Enter* KUCHÚMOV.]

KUCHÚMOV. [*Hums*] *Pace e gioia son con voi!**

MRS. CHEBOKSÁROVA. I'm so glad to see you. Please, be seated.

KUCHÚMOV. [*Sitting down*] *Pace e gioia* . . . And where is our dear nymph?

MRS. CHEBOKSÁROVA. She's flown off on visits. She'll be back soon.

KUCHÚMOV. And the satyr who snatched her away from us?

* From Rossini's opera, *The Barber of Seville*.

Mrs. Cheboksárova. He's gone off on business. He's always preoccupied with his business.

Kuchúmov. A tight-fisted fellow! Still, what has he to worry about? It's we who're kept on tenterhooks with our mouths watering at the sight of the sour grapes, like the fox in the fable.

Mrs. Cheboksárova. How you do talk! At your age, too!

Kuchúmov. My heart is still young, dear lady. I'm of a volcanic nature!

Mrs. Cheboksárova. Incidentally, have you received a letter from my husband?

Kuchúmov. Yes, I have. Don't worry, I'll send him the money to-morrow. It's a bagatelle: only thirty thousand. You can safely dismiss it from your thoughts.

Mrs. Cheboksárova. I have another favour to ask you, my dear Grigory.

Kuchúmov. What's that? What's that?

Mrs. Cheboksárova. Could you get a better job for a friend of mine, something big, a trusteeship or the management of a large estate?

Kuchúmov. It depends who it is for.

Mrs. Cheboksárova. [*Shrugging her shoulders*] It's for my son-in-law.

Kuchúmov. I see! So it's as bad as that, is it? I knew it all the time.

Mrs. Cheboksárova. Yes, my dearest friend, it seems we've made a little mistake.

Kuchúmov. What right had he to marry your daughter in that case? He swore he'd buy her the keys of heaven, and now he can't even support her. A man of straw, after all! Do you know he must be a cadger by nature, must have some lawyer's blood in him. What does he want a job for? To take bribes. How do you expect me to recommend him then? He'll probably disgrace me, the rotter!

Mrs. Cheboksárova. But, please, have pity on me. He's my son-in-law.

Kuchúmov. You told me yourself a minute ago that you were mistaken in him. But he didn't deceive me, no, ma'am! I never trusted that ugly face of his.

Mrs. Cheboksárova. Please, don't talk like that. Don't you like to be the benefactor of a man who is married to such a pretty wife?
Kuchúmov. Who told you I didn't? On the contrary, my dear lady, I'd be glad to help him.
Mrs. Cheboksárova. You probably think that women can't show their gratitude. No, my dear Grigory, if they want to . . .
Kuchúmov. Of course, of course. I'm off at once. Only tell me how, what and where?

[*Enter* Lydia.]

Kuchúmov. In the presence of such beauty, I am dumb.
Lydia. I'm sorry to hear that. Please, don't go dumb, you talk so nicely. [*Sits down in an arm-chair*] I'm so fagged out. I've been rushing about like mad all over Moscow.
Mrs. Cheboksárova. You're quite right, Lydia. Mr. Kuchumov not only talks well, he also acts well. He's sending thirty thousand to your father to-morrow to save our estate and he's also doing us a personal favour. We should be very grateful to him.

[*Looks significantly at her daughter.*]
[Andrey *comes in.*]

Andrey. Mr. Glumov, ma'am.
Mrs. Cheboksárova. Show him into my sitting room.

[*Goes out, followed by* Andrey.]

Lydia. Really, Mr. Kuchumov, what's come over you? Since when have you become a benefactor of humanity? To help others means to deprive oneself of something. What on earth could induce you to do that?
Kuchúmov. And is it you, my dear, who ask me that?
Lydia. Why shouldn't it be me?
Kuchúmov. Why, don't you know that I'm ready to sacrifice not only my wealth, but my life for you?
Lydia. It's hardly likely that I'd require so big a sacrifice, but is it really true that you're sending money to my father?
Kuchúmov. To-morrow, to-morrow, my dear.
Lydia. That is really noble of you. It's impossible not to value such friendship
Kuchúmov. It's much more than friendship, my dear

Lydia. Shall I tell you what? I'm going to buy that estate from your father and make you a present of it.

LYDIA. Fine! Please, buy it as a present for me. I like presents so much.

KUCHÚMOV. To-morrow I'm going to write to your father and tell him that I've decided to buy his estate. I'll send him thirty thousand as a deposit. Money is no object with me. All I care for, my dear, is your goodwill, just your goodwill.

LYDIA. How can I show my goodwill to you? You are already practically a member of our family.

KUCHÚMOV. Hear, hear! A member of your family . . .

LYDIA. However, what member of my family can you be? You're a little too old to be my brother. Would you like to be my pappie for the time being?

KUCHÚMOV. [*Kneels at her feet and kisses her hand*] Yes, your pappie, your pappie . . .

LYDIA. Don't be too naughty, pappie.

KUCHÚMOV. I want to be naughty, I want to be naughty!

[*Kisses her hand again.*]

[GLÚMOV *appears in the doorway and withdraws quickly.*]

LYDIA. [*Gets up from arm-chair*] You ought to be ashamed of yourself to behave like that. You're not a baby.

[KUCHÚMOV *gets up.* ANDREY *enters.*]

ANDREY. Mr. Telyatev, ma'am.

LYDIA. Ask him to come in.

[ANDREY *goes out.*]

KUCHÚMOV. Addio, mia carina! I'm off on your business.

LYDIA. On what business is that?

KUCHÚMOV. I'll tell you later.

[*Goes out.*]

[TELYÁTEV *comes in.*]

TELYÁTEV. Pronounce my death sentence, old girl, but be quick about it. If you decide to be cross with me, I'll retire to a primeval forest and end my miserable life there. But I'd rather you knocked me on the head now and then forgave me. I can't live without you, Lydia. I'm beginning to suffer from spleen like an Englishman and I'll end up by shooting myself.

LYDIA. Why should I be angry with you?

TELYÁTEV. Your words are daggers, old girl.
LYDIA. How are you worse than anybody else? There are many men who are worse than you.
TELYÁTEV. Take pity on me. Do you enjoy torturing me? Tell me straight that I am a cad.
LYDIA. I should hate to contradict you. You're much to blame. You're very much to blame. You are the cause of my marrying a man I don't love.
TELYÁTEV. You don't love him? That's fine.
LYDIA. It seems he doesn't love me, either.
TELYÁTEV. He doesn't love you! Wonderful!
LYDIA. What's wonderful about that?
TELYÁTEV. I don't know how you feel about it, old girl, but to me, a sinful bachelor, such a situation is heaven. Don't we, poor, homeless fellows, wander about the whole world in search of just such situations?
LYDIA. You're immoral to the very marrow of your bones.
TELYÁTEV. If you want to call me names, old girl, I don't object.
LYDIA. Why call you names? Because you love me? Why should I abuse someone who loves me? Or because you refused to marry me although you loved me? But that's an old story already. You can't do anything about it now.
TELYÁTEV. I can't marry you, that's true enough. But I can love you, can't I?
LYDIA. I can't very well forbid you that. It flatters a woman's vanity. The more admirers, the merrier.
TELYÁTEV. What do you want many admirers for? Be satisfied with one for the time being.
LYDIA. You don't seem to know life at all. One admirer is dangerous, people will start to gossip at once, but many admirers kill suspicion, for how are they to tell which is her lover?
TELYÁTEV. Let *me* be your lover, old girl. You can have four others as decoys for prying eyes.
LYDIA. [*Laughing*] You're such a silly idiot that one can't be angry with you.
TELYÁTEV. The clouds have cleared away. Can I now start saying sweet nothings to you?

LYDIA. Do. I like listening to you. You're a darling really, aren't you?

TELYÁTEV. Of course I'm a darling, old girl. How wonderful you look! You've certainly changed for the better, such a change always . . .

LYDIA. No, perhaps you'd better spare me. I've been a married woman such a short time that I'm not used to your talk yet.

TELYÁTEV. What a pity you're not used to it. Do get used to it quickly and save me from boredom. Let's start again. Do you intend to take a lover soon? It's an old Italian custom, you know, for a married woman to have a *cavalier servente*.

LYDIA. But the question is, surely, is it done here?

TELYÁTEV. It's high time we introduced this admirable custom. One ought never to be ashamed of importing anything that's worthy of imitation.

LYDIA. And what will the husbands say?

TELYÁTEV. They'll get used to it with time. Of course, at first many of us cavaliers will get a beating, even a very bad beating, especially from our shopkeepers and tradesmen, and some may even be dragged to the courts, but with time the custom is sure to take root. The first in the field will have to run the risk of a beating, so as to pave the way for the others. No reform is possible without a certain amount of sacrifice. Somebody will have to sacrifice himself for the good cause.

LYDIA. Sounds lovely, but, I'm afraid, it will take a long time before we adopt this custom.

TELYÁTEV. It's already on the way, old girl. A few of us have already sacrificed ourselves. One I saw walking about with a peach of a black eye, another had had even worse luck, poor fellow.

LYDIA. All right, when this admirable custom does take root . . .

TELYÁTEV. Then you'll give me a chance, won't you, old girl?

LYDIA. If you prove worthy. You're such a windbag.

TELYÁTEV. Why a windbag?

LYDIA. Because there's nothing but wind in your head, darling.

TELYÁTEV. Not at all, old girl. I'll tell you why. Because I have no one to whom I could be constant. Command me and I'll be as constant as a telegraph pole.

LYDIA. I'll give you a trial.

TELYÁTEV. You will? Shall I kneel at your feet?

LYDIA. No, don't do that. Spare me the ceremony, I can do very well without it.

TELYÁTEV. Just as you say, old girl. However, I feel I must show my devotion in some more tangible way.

LYDIA. [*Giving him her hand*] You may kiss my hand.

[GLÚMOV *enters and remains in the background.*]

TELYÁTEV. [*Without noticing* GLÚMOV] Won't you take your glove off first? What kind of a kiss is that? The electricity with which my whole being is charged won't reach your heart through the glove. Kid is a very bad conductor, old girl.

[*Kisses her wrist above glove.*]

LYDIA. That'll do. You can't be allowed to take any liberties. Give you an inch and you'll take an ell.

TELYÁTEV. Only half an inch, old girl. This . . . [*Seeing* GLÚMOV] Hullo, George. I didn't notice you.

GLÚMOV. Don't mind me, carry on.

LYDIA. What do you mean? What's there to carry on? Do you want to suggest that there's something between us? I've only let Johnnie, who is an old friend of mine, kiss my hand. I'd gladly let you do the same.

[*Extends her hand to* GLÚMOV.]

GLÚMOV. Thank you very much, but I'm not in the habit of kissing anybody's hand. I only kiss the hand of my mother or my mistress.

LYDIA. In that case you'll never kiss my hand.

GLÚMOV. Who knows? All sorts of things can happen in life. If Mahomet doesn't go to the mountain . . .

LYDIA. Let's go, Johnnie. [*Offers her arm to* TELYÁTEV] He's a very rude man. [*To* GLÚMOV] Are you waiting for my husband? He'll be back soon.

GLÚMOV. Yes, madam, I am waiting for your husband. I've a lot to tell him.

LYDIA. Do me a great favour, tell him something funny. He's grown particularly morose lately. No one in the world can make people laugh as much as you: you're so excruciatingly funny yourself. [TELYÁTEV *and* LYDIA *go out.*]

GLÚMOV. I'll make all of you laugh all right. Bravo, my dear Lydia, bravo! I came intending to make love to you, but I find that two others have preceded me. All that remains now is to get them all at each other's throats with the husband to make up the quartet. Vassily! [VASSILY *enters.*]

VASSILY. Did you call, sir?

GLÚMOV. Yes. When is Mr. Kuchumov usually here?

VASSILY. He's always to be fahnd 'ere at two o'clock, sir. Master ain't at 'ome as a rule then.

GLÚMOV. Where is he?

VASSILY. In conference at 'is hoffice, with a great many other rich people, talkin' business, sir.

GLÚMOV. What sort of business?

VASSILY. As 'ow to get more money for theirselves, sir.

GLÚMOV. Is your master rich?

VASSILY. Course 'e is, sir.

GLÚMOV. I suppose to you anyone who has a hundred-rouble note is a rich man.

VASSILY. Maybe not only an 'undred or a thousand but more'n that, sir.

GLÚMOV. That's nothing, my man, nothing.

VASSILY. Maybe it's nothin' to you, sir, but we 'ave only to look for more and we'll find it. I didn't ought to be talkin' to you, sir. Master don't approve of it and you mayn't understand nothin' of it, neither. 'E's a scholar, 'e is, sir, and 'e ain't lyin' on 'is back all the bloomin' day, neither. Many a night he ain't slep' not a wink, sir, workin' all the time, burnin' the midnight oil, in a manner o' speakin'. You don't understand much what I'm talkin' abaht, do you? I was on me way to London to join me master, but ten miles from there I 'ad to go back with 'im, came back in a train with a hengine, sir. But it's a bloomin' waste o' time talkin' to you at all, sir. [*Goes out.*]

GLÚMOV. What the hell is he talking about? Kuchumov is here every day at two. I'll make a note of that.

[*Enter* VASSILKÓV, LYDIA, TELYÁTEV *and* MRS. CHEBOKSÁROVA.]

GLÚMOV. [*To* VASSILKÓV] Good morning.
VASSILKÓV. How are you?
GLÚMOV. What are you looking so worried about?
VASSILKÓV. I'm very busy. I don't go about all day long chasing dogs in the street as you do. Gentlemen, make yourselves at home, be nice to the ladies, but you must excuse me. I haven't much time. I've important business to attend to. TELYÁTEV and GLÚMOV. Carry on. Don't mind us.
VASSILKÓV. I shall be free at lunch. If you like to stay to lunch, do so, if not, be off. Good-bye.
[*Goes into his study.*]
MRS. CHEBOKSÁROVA. How very polite, I must say.
TELYÁTEV. We don't mind, he's a good fellow.
GLÚMOV. Let's go. I don't like to lunch in private houses: they've always something homely for you, either it is some rhubarb wine* in a large decanter in the middle of the table or some home-made brandy or a cup without a handle or pasties tasting of tallow. Of course, at your house everything is first-class, but I still prefer to have lunch either at an hotel or at the club.
TELYÁTEV. Let's go to the English Club. They're serving a special lunch there to-day.
GLÚMOV. All right. [*They bow and go out.*]
MRS. CHEBOKSÁROVA. Darling, your husband is either a miser or he hasn't any money at all.
LYDIA. [*Frightened*] What do you mean, mother?
MRS. CHEBOKSÁROVA. He told me himself a little while ago that he can't afford to live as we do and that he'll have to cut down expenses. What shall we do if he finds out that we borrowed right and left before your marriage and that he'll have to pay the bills?
LYDIA. And what about the goldmines?
MRS. CHEBOKSÁROVA. It's a story invented by Glumov.
LYDIA. Mother, I'm done for. Like a butterfly I can't live without gold dust. I'll die, I'll just die, mother.
MRS. CHEBOKSÁROVA. I still believe, dear, that he has plenty of money, but he's stingy. If you could be nicer to him . . . Do try to overcome your aversion for him, dear.

* In the text "kvass," a Russian soft drink made out of bread.

LYDIA. [*Thoughtfully*] Be nicer to him? Nicer, did you say, mother? Oh, if it is really necessary I shall be so nice to him that he'll die of sheer happiness and leave me a rich widow. It would be fun to find out what each caress of mine is worth in gold. I may as well start straight away.

MRS. CHEBOKSÁROVA. Don't talk like that, Lydia, you make me frightened.

LYDIA. There's nothing more frightening than poverty, mother.

MRS. CHEBOKSÁROVA. You're wrong, Lydia. Vice is more terrible than poverty.

LYDIA. Vice? What is vice? To be afraid of vice when everybody is vicious is both stupid and unprofitable. The greatest vice in the world, mother, is poverty. Never, never shall I be poor. A woman must have courage to make use of her beauty. Till now I did not bother to attract him, I was reserved, frigid, I kept myself aloof, but now I'll see what I can do when I fling shame to the winds.

MRS. CHEBOKSÁROVA. Stop raving, Lydia. I'm terrified to hear you talk like that.

LYDIA. You're old, mother, and poverty has lost its sting for you, but I am young and I want to live. Life to me means glitter, men's adulation, dazzle and splendour.

MRS. CHEBOKSÁROVA. I refuse to listen to you.

LYDIA. Who is richer, mother, Telyatev or Kuchumov? I must know for I hold them both in the hollow of my hand.

MRS. CHEBOKSÁROVA. Both of them are rich, dear, and both fling their money about, but Kuchumov is richer and more good-natured.

LYDIA. That's all I want to know. Where are the bills from the shops? Give them to me!

MRS. CHEBOKSÁROVA. [*Produces the bills from pocket*] Here they are, all of them.

[*Goes out.*]

[LYDIA *grasps bills in her hand and goes with determined step towards the door of her husband's study.* VASSILKÓV *comes out at the same time and they meet half way.*]

LYDIA. I wanted to see you.

VASSILKÓV. And I wanted to see you.

LYDIA. That's excellent then. We met half way. Where shall we go, to your study or to my room? [*Pointing to her room*] There, darling? Tell me, please.

VASSILKÓV. Let's for the time being stay where we are: half way. I want to have a serious talk to you before lunch. You must forgive me, Lydia, for leaving you so much to yourself.

LYDIA. The less I see of you, the more I want you, darling. [*Embraces him.*]

VASSILKÓV. What's the matter with you? What's come over you? Why this sudden change?

LYDIA. But, darling, am I a doll or what? Am I not a woman? What did I marry you for? Why should I be ashamed to show my love for you? I'm not a little girl. I'm a grown-up woman of twenty-four. I don't know how other women feel about it, but to me my husband is everything. Do you understand, darling, everything! I kept too long aloof from you. I can see now that I was wrong.

VASSILKÓV. *Quite* wrong, my dear.

LYDIA. When I feel like strangling you in my arms, I shall strangle you. I warn you in time, darling, in case you'd like to prevent me.

VASSILKÓV. Why should I?

LYDIA. I don't know what's come over me so suddenly. I didn't care for you before, but now I feel such a violent attraction to you. Can you feel my heart pounding, darling? I love you so much! [*Cries.*]

VASSILKÓV. But why are you crying?

LYDIA. Because I'm so happy.

VASSILKÓV. It's me who should be crying. I expected to possess only a beautiful body and I found a loving, devoted heart. Do love me, Lydia, I think I am worthy of your love.

LYDIA. I'd love you anyway, my strong, wild man.

VASSILKÓV. Yes, I am a wild man, but with a tender heart and cultivated tastes. Let me hold your lovely hand, darling. [*Takes* LYDIA's *hand*] How lovely it is! What a pity I'm not a painter!

LYDIA. Everything I have is yours, darling, not only my hand. [*Clings to him.*]

VASSILKÓV. [*Kisses her hand*] Give me both your hands. [LYDIA *hides bills in her pocket*] What are you hiding there?
LYDIA. Don't ask me, darling, please don't.
VASSILKÓV. Why implore me so much? If you have a secret, you can keep it. I am not interested in other people's secrets.
LYDIA. How can I have any secrets from you, darling? Aren't we one, body and soul? I'll tell you my terrible secret. I have in my pocket the bills for my trousseau which mother should have paid. But she is in financial difficulties now. Father can't send her any money, he seems to have invested it all in some business deal. I wanted to settle them out of my own pocket, but I don't know if I can raise enough money just now. That's all there is to it, darling. You see, it isn't really important.
VASSILKÓV. Show me your bills.
LYDIA. [*Gives him the bills*] Here they are, darling. Do you really want to see them?
VASSILKÓV. Yes. I'm going to pay for your trousseau because you've made me so happy. If I had married a poor girl, I should have had to pay for her trousseau and she might not have loved me as much as you do.
LYDIA. No, no. I will settle everything myself. I must repay mother for all she's done for me.
VASSILKÓV. Keep your money for your own needs, darling.
 [MRS. CHEBOKSÁROVA *enters.* VASSILKÓV *sits down at the table and begins to add up the bills.*]
LYDIA. [*Softly to* MRS. CHEBOKSÁROVA] He'll pay for everything. [*Lies down on couch and takes book. Aloud*] Mother, do be very quiet. Savva is busy. [*Softly to* MRS. CHEBOKSÁROVA *who sits down at the head of the couch*] He's entirely in my hands.
VASSILKÓV. [*Stops in his adding up*] Lydia, there's a bill here for the new wallpapers and curtains which are hardly part of your trousseau.
LYDIA. But, darling, we had to have everything new for the wedding. We had such crowds of people. But for the wedding we shouldn't have bothered about it.
MRS. CHEBOKSÁROVA. The old ones would have been good for another winter.

VASSILKÓV. All right, all right.
[*Goes on adding up figures.*]
LYDIA. [*Softly to* MRS. CHEBOKSÁROVA] Yes, I'm telling you he's going to pay for everything, absolutely for every damn thing.
[*A fashionably dressed* MAID *enters and gives* LYDIA *a bill.* LYDIA *motions her to give it to her husband.* MAID *hands bill to* VASSILKÓV, *who glances at it, nods to his wife and goes on counting. The* MAID *comes in again and hands another bill to* LYDIA *who gets up and throws it negligently on the table. The* MAID *goes out and* ANDREY *comes in with two more bills and the same scene is repeated.* ANDREY *goes out.* VASSILY *comes in with a large bundle of bills and gives it to* VASSILKÓV.]
VASSILY. There are 'undreds of 'em, sir. All from the French shops.
VASSILKÓV. Give them to your mistress.
[VASSILY *hands them to* LYDIA *who drops them on the floor.*]
VASSILY. [*Picking them up*] Why throw 'em on the floor, ma'am. Them's kind of documents, them's got to be paid.
LYDIA. Go away! I can't stand the sight of you!
[VASSILY *puts the bills carefully together, places them on the table in front of* VASSILKÓV *and goes out.*]
VASSILKÓV. [*Gets up and paces room*] I've finished. The bills come altogether to thirty-two thousand five hundred and forty-seven roubles and ninety-eight copecks. This is rather a large sum for me, but, as I've given you my word, I'm going to pay the lot. I'll borrow the money to-day, but to balance our budget we'll have to cut down expenses drastically for a long time. There is a small, one-storied house opposite. It has only three windows looking out onto the street. I've already been to see it and I think that it will do very nicely for us. We're going to dismiss our servants: I'll keep Vassily and you'll have one maid only, an inexpensive one. We'll dismiss the chef and engage a cook. We'll also sell our horses.
LYDIA. [*Laughs*] How can we manage without horses? Aren't horses made to take us from one place to another? How are we going to go out? Are we going to fly in a balloon?
VASSILKÓV. When it's dry, we shall use our feet, and when it's wet or slushy, we shall hire a cab.

LYDIA. So that's what your love really amounts to!
VASSILKÓV. I don't want to go bankrupt because I love you.
LYDIA. You'd better hurry up and pay the bills. The shopkeepers are waiting, they at least are respectable people. It's not nice to keep them waiting. They must be paid.
VASSILKÓV. Why not pay them yourself? You have money of your own, haven't you?
LYDIA. I shan't pay.
VASSILKÓV. They can summons you, you know.
LYDIA. But I have no money! Oh, God!
MRS. CHEBOKSÁROVA. [*Excitedly*] Why do you torture us? We deserve better treatment. We've made a mistake. You're a poor man, but we're doing our best to rectify our mistake. Of course, a boor like you cannot be expected to appreciate the delicacy of our feelings. Take my husband, for example. He had a very important and responsible position in the Civil Service. Lots of money passed through his hands, and—do you know?—he cared so much for me and my daughter that whenever a large sum was required to keep up our social standing or simply to meet some whim of ours, he . . . he never bothered to make any distinction between his money and public money. Do you see? He didn't hesitate to sacrifice his career on the altar of his home and family! Eventually, he had to stand his trial and was forced to leave Moscow for the provinces.
VASSILKÓV. And serve him jolly well right!
MRS. CHEBOKSÁROVA. If you can't appreciate what he did for us, try at least to appreciate our present position. You are poor, but we shan't let you remain poor. We have good connections. We are looking for and we shall find a lucrative trusteeship or some other good job for you. All you'll have to do is to follow my husband's example and be as exemplary a family man as he. [*Goes up to* VASSILKÓV, *puts hand on his shoulder and whispers*] Don't be squeamish, you understand? [*Points to his pocket*] Leave it to me to see to it that those in authority look the other way. Just help yourself to what's going.
VASSILKÓV. Go to the devil with your infernal advice! No poverty and no beautiful woman will ever make a thief of

me. If you dare speak to me again of thieving, I'll throw you out of my house. Lydia, stop crying! I'll pay your bills, but for the last time and on condition that to-morrow we move to that small house with the three windows. There's a small room for your mother there. We're going to live modestly. We shall do no entertaining and you will receive no visitors.
[*Begins to check the bills again.*]
LYDIA. [*Leaning against her mother's shoulder*] We must accept his offer. [*Softly to her mother*] We'll get all the money we want and we'll live as before. [*Aloud to husband*] I agree, darling. I can't very well oppose you when I ought really to be grateful to you. [*Softly to her mother*] Watch me pull the wool over his eyes. [*Aloud to her husband*] All right, darling, we shan't receive anyone.
VASSILKÓV. [*Going over his accounts again*] I knew I could depend on you.
LYDIA. But what about old Kuchumov, darling? He's almost a member of the family.
VASSILKÓV. [*Counting*] All right, we'll make an exception for Kuchumov. [LYDIA *presses her mother's hand convulsively.*]
MRS. CHEBOKSÁROVA. [*Softly*] What's in your mind?
LYDIA. [*Softly*] No one has ever humiliated me as much as he. I'm no longer a woman, I'm a serpent. I'm going to sting him till he howls with pain.
VASSILKÓV. [*Immersed in his calculations*] You're a frightful spendthrift, darling.
LYDIA. [*Goes over to him and embraces him*] Please, forgive me, dearest. I'm a mad, spoilt woman, but I'll do my best to reform. I want you to teach me a lesson, angel, don't spare me.
VASSILKÓV. Then it's peace?
LYDIA. Yes, darling, peace for ever and ever.
VASSILKÓV. That's fine, darling. At least we understand each other perfectly now. You know that I am thrifty to a fault and I know that you are spoilt and improvident, but that you love me and that you'll do your best to make me happy. A plain business man like me, could hardly have hoped for such happiness from a spoilt society woman like you, and that's why this happiness is so dear to me, Lydia, my angel. [*He embraces his wife.*]

ACT FOUR

[*A very modestly furnished room, which also serves as* Vassilkov's *study; at each side windows, at the back to the right of the spectators a door leading into the hall, to the left a door leading to the inner rooms; between the doors a tiled stove; the furniture is poor: a writing desk, an old piano.*
Vassilkóv *sits at desk and arranges papers,* Vassily *stands in front of him.*]

Vassilkóv. Well, Vassily, it seems your mistress is getting used to the new house and to you.

Vassily. I ain't sure abaht 'er gettin' used to the 'ahse, sir. When you're aht, sir, they ain't 'alf carryin' on, 'er and 'er ma, burstin' aht laughin' as if enjoyin' some joke agin somebody. As for me, sir, I ain't 'alf surprised I ain't long gawne and drownded meself, it's so fed up I am, sir, with everythin' 'ere.

Vassilkóv. Why, what's wrong?

Vassily. It's the missus and 'er ma, sir. They will hinsist, sir, that I be wearin' them tails and white shirt an' collar of an evenin' and that carst orf blue liverie with them brass buttons and fancy trahsers in daytime, sir. But I keeps on refusin', for I ain't no bloomin' butler, sir, nor no blinkin' footman, neither. I am your valet, sir, been kind of hassistant to you, if I may so, sir, travellin' together all rahnd the world, in a manner of speakin'. Why, sir, we almost drownded together in the sime boat like for the good of yer business.

Vassilkóv. [*Gets up*] Of course, of course, Vassily.

Vassily. And she nearly devahred me alive for them fruit, sir.

Vassilkóv. Which fruit?

Vassily. In a manner of speakin', sir. There weren't more'n this much of it, sir.

[*Shows on finger how little there was of it.*]

Vassilkóv. Of what?

Vassily. Of a piece o' radish, sir. I ain't 'alf fond o' radishes, sir. There weren't more'n that, sir. I was sittin' in the hall, havin' a good time like, sir, eatin' me bit o' radish.

VASSILKÓV. Well, Vassily, I don't think you ought to, you know.
VASSILY. But we workin' folk, sir, ain't 'alf fond of a tasty bit o' radish!
VASSILKÓV. Don't forget, Vassily, what I told you: while I am away you are not to let anyone into the house except Mr. Kuchumov.
VASSILY. Very good, sir. You can rely on me, sir.
[VASSILKÓV *and* VASSILY *go out.*]
[*Enter* LYDIA.]
LYDIA. Where's that repulsive, doddering old fathead? For three days I've been imprisoned in this ghastly hole. I can't go near the windows even for fear of being spotted by some of my old friends who are no doubt driving past the house purposely to catch sight of me. Glumov, I suppose, has his verses all written. Dearest Kuchumov, my darling pappie, please get me out of this hovel! Mummy and I could go back to our old apartment and have a nicer time than ever before. If only I could have some music to distract me. There's great comfort in a waltz! Say what you will, but Johann Strauss is the greatest connoisseur of a woman's heart. [*Opens piano and plays a few bars*] What a rotten piano! He got it on purpose to humiliate me. Wait, my precious one, I'll lead you such a dance! [*Listens to the sound of a carriage outside*] I wish I could go up to the window, but how can a society girl even show herself at such a crazy peep-hole. Is it Kuchumov? He usually comes at two. It's him! It's him! He's at the door now. Yes, I can recognize his steps. I wonder what's going to happen now?
[*Behind the scenes* KUCHÚMOV'S *voice is heard asking:* "*Is your mistress at home?*" *and* VASSILY'S *voice answering:* "*Yes, sir.*"] [KUCHÚMOV *comes in.*]
LYDIA. At last, dear pappie. Aren't you ashamed of yourself to have been away so long?
KUCHÚMOV. [*Kisses* LYDIA's *hand and looks round the room angrily*] What's all this? What's all this? Where has he dragged you to? What furniture! It's like a low-class village inn. What does it all mean, I ask you? My angel, don't be angry with me for talking to you like that. In such rooms one can't

153

help being rude. How did it all happen? How did you allow yourself to be placed in such a humiliating situation? You are dragging the name of the Cheboksarovs in the mud, madam!

LYDIA. Don't blame me, pity me rather.

KUCHÚMOV. It's impossible to pity you, madam. You are disgracing your family. What would your poor father say if he knew of your humiliation?

LYDIA. But what am I to do?

KUCHÚMOV. You must run away, madam, run away at once.

LYDIA. But where? Mother has no money. He paid all our debts.

KUCHÚMOV. That was only his duty. For the possession of such a treasure as you, for the happiness which you bestowed on this . . . this sea-lion, he is in duty bound to carry out your slightest whim.

LYDIA. He doesn't seem to regard me as such a treasure or to value the happiness I gave him.

KUCHÚMOV. If he doesn't, all the better. You ought to know your own worth. Go back to your old apartment with your mother. There's nothing wrong about that. To live in this hencoop is a disgrace.

LYDIA. But, pappie, what are we to live on? Mother hasn't a bean, neither have I. We can't even hope to get anything on credit.

KUCHÚMOV. Credit! What do you want credit for? You ought to be ashamed of yourself to talk like that. You should have come to me. You are ashamed to ask me for money, but you aren't ashamed to live in such a hovel. You, our queen of fairies, seem to have forgotten how to command. You have only to wave a wand and this hovel will be transformed into a palace.

LYDIA. Which wand, pappie?

KUCHÚMOV. You, as a fairy princess, ought to know that better than us mortal men. Fairy princesses and lovely women have many magic wands they can wave.

LYDIA. [*Throwing her arms round his neck*] Do you mean that, pappie?

KUCHÚMOV. Yes, yes . . . [*He has a sudden attack of giddiness and sits down quickly on a chair*] Will forty thousand be enough for a start?

LYDIA. I don't know, pappie.

KUCHÚMOV. You don't want much for the time being. You'll go back to your old apartment. It is beautifully decorated and it isn't taken yet. You have plenty of fine dresses and things. Forty thousand should be quite enough for a start. Listen, my dear, if you refuse, I shall throw it out of the window of my carriage or lose it at cards at my club. I'll get rid of it in one way or another if you won't take it.

LYDIA. Then let me have it, pappie.

KUCHÚMOV. [*Searches his pockets*] Good heavens, such a thing happens only to me. I put the money in my wallet to give it to you, but I must have left my wallet at home. Forgive me, child. [*Kisses her hand*] I'll be certain to bring it to-morrow for your house-warming party. I hope you'll move to-day. I'll order a special pie at the best pastrycook's in Moscow and I'll buy a gold salt-cellar, a very large one, five pounds in weight, at the best jeweller's in Moscow and place the money there. I wish I could change it all for gold coins, but I could hardly get so much gold at the bank. I will, however, get about one hundred gold half-imperials and add it to the forty thousand for luck.

LYDIA. Thank you, thank you, pappie!

[*Strokes his head.*]

KUCHÚMOV. What bliss! What bliss! What does money matter? If I possessed millions, life without such a pair of eyes as yours and without your caresses, my dear, would be pure misery!

[*Enter* MRS. CHEBOKSÁROVA.]

LYDIA. Mother, darling, dear Grigory advises us to go back to our old apartment.

KUCHÚMOV. Naturally, you can't stay here, my dear, you can't stay here.

MRS. CHEBOKSÁROVA. Oh, dear Grigory, you can't imagine what I've been through! How I suffer! How I suffer! You know the kind of life I led when I was younger. I get a heart attack at the very memory of it. I would have taken Lydia to her father, but he doesn't want us to come. He doesn't mention having received any money from you, either.

KUCHÚMOV. I don't suppose he's got it yet. [*Counts on his fingers*] Tuesday, Wednesday, Thursday, Friday . . . He must have got it last night or this morning.

LYDIA. We ought to go back immediately, mother.

MRS. CHEBOKSÁROVA. We must think it over, Lydia. I can't help feeling that your husband is really very rich and that he is only pretending to be in difficulties.

LYDIA. Whether he is rich or poor, he has so humiliated me that everything between us is finished. Dear Grigory has done so much for us already and he doesn't want me to stay with my husband. We shall have money for all our expenses, pappie has promised me.

MRS. CHEBOKSÁROVA. Pappie! Fie, Lydia, where did you learn to talk like that? A mother can't bear to listen to you.

LYDIA. How do you like that? Are you ashamed of me? Then, please, don't be ashamed of me any more. I've made up my mind, mother, that the only thing I shall be ashamed of in future is poverty. I shall be ashamed of nothing else . . . Think, mother! We are both women. We haven't the means to live decently and to live decently means to you to live in luxury, doesn't it? How can you therefore demand that I should be ashamed of anything? No, mother, whether you like it or not, you'll have to close an eye to certain things in future. Such is the fate of all mothers who bring up their daughters in the lap of luxury and leave them without a penny.

KUCHÚMOV. *Benissimo!* I can hardly believe that so young a woman possesses so much commonsense.

LYDIA. Mother, pappie promises to give us forty thousand as soon as we have moved out of here.

MRS. CHEBOKSÁROVA. [*Overjoyed*] Really? [*To* KUCHÚMOV] You are a very, very generous man. But, nevertheless, dear, don't you think we'd better sleep on it?

LYDIA. Why sleep on it? All we can expect here is humiliation, but there is happiness!

MRS. CHEBOKSÁROVA. Come to my room, dear. Let's discuss

this thing properly. The chief thing that we simply mustn't forget is that we have to keep up appearances.

LYDIA. You can rely on me for that, mother.

KUCHÚMOV. I am not a little schoolboy, I know how to enjoy happiness without trumpeting it abroad, I know how to hold my tongue.

[VASSILY's *voice is heard behind the scenes:* "*No, sir. Master's orders were not to admit no one.*" GLÚMOV's *voice:* "*Don't be a fool, man!*"]

[KUCHÚMOV, LYDIA *and* MRS. CHEBOKSÁROVA *go out.* KUCHÚMOV's *hat remains on table. Enter* GLÚMOV *and* VASSILY.]

GLÚMOV. What are you talking about, you old idiot? Did he give you orders not to admit me? That's impossible.

VASSILY. I ain't no idiot, sir. I shan't let no one call me an idiot, sir. It ain't my fault if I been told to admit no one.

GLÚMOV. Who told you not to admit me, your master or you mistress?

VASSILY. Never mind that, sir. Orders is orders and I ain't making no hexception for nobody. But if you hinsist on knowin' I don't mind tellin' you: it's master who told me not to let you in and mistress don't want to see you, neither.

GLÚMOV. You're a born fool, your folly is quite incurable, but you probably know the reason why your master ordered you not to admit me. What is it? Even an ass like you ought to know it. So out with it, and to help your memory here's a silver rouble for you; it's more than your information is worth.

VASSILY. Thank'ee, sir. [*Takes coin and puts it in his pocket*] Wot'll I tell ye like? You know 'ow it is 'ere, sir. If you come, somebody else'll come, and another and another. There won't be no end of visitors, sir. One glass of vodka for you, that's gone, then two more are gone, then four, six, eight, ten, and all that costs an 'eap o' money, sir. And master, 'e says our business's gettin' not 'alf slack like. You'd feel the sime way yerself, sir. Why should we feed all them good-for-nothin' wastrels, sir? It's all gone dahn the drain like and nobody the better for it. Of course, if missus's friends were all respectable business men, it wouldn't 'alf make a difference, but with all them rough customers, sir . . .

GLÚMOV. That'll do. Give me a piece of paper and get out of here. I want to write a note for your master and then I'll go.

VASSILY. The piper's on the table, sir. Only don't wiste much of it, it's very hexpensive. I'll be leavin' you now, sir.

[*Goes out.*]

GLÚMOV. [*Takes pen and paper*] What shall I say? [*Notices* KUCHÚMOV's *hat*] Hullo! Whose may this be? [*Examines hat and whistles significantly*] It's Kuchumov's, by gad! The dear princeling is already here, is he? Excellent! Vassilkov has already got his letter. Telyatev, too. They'll meet here together, the whole bunch. What a party! What a situation! Let me say a few words, so that they'll not suspect me. [*Writes and reads aloud*] "My dear Savva, I looked in for a moment to talk a certain business over with you. I am very sorry you were out. I'll look in a little earlier to-morrow. Yours, Glumov." That's right. Written clearly, in large characters. Let me place it here, in the middle of his desk, so that he'll see it at once.

[TELYÁTEV's *voice is heard behind the scenes:* "*You can't keep me out, old fellow me lad.*" *Enter* TELYÁTEV *and* VASSILY.]

TELYÁTEV. [*To* GLÚMOV] Have you seen Lydia?

GLÚMOV. I have not. What do I want to see her for? I came in to see Savva, but missed him and left him a note. Good-bye, if you want Vassilkov, you'd better go to the Stock Exchange. He knocks about there all day long.

TELYÁTEV. So much the better.

GLÚMOV. It seems he has taken up a new kind of business, buying and selling silk.

TELYÁTEV. An excellent line, old fellow.

GLÚMOV. On a lucky day, he may make as much as five roubles.

VASSILY. That ain't true, sir.

GLÚMOV. There's a typical business man for you. Comes to Moscow and throws his money about as if he owned all the goldmines in the world, but after six weeks all his money is gone, he either joins the army or is sent home by the police by foot convoy, or else his dear daddy arrives, finds him in a pub, takes hold of him by the hair and drags him home four hundred miles. [*Looks at his watch*] However, it's time I went. Been talking too long. [*Goes out quickly.*]

TELYÁTEV. [*Sits down at desk with his hat in left hand*] Well, old fellow me lad, so you still insist that I am not to be admitted to this house!

VASSILY. Yes, sir.

TELYÁTEV. Are you quite sure it isn't your own bright idea?

VASSILY. No, sir. Strewth, it ain't. I durstn't do no such thing, sir

TELYÁTEV. And aren't you sorry for me, old fellow me lad?

VASSILY. I ain't 'alf sorry for you, sir. You ain't like the rest of 'em, sir.

TELYÁTEV. Better, eh?

VASSILY. Much better, sir.

TELYÁTEV. Sit down, old fellow me lad, sit down. [VASSILY *sits down with hands on his knees*] Let's have a jolly old palaver, old fellow me lad.

VASSILY. If it's talkin' you want, sir, I don't mind obligin' you.

TELYÁTEV. That's fine. I understand you've been in London, but have you ever been in Morocco?

VASSILY. Never 'eard of no such country, sir. Wot would I be wantin' in Morocco, sir? I've 'ad enough wanderin' rahnd the world, sir. All I wants to know is 'ave they enough bread in their bellies and warm clothin' to their backs for a cold day like?

TELYÁTEV. I can't tell you whether they have enough to eat there, but they don't want any warm clothes because it's jolly hot there all the year round.

VASSILY. Wot I says, sir, is let everybody mind 'is own business, so long as we 'ere 'ave good hexpectations.

TELYÁTEV. But what kind of expectations?

VASSILY. Good hexpectations, sir. In ahr business we've 'ad plenty of trouble of one kind and another. We've known 'unger and cold, sir. Of course, it's been like that since the flood, sir, but the good Lord feeds his sparrers, sir.

TELYÁTEV. I see you're quite a philosopher, old fellow me lad, but do you think it's wise to peer too deeply into every bally thing?

VASSILY. I don't mind talking abaht somethin' else, sir.

TELYÁTEV. That'll do, old fellow me lad. I'll have another chat with you another time. [*Absentmindedly takes* KUCHÚMOV's *hat from desk and tries to put it on at the same time as his own*] What's this, old fellow me lad?

VASSILY. It can 'appen to heverybody, sir. We ain't 'alf sinners, all of us, sir.

TELYÁTEV. What sin are you muttering about?

VASSILY. Sometimes one can't 'elp pinchin' even an 'at that don't fit one's head, sir.

TELYÁTEV. You're talking through your hat, old fellow me lad.

VASSILY. You'd better try 'em on, sir. The one that fits is yourn.

TELYÁTEV. That's better, old fellow me lad. Now you're talking jolly old horse-sense. [*Tries on his own hat first*] This is mine. And whose is this? Well, well, well . . . if it isn't the good old princeling's! Is the old boy here?

VASSILY [*Mysteriously*] 'E is 'ere, sir.

TELYÁTEV. Where is he?

[VASSILY *silently and solemnly points to the door leading to the inner rooms.*]

TELYÁTEV. Why is he admitted and not I?

VASSILY. 'Cause he's a relation, sir.

TELYÁTEV. He is as much a relation as yourself, old fellow me lad. You'll have to excuse me now. I'll stay here and you'd better go back to your cubbyhole in the hall.

VASSILY. Master anyways ain't usually at 'ome at this time, sir, otherwise . . .

TELYÁTEV. That'll do, old fellow me lad. Don't wait for me to chuck you out of here.

VASSILY. I suppose, sir, you ain't 'alf goin' to, if you say so.

[*Goes out.*]

TELYÁTEV. [*Takes out letter from pocket and reads*]:

> "Do not, Telyatev, be conceited,
> Such miracles are not unknown,
> The princeling will not be defeated,
> At two Lydia will be his own."

And so it seems, he will not be defeated! He's a relation, and I'm held at bay by that precious ass of a philosopher. What am I to do? To give her up without a fight is hardly gentlemanly, besides, I'm damned if I will. Let's wait and see how she sees him off. I'd like to see their faces when they find me here in the role of avenging fate. What a situation for them! Maybe I'd better take the bull by the horns and see what's going on in there. It's not very nice, to be sure, but . . . Where the hell are they? [*Goes up to a door and listens at the keyhole*] Nobody there. Let's investigate.
[*Opens door carefully, goes out and closes it as carefully.*]
[VASSILKÓV *and* VASSILY *come in.*]
VASSILKÓV. [*Hurriedly*] Did anyone call here while I was out?
VASSILY. Mr. Glumov, sir. He left a note.
VASSILKÓV. [*Sternly*] And who else?
VASSILY. Mr. Kuchumov, sir . . .
VASSILKÓV. All right, you can go.
[VASSILY *goes out.*]
VASSILKÓV. Kuchumov is so old that it's impossible even to suspect him; after all, my wife has some taste. [*Stops in front of desk and sees* GLÚMOV'*s note. Takes out letter from pocket and compares the two handwritings*] Not at all alike, and I thought it might be he. [*Reads letter*]:

"To 'Change the husband does repair,
For all his interests are there,
His lovely wife at home he left,
She is of interest bereft.
Does she do naught or nowhere go?—
'Praps 'tis as well he does not know.
Alas, poor husband!

He'll meet some friends during the day,—
At business, lunch, may be at play,
They'll bargain, chatter, joke and laugh,
Maybe a drink or two they'll quaff,
Schemes they will plan and stories tell,—
Maybe his *wife's* a friend as well!
Alas, poor husband!

"Be at home at two o'clock for certain and you'll understand the meaning of these words." [*Short pause*] What is it, a leg-pull or a calamity? If a leg-pull, then it is stupid and inexcusable to laugh at a man without regard to his feelings. If a calamity, then why does it break so soon and so unexpectedly? If I knew my wife, I shouldn't have been at a loss. I know how a simple girl or woman loves, but I'm hanged if I can tell what a society girl feels at heart. I don't know her at all. I can't penetrate her mind. I am a stranger to her and she is a stranger to me. She doesn't care what a man feels, all she is interested in is what he says. She wants fine speeches and I can't make fine speeches. Damn fine speeches! How easily we adopt some stranger's way of speaking and how slow we are to change our way of thinking. Everybody seems to be making speeches now as they do in the English Parliament, but they still think as they used to think in the days when no English Parliament was even thought of. And as for doing anything . . . They just do nothing . . . What the hell can this letter mean? I'll show it to Lydia. But if . . . if . . . my God! What am I to do then? How am I to behave? It's silly to try to prepare oneself for such an eventuality, it's silly to play-act. What my stupid provincial heart tells me, I'll do. [*Opens box with pistols, examines them, and replaces in box, which remains open. Goes to door which opens from inside.* TELYÁTEV, *walking backwards, comes in*] Telyatev, real friends don't behave like that!

TELYÁTEV. Hullo, old fellow. [*Softly*] Wait a minute, they'll be coming out presently.

VASSILKÓV. Answer my questions, or I'll kill you on the spot!

TELYÁTEV. Sh . . . Quiet, I tell you. [*Listens*] What do you want to know?

VASSILKÓV. Have you come to see my wife?

TELYÁTEV. Yes.

VASSILKÓV. Why?

TELYÁTEV. To spend a jolly hour or two, old fellow. A little flirtation, you know, doesn't do anyone any harm.

VASSILKÓV. Why should you pick out my wife to flirt with, aren't there any others?

TELYÁTEV. Because, old fellow, I've got good taste.

VASSILKÓV. We are going to fight a duel!
TELYÁTEV. All right, old fellow, all right. Don't make such an infernal noise. I can hear voices.
VASSILKÓV. I don't care a damn whether you hear voices or not. The pistols are ready.
TELYÁTEV. Don't be a silly ass, old fellow. Cool down. Have a drink of cold water.
VASSILKÓV. Look here, Telyatev, I am a quiet, peaceful man, but there are times when . . . I can't tell you the hell I'm in now. I . . . You see, I'm nearly crying. Here are the pistols. Choose which you like.
TELYÁTEV. If you want to make me a present of them, let me have the two. Why separate them? But if you really want to fight, then why be in such a confounded hurry, old fellow? I am going to have a lovely dinner to-day. After a good dinner I always feel a bit heavy; I shouldn't mind being killed then.
VASSILKÓV. No, we're going to fight it out now, right here, without any seconds.
TELYÁTEV. No, sir. I also can be obstinate. I am not going to fight any duels. What an awful place you have here, old fellow. Everything, you know, must be done properly. Wait! Wait! You'd better tell me first why you moved to this frightful hole.
VASSILKÓV. I haven't enough money to live anywhere else.
TELYÁTEV. Why didn't you say so before, old fellow? Here [*takes out wallet*], how much do you want? You'd better take the lot, I can get on very well without money in Moscow.
VASSILKÓV. Do you want to buy me off with your money? Do you want to buy my wife from me?
TELYÁTEV. Listen, old fellow. Better kill me, but don't insult me. I respect you more than you think or than you deserve.
VASSILKÓV. I'm sorry. I seem to have gone mad.
TELYÁTEV. I'm offering you the money simply because I'm good-natured or rather because of the general improvidence about money matters all round. When you have money, give it all to the first man you meet, when you haven't any, borrow it from the first man you meet.

VASSILKÓV. All right, let me have the money. How much have you got there?

TELYÁTEV. Count them later, old fellow. About five thousand, I think.

VASSILKÓV. I must count them now and give you a receipt.

TELYÁTEV. Don't bother, old fellow. I usually give receipts to people, I don't accept any from anybody. Even if I did, I'd lose them.

VASSILKÓV. Thanks. I'll pay you good interest on your loan.

TELYÁTEV. Pay me with champagne, old fellow. I take no other interest.

VASSILKÓV. Nevertheless, we'll have to fight, you know, because you are making love to my wife.

TELYÁTEV. It isn't worth while, old fellow, not worth while. Just consider: if your wife is an honest woman, all my love-making will be a waste of time, though, as far as I'm concerned, a jolly pleasant waste of time, but if she is not honest, she isn't worth endangering anyone's life for.

VASSILKÓV. What do you advise me to do then if she is unfaithful? [*In despair*] What am I to do?

TELYÁTEV. Send her packing, old fellow. That's all.

VASSILKÓV. I was so happy. She pretended so well that she was in love with me. Think how much the love of such a beautiful woman means to a man like me, an awkward provincial business man with no social pretensions of any kind—it's just heaven! And now I find that she's unfaithful to me. My whole world has suddenly collapsed about my ears. I can't bear the thought that she's deceiving me!

TELYÁTEV. All right, old fellow, shoot *her*, why shoot me?

VASSILKÓV. Because it was you who led her astray. She is a good woman by nature, but in your cesspool a woman is capable of losing everything, honour, conscience and shame! And you are the most dissolute man of them all. Take a pistol or I'll beat your brains out with a chair.

TELYÁTEV. To hell with you! I'm sick of the sight of you. Come on, let's shoot it out! [*Makes for the desk with the pistols, but stops to listen at the door*] Listen to me, old fellow, before fighting it out, let's hide behind the stove.

VASSILKÓV. No! Let's fight at once!
TELYÁTEV. [*Takes him by the shoulders*] Quiet, quiet, you silly ass!
[*Drags him behind the stove.*]
[*Enter* KUCHÚMOV *and* LYDIA.]
KUCHÚMOV. [*Sings*] In mia mano al fin tu sei.*
LYDIA. Good-bye, pappie!
KUCHÚMOV. [*Sings*] Kiss me, my darling, your kisses are so sweet . . . *Addio, mia carina!* . . .
LYDIA. With pleasure, pappie!
[*Kisses him.*]
[VASSILKÓV *and* TELYATEV *come out from behind the stove.*]
LYDIA. Hell!!!
[*Runs off into a corner.*]
KUCHÚMOV. [*Waving a finger*] Gentlemen, gentlemen! I . . . Just as an old friend of the family, you know . . . *Honi soit qui mal y pense!*
VASSILKÓV. [*Pointing to the door*] Get out! I'll send my seconds to you to-morrow.
KUCHÚMOV. Don't do that, young man! I'm not going to fight any duels with you. My life is much too valuable to Moscow to put in jeopardy against yours, which, as far as I can see, is of no value to anybody.
VASSILKÓV. I'll kill him!
[*Goes to desk.*]
KUCHÚMOV. Please, young man, please . . . This is no joke, young man.
[*Runs out.*]
[*Enter* MRS. CHEBOKSÁROVA.]
MRS. CHEBOKSÁROVA. What's all this row about?
VASSILKÓV. Take your daughter away from me. I'm quits with you. I'm returning her to you as dissolute as she was when I took her from you. She complained that my name was too common for her own exalted one. It is my turn now to complain that she has disgraced my common but honest name. When she married me, she said that she did not love me. Having lived with her only one week, I can say that I have nothing but contempt for her. She married me a

* From Bellini's opera *Norma*, Act II.

poor girl. I even had to pay for her trousseau and for her dresses. Let her consider that as payment for her caresses, which I was not the only one to enjoy!

LYDIA. What a tragedy!

MRS. CHEBOKSÁROVA. Don't be so excited, Savva. I'm sure it's only a misunderstanding. But even if married couples separate, it is usually done decently, without any scandal.

VASSILKÓV. [*To* TELYÁTEV] Don't leave me, my friend. I have still some arrangements to make. Here's your money. Take it. I merely wanted to earn you good interest for the sake of our friendship. Take it! [*Gives money back to* TELYÁTEV, *who shoves it negligently into a pocket.* LYDIA *looks keenly at the money*] I must make a few arrangements, write to my mother . . . I'm going to shoot myself!

[*Lowers head on chest.*]

TELYÁTEV. Don't be an ass, old fellow. You are an ass, Savva, you know. I had a friend who was married twice and both his wives ran away from him. Do you think he ought to have shot himself twice? Look at me, Savva. Listen to me, I am a sensible chap, I can give you some really good advice. First of all, for heaven's sake don't try to shoot yourself in a room. It isn't done. Gentlemen usually shoot themselves in the Petrovsky park. Secondly, have dinner with me to-night. We'll discuss everything later.

VASSILKÓV. [*To* MRS. CHEBOKSÁROVA] Take your daughter away from me at once. Take her away at once!

LYDIA. Don't you worry. I'll go sooner than you think. We intended to go back to our old apartment to-day, anyway. We've already taken it and we shan't even look from our big windows at this miserable hovel with its miserable owner. You played a comedy and we, too, played a comedy. We have more money than you, but we are women and women do not like to pay anything back. I pretended to love you, I pretended in spite of the disgust I sometimes felt for myself, but, you see, I had to make you pay my debts. I succeeded in making you pay them and I am satisfied. Have you realized what a fine actress I am? With such a talent no woman will ever know want. Shoot yourself! The sooner, the better. Telyatev, don't try to dissuade him! By shooting yourself you will make me a free woman again and I shan't make the same mistake a second time in the choice of a husband or a . . . you know what I mean, don't you? Good-bye! All I want is never to see you again. [*To her mother*] Have you sent for a cab?

MRS. CHEBOKSÁROVA. I have. It's waiting.

[*MRS. CHEBOKSÁROVA goes out, followed by Lydia.*]

VASSILKÓV. This is the end of everything for me.

TELYÁTEV. Don't talk tommy rot, old fellow. You have still plenty to live for.

VASSILKÓV. No, it's the end. If I were as heartless as she is, I'd rave and kick myself for being such a fool, but I would have got over it. If I had been unfaithful to her, I would have forgiven her. But I am a good-natured man. I believed in her, and she merely took an unfair advantage of my good nature. I shouldn't have minded it so much if she had only laughed at me or at my undistinguished origin, but she laughed at something which I consider the most precious part of me: my good heart, my love, the great happiness she herself had given me. It isn't my vanity that she hurt so much, it is the very essence of my whole being, my very soul. My soul is dead, all that is left is to kill my body.

[*Sits down, buries his face in his hands and cries.*]

TELYÁTEV. Listen, old fellow, you'd better stop crying or you'll make me cry, too. Just think what I'd look like! Stop, Savva, for heaven's sake stop! Just let me take you in hand for a few hours. Let's have dinner. Leave it to me to make it a good one.

VASSILKÓV. [*Takes pistol and puts it in pocket*] What's that, old man? [*He runs to window*] It's their carriage. They've gone. [*Looks completely done in*] Take me anywhere you like. I don't care what happens to me.

ACT FIVE

[*A boudoir in the former Cheboksarov apartment, to the left of the spectators a door to the drawing room, in the middle entrance door, to the left a french window.*
LYDIA *in morning dress lies on a settee.* MRS. CHEBOKSÁROVA *enters.*]

MRS. CHEBOKSÁROVA. Hasn't he been yet?
LYDIA. Not yet.
MRS. CHEBOKSÁROVA. I have lost my head completely. What are we to do? A week ago Kuchumov, instead of fulfilling his promise to bring the forty thousand when we moved in here, gave me only six hundred and thirteen roubles, and he pulled such a long face as though he were doing me a great favour. We're up to our necks in debt again. Don't forget that all our furniture has to be paid for. Our old furniture was sold by that scoundrel of a husband of yours.
LYDIA. Kuchumov promised faithfully to bring it to-day. It isn't fair not to believe him when he did such a favour to father.
MRS. CHEBOKSÁROVA. But did he? I have my doubts about that. I got a letter from your father to-day. He tells me he got no money from anyone, that his estate has been sold and that he himself lives with a friend. He says that after the sale of the estate he was left with only very little money and that he intends to start a dairy business in partnership with some tartar or bashkir.
LYDIA. I see it now! Do you know who bought the estate?
MRS. CHEBOKSÁROVA. Who?
LYDIA. Kuchumov. He promised to buy it and give it to me as a present.
MRS. CHEBOKSÁROVA. I don't think so, dear. Your father writes that at the auction a certain Yermolayev, an agent of Vassilkov, made the largest bid. Isn't that him?
[*Points to window.*]
LYDIA. Don't try to be funny, mother. How could he buy the estate? You saw yourself that he was borrowing money

from Telyatev and promised him a high rate of interest for it, and people offer high rates of interest only if they want money badly. Besides, he is too stupid for such a deal. Don't let us even discuss him.

Mrs. Cheboksárova. All right. I won't.

Lydia. I consider myself disgraced, mother, because I married him. I must wipe all memory of him from my mind. I should have returned all his presents if they were not so valuable. I ordered my jewels to be reset so that they shouldn't remind me of him.

Mrs. Cheboksárova. I'll go see if the carriage has arrived. I managed to get it on credit from a coach-maker and have even got our coat-of-arms painted on it. We'll have to hire the horses, but at least we shall have our own carriage. A hired carriage can always be recognized.

[*Goes out.*]

Lydia. Yes, experience is a great thing. I am still too credulous and credulity can lead to some irreparable mistake.

[*Enter* Andrey.]

Andrey. Mr. Kuchumov, ma'am.

Lydia. Show him in!

[Andrey *goes out.* Kuchúmov *comes in.*]

Kuchúmov. [*Kneels and kisses* Lydia's *hand*] *Il segretto per esser felice.**

Lydia. Don't be naughty. Sit down. I want to talk to you.

Kuchúmov. What frigidity! What icy chill in your voice, child.

Lydia. I've had enough of your jokes! Listen to me. You forced me to leave my husband, we are running up big debts. I am ashamed to remind you of the money as though I were your mistress, but you promised it to us yourself.

Kuchúmov. [*Sits down*] You must either kill me or you must forgive me for being so absentminded. I was counting the money and putting it in my wallet to bring it to you, when suddenly my wife came into the room. I put it into a drawer, started talking to my wife and . . . it slipped my memory! I'll bring it in half an hour.

Lydia. Who bought my father's estate, pappie?

* From Donizzetti's opera, *Lucretia Borgia*, Act II, Sc. 5.

KUCHÚMOV. I did, of course.

LYDIA. Father writes that an agent of Vassilkov bought it.

KUCHÚMOV. That's quite true. I asked a certain Vassilkov, a business man I know, to effect the purchase for me. I stood godfather to his son. He must have got someone else to go to Kazan as his agent. What a funny letter he sent me! I'll bring it to you in less than ten minutes! [*Gets up and looks round the room. Sings*] Io son rico, tu sei bella.* Yes, this is nice, and that is not so bad. What a perfect taste you have, my dear. You want some greenery here. I'll send you a large palm and some tropical plants. Under the palm we shall exchange our intimate secrets. I'll send it to you to-day.

[*Sits down near* LYDIA.]

LYDIA. [*Moving away*] When you bring us the money, I shall again call you pappie and, maybe, I shall even learn to love you.

KUCHÚMOV. [*Sings*] Io son rico, tu sei bella! As you can scarcely have any doubts about my honesty, you needn't be so parsimonious with your love, darling.

LYDIA. Do you think so? I'm afraid I am in a very bad temper to-day, I am not in the mood for love. For some time now I've heard of nothing but riches, my husband owns goldmines, you own mountains of gold. Telyatev is almost a millionaire and, they say, even Glumov has got very rich. All my admirers extol my beauty, all of them promise to heap riches on me, but neither my husband nor my admirers can oblige me even with pin-money. I have nothing to drive out in, I have to hire a hackney carriage drawn by a couple of dray-horses.

KUCHÚMOV. That's terrible! But in half an hour, my love, everything will be in order. It's my fault, I admit it. I alone am to blame.

LYDIA. I live apart from my husband and you come to see me every day at a certain hour. What will people say?

KUCHÚMOV. It's too late to stop people talking now, my child. The harm's done, however virtuously you've behaved. In my opinion, if you have to become the object of gossip, then why not give the gossips something real to talk about?

* From Donizzetti's opera, *The Love Potion*, Act II, Sc. 1.

To be slandered for nothing is the worst thing that can happen to anyone, my darling. I tell you, in half an hour . . . Of course, unless something unforeseen happens . . . There may not be so much money at my office, or something simply has to be paid immediately, then, of course, it may take a day or two . . . in any event, not more than a week and then you can have everything that your heart desires.

LYDIA. [*Gets up*] In a week? In ten minutes it must be here! Do you hear? I shan't let you into the house if you don't bring me all the money in ten minutes!

KUCHÚMOV. Ten minutes? Am I the god Mercury to fly so fast? I may be detained by business.

LYDIA. No one is going to detain you: your money is in your drawer, the letter from Vassilkov, I suppose, is in another. Good-bye!

KUCHÚMOV. I'll clear myself in your eyes, but [*points his finger accusingly at her*] I shan't forgive such behaviour towards me for a long time. [*Goes out.*]

LYDIA. This is where all my confidence is beginning to forsake me. A shiver runs down my spine. Is Kuchumov deceiving me or not? [*In a determined voice*] He is! So far he hasn't carried out even one of his promises. What is there left for me to do? Despair and suicide or . . . No, that's also suicide, only more slow and more painful . . .

[*Enter* ANDREY.]

ANDREY. Mr. Telyatev, ma'am.

LYDIA. [*Thoughtfully*] Show him in.

[ANDREY *goes out.* TELYÁTEV *comes in.*]

LYDIA. Where have you been all this time? Why didn't you come to see me?

TELYÁTEV. A man who has no business is usually very busy. Why so serious, old girl? [*Looks at her closely and makes a clucking noise with his tongue*] Tch-tch-tch . . .

LYDIA. What's the matter?

TELYÁTEV. A wrinkle, old girl. There, on your forehead. A little one, a very little one, but definitely a wrinkle.

LYDIA. [*In dismay*] It's not true!

TELYÁTEV. Look at yourself in the glass. Tch-tch-tch . . . At your age, too! What a shame!

LYDIA. [*In front of the glass*] Stop tch-tch-tch-ing! I'm sick of you!

TELYÁTEV. Don't think too much, old girl. Above everything else don't overdo thinking. May the good God save and preserve you from thought. Our women preserve their beauty so long because they never think at all.

LYDIA. Oh, Johnnie, anyone else in my place would have gone grey by now! How can I help thinking? Who else will do the thinking for me?

TELYÁTEV. Why, old girl, what do you want? Your position is assured: you live alone, in a beautiful apartment, you are absolutely free to do what you like, you are rich, as I heard you say yourself, you have crowds of admirers, your husband has gone out of your life . . .

LYDIA. [*Happily*] Has he shot himself?

TELYÁTEV. No, he changed his mind.

LYDIA. What a pity! Can I trust you with a secret?

TELYÁTEV. Very much so, old girl.

LYDIA. You won't tell it to anyone?

TELYÁTEV. I can't promise you that, but I usually forget all about it, and that's even better. Tell me a secret at one ear and it is sure to fly out at the other immediately. In an hour I shan't for the life of me be able to remember what the secret was about.

LYDIA. Our position is desperate. We have simply nothing to live on.

TELYÁTEV. There is hardly a family that hasn't got the same kind of secret.

LYDIA. Listen to me! You are quite impossible. I left my husband only because . . . No, I'm too ashamed to tell it to you.

TELYÁTEV. Why be ashamed, old girl? Go on, tell me. I am a particular kind of a bloke, no woman is ever ashamed before me.

LYDIA. All right, I shan't be ashamed before you, either. I left my husband because Kuchumov promised to lend me forty thousand.

TELYÁTEV. What a funny old boy! Why didn't he promise you eighty thousand?

LYDIA. Could he lend me eighty thousand?

TELYÁTEV. Of course. He could lend you two hundred thousand, that is to say, he could promise to lend it to you, but whether he'd ever give you the money is a different proposition. He rarely has as much as ten roubles in his pocket.

LYDIA. You're slandering him. He bought my father's estate for a lot of money. I saw him give six hundred roubles to my mother myself.

TELYÁTEV. I can't tell you anything about the estate, but I know where he got the six hundred roubles from. For five days he was running all over Moscow trying to raise that money and after a lot of trouble he got it from some money-lenders who charged him two thousand for it for one month. I thought he was trying to get the money for your husband to whom he lost it ages ago at cards.

LYDIA. [*In despair*] You're killing me!

TELYÁTEV. Why? Kuchumov is a very nice man. Don't be afraid for him. We all love him, but he is very forgetful. He did have a large fortune a long time ago and he very often forgets that he squandered it years ago. Mind you, there is no reason why he shouldn't forget it: he still gives wonderful receptions, balls and dinners, he still drives about in splendid carriages, only all that is his wife's and is held in trust for her nieces. He himself gets no more than ten roubles for his club expenses. On his birthday or during holidays he usually gets thirty roubles and sometimes even a hundred. That's when you ought to see him! He comes to the club, sits down at the head of the table, orders oysters and champagne, and how pernickety he is! He runs the waiters off their feet, he keeps five waiters fussing round him and, as for the chefs, it is a real black day for them!

LYDIA. [*Going pale*] What am I to do? I owe so much money!

TELYÁTEV. Why be so alarmed about it? Who doesn't owe money to-day?

LYDIA. Johnnie, you have a large fortune, have pity on me! Don't let me perish! [TELYÁTEV *bows his head*] Please, help me to save the honour of my family. You are such a good sport, Johnnie. Please, save me!

[*Puts her hands on his shoulders and bows her head.*]

TELYÁTEV. All this is very nice of you, old girl, and I'd be glad to help you, only I'm hardly myself to-day.

LYDIA. [*Looks into his eyes*] What's the matter? Are you getting married or are you already married?

TELYÁTEV. I am neither married nor am I getting married, but to-morrow I expect to be taken to the debtors' jail.

LYDIA. That's impossible! Where's all your money? I saw you yourself lending money to my husband.

TELYÁTEV. Why shouldn't I? It wasn't my money.

LYDIA. But haven't you any money of your own?

TELYÁTEV. I can't remember the time when I had any money of my own. Yesterday I learnt that I owed about three hundred thousand. Everything you have ever seen in my possession belongs to someone else: my horses, my carriages, my apartment, my clothes. Nothing has been paid for. At first I received bills, then summonses, then orders of execution. I must have borrowed huge sums from moneylenders. All my creditors will do me the honour of paying me a visit to-morrow. It will be a wonderful scene. My furniture, carpets, mirrors and pictures were all on hire and have already been removed. My carriage and horses have also gone, and the tailor is coming early to-morrow morning to fetch my clothes. I am quite sure that my creditors will be tickled to death. I shall receive them in my dressing gown, for that is the only thing in the world that is mine, and I shall offer them a cigar each. They will look at my empty walls and will say: "Go on, have a good time, old fellow!" One of them, who is angry with me because of an affair with his wife, may insist on being paid, which, of course, means that I shall have to spend two months in jail, but he'll soon get fed up paying for my food. In time they will let me out and I shall be free again and I shall have plenty of credit again, because I am a nice chap and because I have about eleven grandmothers and old aunts whose sole heir I am. You can't imagine, old girl, how much money I had to spend on stamped paper for bills of exchange alone! If I were to sell it by the hundredweight, I should get more money than my creditors will get from me to-morrow.

LYDIA. And you are so unruffled?

TELYÁTEV. Why should I worry? My conscience is clear of blame as my pockets are of money. All my creditors have got three times the money I owed them long ago. They are suing me merely as a matter of form.

LYDIA. But where am I to get money, a lot of money, heaps and heaps of money? Can't I get it from anybody?

TELYÁTEV. Yes, of course.

LYDIA. From whom?

TELYÁTEV. From business men who are not in the habit of throwing it to the winds.

LYDIA. What a pity!

TELYÁTEV. It is a great pity, old girl. Even money seems to have got more sense now: it all goes to the business men, and not to us. Before money was not so hard to get, it was easy money. I, too, got easy money, money that came easily and went easily. Only recently I understood why your money and my money was easy money. It was because we did not earn it ourselves. Money which you earn by hard work is sensible money. It keeps still. You and I whistle for it, but it doesn't come. Such money, if granted the gift of speech, would say: "We know the kind of money you want, we shall have nothing to do with you." And, however much you begged, it wouldn't come to you. Which is really unfair, for we are all such charming people.

LYDIA. I'm going to become an actress.

TELYÁTEV. You need talent for that, old girl.

LYDIA. I'll go to the provinces.

TELYÁTEV. Hardly worth while, old girl. You won't meet any man there worth catching. What kind of a career is that?

LYDIA. But, Johnnie, please help me. I want money!

TELYÁTEV. Come here, I'll show you something. [*He takes her to the window*] Do you see that little tumbledown house in the street, looking at the world with its three tiny windows? That's where there is lots of money.

LYDIA. My husband has lots of money?

TELYÁTEV. Yes, he has. He is not only richer than any of us, but he is so rich that it makes you dizzy only to think of it. To-day the rich man is not he who has a lot of money, but he who knows how to make money. If your husband to-day has three hundred thousand in ready money, then you can bet your life that in about a year he'll have a million and in five years—five million.

LYDIA. It's impossible! I don't believe you. Go away! It's he who sent you to me.

TELYÁTEV. But, please, listen to me first. After you left him, we had dinner at the Troitzky restaurant. He sat there without looking at anyone, without eating or drinking. Then a few queer customers came up to him, whispered something in his ear, and he got a little livelier. Then they brought him a telegram, he read it and his eyes began to shine. "No," said he, "it's silly to shoot myself. Let's have a good time instead. Congratulate me." Well, of course, I congratulated him, we embraced and off we went to have a good time. I introduced him to a few of my old friends, they are not really old, you understand, they are, in fact, still very, very young and pretty, but I've known them for some time.

LYDIA. [*At the window*] Look, whose carriage is that? What a lovely thing, how luxurious! Could it be the one mother has got?

TELYÁTEV. No, old girl, you're mistaken. That's the carriage your husband has given to one of my pretty friends. He also bought her the horses and hired a coachman you might exhibit at the Zoo. There she is, leaving his house, a pretty little blonde with cornflower-blue eyes.

LYDIA. Oh, I'm going to faint! That isn't a carriage, it's a dream! One could die of happiness merely to sit in it. What's happened to me? I seem to hate him now and even to be jealous. I could kill that blonde! Look at her, turning up that snub nose of hers!

TELYÁTEV. That isn't jealousy, old girl, it's envy.

LYDIA. Does he love her?

TELYÁTEV. Whom?

LYDIA. That blonde.

TELYÁTEV. Why should he? To love her and to give her

money is a bit too much of a good thing. Would you like to hear what your husband told me about himself?
LYDIA. Yes, tell me. I'd like to know.
TELYÁTEV. He went abroad, spent some time studying the railway system, came back to Russia, got a small job of railway construction and set to work. He lived in barracks with his workers and Vassily. You've met Vassily, haven't you? A jolly fellow.
LYDIA. Really!
TELYÁTEV. After building his first stretch of railway, he undertook to build another, a much bigger one, and then another, bigger and bigger. And now when he got that telegram, he said to me, "Well, old chap, I shan't take less than a million for that!" And I said to him, "Of course not, old fellow!" It didn't matter to me either way, I wasn't going to lose anything.
LYDIA. I'm going to die!
TELYÁTEV. What's the matter?
LYDIA. [*Lies down on the settee*] Call mother, call her quickly!
TELYÁTEV. [*Opens door*] Mrs. Cheboksarova!

[*Enter* MRS. CEBOKSÁROVA.]

LYDIA. Mother, for heaven's sake!
MRS. CHEBOKSÁROVA. What's the matter, Lydia? What's happened, my darling?
LYDIA. For heaven's sake, mother, go to my husband and tell him to come here at once. Tell him I'm dying!
MRS. CHEBOKSÁROVA. [*Looks closely at her daughter*] All right, dear, I can see that you are very ill. I'll go at once.

[*Goes out.*]
[ANDREY *comes in.*]

ANDREY. Mr. Glumov, ma'am.
LYDIA. [*Raising herself*] Shall I receive him or not? I don't know whether my husband will agree to take me back. A drowning man catches at a straw. [*To* ANDREY] Show him in.

[ANDREY *goes out.* GLÚMOV *comes in.*]

GLÚMOV. Hullo, what's the matter?
LYDIA. I am a little out of sorts. And how are you? I hear you're rich.
GLÚMOV. Not yet, but I have hopes. I've got a very good job.

TELYÁTEV. You've all the qualifications for it, old fellow.

GLÚMOV. I was lucky, that's all. An old lady has been looking for a long time for . . . how shall I put it?—not a manager exactly, but a . . .

LYDIA. A confidential secretary?

GLÚMOV. Yes, madam, a confidential secretary. She wants an honest man to whom she can entrust . . .

TELYÁTEV. Herself and her fortune?

GLÚMOV. Almost. She owns houses, estates, companies and what not. She can't possibly look after it herself! She has quarrelled with all her heirs. I am trying to convert it all into money and I receive a big commission on all the deals.

TELYÁTEV. A noble, trusting woman. You must admit, old fellow, you can't find many more like her.

GLÚMOV. Hardly. I suppose she is the only one left in the whole world: I know them all by heart.

TELYÁTEV. We were just talking of easy money and how difficult it is to find it now. But you are luckier than any of us: you have found it!

GLÚMOV. But think, old man, how long and how persistently I looked for it!

LYDIA. So you have plenty of money now, haven't you?

GLÚMOV. Plenty is always relative. The Rothschilds would probably consider it little, but to me it is a lot.

LYDIA. Lend me twenty thousand, please.

GLÚMOV. No one lends money to young, pretty ladies, for it would be highly indelicate to remind them, should they forget about their debt, and to summons them for it, is even more indelicate. Either you politely refuse to give it to them or you make them a present of it.

LYDIA. All right, I don't mind, make me a present of it.

GLÚMOV. I'm afraid I can't give it to you. You remember you told me that I should never kiss your hand. I don't forget an insult.

LYDIA. Kiss it.

GLÚMOV. Now it's too late, or rather too early. Wait a year for me, then I'll come to kiss your hand. To-morrow I'm leaving for Paris with my boss. She hasn't the faintest idea of money and I'm going to be her cashier. She is suffering from asthma and fatty degeneration of the heart. Here the doctors don't give her more than a year to live and in Paris with the travelling to the different spas and the help of the latest medical advice she is sure to die long before that. So you can see that I have no time to waste. For the next year I shall have to nurse a very sick woman, but afterwards I shall be able to enjoy the fruits of my labour and spend a lot of money, with your active participation, if you want.

LYDIA. You are a really wicked man!

GLÚMOV. Before you seemed to admire this trait in my character,—we seem to share it.

LYDIA. Yes, when you didn't overstep the borderline, but now—good-bye!

GLÚMOV. Good-bye. I leave in the pleasant hope that in about a year you'll change your mind, you'll learn to value me and we shall probably meet again like two kindred souls.

LYDIA. That's enough. I don't want to hear any more.

GLÚMOV. *Au revoir*, then.

TELYÁTEV. Good-bye, old fellow. Pleasant journey. Remember me to Paris: my poor ghost still wanders there at every street crossing.

GLÚMOV. Good-bye, Telyatev.

[*Goes out*]

[MRS. CHEBOKSÁROVA *comes in with medicine bottles, followed by a* MAID *with pillows.* MAID *puts pillows on couch and goes out.*]

MRS. CHEBOKSÁROVA. You must lie down, Lydia. Please, don't exhaust yourself. I can see by your look that you are very ill. I told your husband of your sudden illness. He'll be here presently. Here are the smelling salts and the drops which did you so much good before.

LYDIA. [*Reclines on the pillows*] How did he receive you?

MRS. CHEBOKSÁROVA. Very politely, though I'm afraid rather coldly. He asked whether you were seriously ill and I said, yes, very seriously. What are you laughing at, Mr. Telyatev?

TELYÁTEV. I'm afraid, ma'am, I can't remain unaffected: I have either to cry or to laugh.

MRS. CHEBOKSÁROVA. You don't know Lydia's nature or

her constitution. She is such a nervous child. Even as a baby she was very nervous.

TELYÁTEV. Pardon me, m'am, but I haven't the faintest idea of her constitution. It is a mystery to me.

LYDIA. Johnnie, you are such a clown, you'll make me laugh.

MRS. CHEBOKSÁROVA. Really, Mr. Telyatev, you will make her laugh and he may come in any moment.

TELYÁTEV. Shall I hide somewhere?

LYDIA. [*Languorously*] No, stay here, Johnnie. I like to see you. You give me such strength.

TELYÁTEV. If you wish, old girl, I shall not only stay here, but I shall remain standing before you rooted to the ground. Look at me as much as you like, but in this comedy I crave only a walking on part.

[*Enter* ANDREY.]

ANDREY. Mr. Vassilkov, ma'am.

LYDIA. [*In a weak voice*] Show him in.

[ANDREY *goes out.* MRS. CHEBOKSÁROVA *adjusts the pillows.* TELYÁTEV *puts handkerchief to his eyes. Enter* VASSILKÓV.]

VASSILKÓV. [*After a general bow*] You sent for me?

LYDIA. I am dying.

VASSILKÓV. In that case you should have sent either for a doctor or a priest. I'm neither the one nor the other.

LYDIA. You abandoned me and mother.

VASSILKÓV. I did not abandon you, it's you who left me without even saying good-bye.

LYDIA. So you want us to part?

VASSILKÓV. Just as you like.

LYDIA. Do you want me to ask you to forgive me?

VASSILKÓV. By all means.

LYDIA. I am to blame only for having left you without realizing how little money I have. You are to blame for everything else.

VASSILKÓV. We are quits then: I was to blame and you left me. What else is there to discuss? Good-bye!

LYDIA. No, no! Wait, please!

VASSILKÓV. What do you want?

LYDIA. You haven't paid anything for your share of the blame, but I can be made to pay cruelly for mine. I am in debt all round and I might be put in prison together with all sorts of shopkeepers and tradesmen.

VASSILKÓV. Oh? So that's what you're afraid of? That's the sort of dishonour that you dread? Don't be afraid. Many an honest man finds his way to the debtors' jail. From there it is possible to escape. It is right to dread the Moscow Pit, as the debtors' jail is called, but you should dread more that bottomless pit which is called vice and in which the good name, honour and decency of a woman perishes. You're afraid of the pit, but you're not afraid of that abyss from which there is no return to the straight and narrow road.

LYDIA. Who bade you preach to me?

VASSILKÓV. He who bids those who can see help the blind to find the way, who bids the wise to warn the foolish ones and who bids the learned to teach the ignorant.

LYDIA. You have no right to teach me.

VASSILKÓV. I have a right to teach you, the right of pity.

LYDIA. Are you talking of pity? You find your wife in such a hopeless predicament and you refuse to pay some miserable debts for her.

VASSILKÓV. I don't throw my money away, not for anything in the world!

MRS. CHEBOKSÁROVA. I can't understand your philosophy. All this sounds strange to me. Do you mean to say, sir, that to pay a wife's debt is throwing your money away?

VASSILKÓV. What kind of a wife is she to me? Besides, she told me herself that she had more money than I.

MRS. CHEBOKSÁROVA. She told you! What will a woman not say in anger? However much a wife may insult her husband, the wife is always more to be pitied than the husband. We are such weak, nervous creatures, every quarrel takes so much out of us. A quick-tempered woman may commit some foolishness rashly, but she is also quick to repent.

VASSILKÓV. But she doesn't say that she repents.

LYDIA. But ·I do repent. I'm sorry for what I've done.

VASSILKÓV. Isn't it a bit late?

Mrs. Cheboksárova. No, no! She may have been carried away, but she was not unfaithful. She will never be unfaithful.

Vassilkóv. I know she has not been unfaithful to me. I paid your servants more than you paid them. But I don't know what saved her from being unfaithful: her honour or the fact that Kuchumov could not raise the money. [*To* Lydia] What do you want?

Lydia. I should like to live with you again.

Vassilkóv. That's impossible. You change your mind so quickly that you may decide to leave me again to-morrow. I've had quite enough with one dishonour, I do not want another.

Lydia. But you must save me.

Vassilkóv. There is only one way of saving you: I shall offer you honest work and I shall pay you for it.

Lydia. What kind of work and what pay?

Vassilkóv. I offer you the job of my housekeeper. I'll pay you a thousand a year for it.

Lydia. [*Gets up from couch*] Get out!!!

[Vassilkóv *goes out.*]

Telyátev. [*Removes handkerchief from eyes*] Now that you're well again, I can stop crying.

Lydia. I'm not in the mood for your jokes now. Quickly, run and bring him back! [Telyátev *runs out.*]

Mrs. Cheboksárova. What an obstinate mule he is! What an awful man! A real gentleman would never have behaved like that. He'd rather kill his wife than make such a proposal to her. [Vassilkóv *and* Telyátev *come back.*]

Lydia. Please, forgive me. I didn't quite understand. Tell me what does "housekeeper" mean and what are a housekeeper's duties?

Vassilkóv. With pleasure. I will explain it to you, but I must warn you that if you don't accept my offer, I shall never come back to you. A housekeeper is a woman who looks after a house. There is nothing humiliating about such work. These will be your duties: I have an old mother in the country who is an excellent housewife. You will be entirely at her beck and call: she'll teach you how to pickle mushrooms, how to make all sorts of household drinks, jams and so on, she'll give you the keys of the pantry and the cellar, and she will keep you under her eye. I need such a housekeeper, as I'm often away on business.

LYDIA. This is terrible, terrible!

VASSILKÓV. Shall I conclude?

LYDIA. Go on!

VASSILKÓV. When you have learnt how to run a house, I'll take you to our county town where you will be able to dazzle all our provincial ladies by your fine dresses and your exquisite manners. I shan't be niggardly with my allowance for you, but I shall never live beyond my income. As a business man with ever expanding interests in every part of our vast country, I badly need such a wife as you. If, later on, you are nice to me, I'll take you to Petersburg. There we'll have our box at the opera to hear Patti, I shouldn't mind spending a thousand for it. I have very influential business connections in Petersburg, but I'm rather uncouth and raw in my manners. I want a wife who could receive and entertain important people, including a Cabinet minister or two. You have everything I need in a wife, but first you will have to unlearn certain habits which you've acquired from Telyatev and the rest.

TELYÁTEV. But I never dreamt that dear Lydia would get such a marvellous chance of rising from a kitchen maid to a Petersburg leader of fashion!

VASSILKÓV. [*Looking at his watch*] Do you accept my offer or not? But I warn you, that, to begin with, you will be my housekeeper and that for a very long time.

LYDIA. Please, take pity on me! Take pity on my pride! I am a lady, a lady born and bred, a lady from the crown of my head to the soles of my feet! Please, make some concession to me!

VASSILKÓV. I shall make no concessions whatever. Why should I have pity on your pride when you refused to have pity on my simplicity and good nature? Even in making you the offer of becoming my housekeeper I do it out of love.

LYDIA. At least don't call it housekeeper! It's such a horrid word!

VASSILKÓV. Not at all, I think it's an excellent word.

LYDIA. You must give me time to think it over.
VASSILKÓV. All right, you can think it over.
[*Enter* ANDREY.]
ANDREY. The broker's men are here to make an inventory of the furniture, ma'am.
LYDIA and MRS. CHEBOKSÁROVA. Good God!
[LYDIA *buries her face in a pillow.*]
TELYÁTEV. What's all the fuss about? Calm yourselves. The furniture of two of my friends was distrained by bailiffs yesterday, to-day it will be your furniture, to-morrow mine, the day after to-morrow Kuchumov's. It's a kind of epidemic now.
LYDIA. [*To her husband*] Save me from disgrace! I accept your offer! I agree to everything. What can I do? I wanted to shine like an inextinguishable star, but you want me to be a meteor which bursts into dazzling light for a moment and flickers out in some swamp. But I agree, I agree, only, please, I implore you, save me!
[VASSILKÓV *goes out with* ANDREY, *who comes back.*]
ANDREY. Mr. Kuchumov, ma'am.
LYDIA. I think I'd better receive him.
TELYÁTEV. Yes, you should receive him.
LYDIA. Show him in.
[ANDREY *goes out, enter* KUCHÚMOV, *followed a little later by* VASSILKÓV.]
KUCHÚMOV. [*Humming*] Io son rico . . . What's the matter?
LYDIA. Bailiffs are making an inventory of my furniture. Have you brought the forty thousand?
KUCHÚMOV. *Io son rico* . . . No, fancy what bad luck! [VASSILKÓV *enters and stops at the door*] My valet, whom I loved like a son, stole all my money and ran off to America, I believe.
TELYÁTEV. I am very sorry for your valet. With the money he stole from you he could not only never reach America, he could hardly reach the next station.
KUCHÚMOV. Don't crack such silly jokes! I don't like it. I've dispatched telegrams all over the country. I suppose they'll catch him soon, return me the money and then, my child, I'll give it to you.

TELYÁTEV. But, surely, he didn't pinch everything, he must have left something behind.

KUCHÚMOV. Of course, he left something. I never leave my house without a thousand in my pocket.

VASSILKÓV. In that case you'd better pay me the six hundred roubles which you lost to me at cards.

KUCHÚMOV. Oh, you're here? Very nice, too. I wanted to pay you back a long time ago. A debt at cards is a matter of first importance to me. [*Takes out wallet*] Goodness gracious! What's that? Where's the money? I must have put it in my left pocket. No? Oh, I see, I've put on another coat! However, you can get the money from Mrs. Cheboksarova.

VASSILKÓV. All right, I'll get it from her. Lydia, I have paid your debts. Now get ready to leave for the country.

LYDIA. As you please.

VASSILKÓV. I am leaving to-morrow. Be ready to leave with me.

LYDIA. [*Offers hand to her husband*] Thank you for granting me a whole day to weep. I have many things to cry over. I have to cry over the lost dreams of my youth, over my mistake, over my humiliation. I have to cry over something which I can never bring back. My goddess of careless joy has been thrown off her pedestal and in her place there stands the rude idol of industry and commerce, whose name is income. Poor, tender creatures! Pretty, happy-go-lucky girls! How my heart bleeds for you! Never again will you have husbands with perfect manners and very bad heads for figures. Ethereal creatures, away with your dreams of unrealizable happiness! Never again dream of men who can squander a fortune with such inimitable grace, but marry men who can make a fortune without a suspicion of grace and who are known as business men!

TELYÁTEV. Spare us, spare us, old girl, those who are good for nothing implore you!

KUCHÚMOV. [*Sings*] *Io son rico* . . .

TELYÁTEV. No, old fellow, you are not rich. You should sing: *Noi siamo poveri*, we are poor.

LYDIA. This is the sacrifice I am making for you.

VASSILKÓV. I don't want any sacrifices from anybody.

LYDIA. I see that I've met my match in you. Very well, I'll make a clean breast of it. I have accepted your offer because I consider it profitable.

VASSILKÓV. But remember, I shall never spend beyond my income!

LYDIA. I suppose I shall never be allowed to forget it.

VASSILKÓV. Only those to whom money comes easily can afford to live beyond their income.

TELYÁTEV. It's gospel truth, old fellow, it's more than that: it's what I've been saying all along!

VASSILKÓV. [*To* TELYÁTEV] Good-bye, old man. I am very sorry for you. To-morrow you won't have anything to eat and no roof over your head.

TELYÁTEV. Would you like to lend me some money? No, old fellow, don't you lend me anything. It will only be a dead loss, for you won't see a penny of it. Moscow, Savva, is a city where the Telyatevs and the Kuchumovs will never go under. Even if we haven't a penny, we shall always have honour and credit. For a long time to come every shopkeeper in town will be honoured to dine and wine us at his expense. The tailors, it is true, do not show much respect for us, but even an old overcoat and an old hat can be worn with such distinction that people will move aside to let you pass. Good-bye, old fellow, don't be sorry for us. Virtue shines through even the meanest rags!

[*Embraces* KUCHÚMOV.]
[LYDIA *goes up shyly to* VASSILKÓV, *puts her hand on his shoulder and buries her head on his chest.*]

CURTAIN

WOLVES AND SHEEP
A Comedy in Five Acts

By
ALEXANDER OSTROVSKY

Translated by
DAVID MAGARSHACK

CHARACTERS

MEROPIA DAVYDOVNA MURZAVÉTZKAYA, a spinster of 65 years of age, owner of a large but insolvent estate, a person of great influence in the county.

APOLLONIUS VIKTOROVICH MURZAVÉTZKY, a young man of 24, a retired lieutenant of infantry, nephew of Murzavétzkaya.

GLAFÍRA ALEXEYEVNA, a young girl, a poor relation of Murzavétzkaya.

EULAMPE NIKOLAYEVNA KUPÁVINA, a rich young widow.

ANFÚSSA TIKHONOVNA, her aunt, an old woman.

MIKHAIL BORISSOVICH LYNYÁYEV, a rich landowner, just under fifty, an honorary Justice of the Peace.

VASSILY IVANOVICH BERKÚTOV, a landowner, a neighbour of Mrs. Kupávina; a bald-headed, middle-aged man, but very much alive and with all his wits about him.

VUKOL NAUMOVICH CHUGÚNOV, a former clerk to a court, about 60.

CLAVDY GORÉTZKY, a nephew of Chugúnov, a handsome young man with wavy hair and good complexion, dressed in a light summer coat, buttoned up to the neck, a coloured Russian shirt without tie, breeches tucked into high boots.

PAVLIN SAVELYICH, butler
VLAS, pantry-boy } Servants of Murzavétzkaya.
KORNILY, footman

FOOTMAN of Mrs. Kupávina.

STOROPILIN, builder.

HOUSEPAINTER.

CARPENTER.

PEASANT, former Village Headman of Murzavétzkaya.

Artisans, Peasants and Poor Relations of Murzavétzkaya.

The first and last acts take place in a county town, in the house of Murzavétzkaya.

ACT ONE

[*A large room furnished in old-fashioned style, to the right (of the spectators) three windows, between them long, narrow mirrors with brackets. Near the first window a highbacked chair and a small table; on the table an open old family Bible and a handbell. At the back, in the right-hand corner, a pair of folding doors leading into a large hall; in the left-hand corner a door leading into* APOLLONIUS'S *room; between the doors a Russian stove. To the left, in the corner, a door leading into a corridor which leads into the inner rooms. Nearer to the front of the stage doors leading into the drawing-room. Between the doors, close to the wall, a large dining table.*

PAVLIN *is standing near the folding doors surrounded by the* BUILDER, HOUSEPAINTER, CARPENTER, VILLAGE HEADMAN, WORKMEN *and* PEASANTS.

PAVLIN. [*Shaking hands with the* BUILDER] Ah, Mr. Storopilin, pleased to meet you. [*To the rest*] Please, gentlemen, please! What a din!

CARPENTER. Every man for himself!

HOUSEPAINTER. We want our money real bad!

VILLAGE HEADMAN. It's holiday time, so havin' nothin' to do like, we've all come for our money.

BUILDER. Holiday time, my lad, is hardly the time to go collecting your money, you mightn't reach home to the wife with it.

CARPENTER. We'll take a chance, only let's get it first.

HOUSEPAINTER. Aye, you won't catch me giving nothing to nobody. I'll clench it in me fist so hard that no man o' yourn will take it off me!

PAVLIN. So you've quite made up your minds to wait for Miss Meropia?

1ST PEASANT. Aye, we don't mind waitin'. We're used to waitin'.

2ND PEASANT. Waitin' does no 'un no 'arm. I took me timber for the bath-house last autumn. [*Pointing to* BUILDER] Ginger yonder did the buildin'.

HOUSEPAINTER. Aye, and I painted the fence, twelve sections of it, and touched up the summer-house in umber.

VILLAGE HEADMAN. Same time as I sold the milkfed bull-calf for saltin'.

CARPENTER. Every man wants to be paid for his work. I 'ere made two fine small walnut tables for the old lady's bedroom.

PAVLIN. And what about you, Mr. Storopilin?

BUILDER. Aye, me, too. I have a little old bill to settle. Left my home on some business this morning, I did, and, well, I says to myself, might as well trot round, I says, a little walk don't do no man no harm.

PAVLIN. What do you want me to do? I can't let you all in. Tell you what, my good people. You'd better go back to your homes. You can look in later again, but not all at the same time.

BUILDER. Nay, you'd better let me see her!

VOICES. We all want to see the old woman! Let's all see her!

PAVLIN. All right, all right. I'll see what I can do, only let's get this straight, gentlemen. In the first place, those who are better dressed [*pointing at the* BUILDER, HOUSEPAINTER, CARPENTER *and* VILLAGE HEADMAN] can stay here, [*to the rest*] while you wait outside. Secondly, as soon as Miss Meropia returns, you'll immediately go up to her and kiss hands and those who want to show their respect can go down on their knees, but you mustn't even mention money to her. You can pay her the compliments of the season, if you wish, but not a word about money!

HOUSEPAINTER. How d'ye mean, not a word about money? We've come here for our money, haven't we?

PAVLIN. Not a word and that's all there is about it. When Miss Meropia has gone into the drawing-room and has had tea, I shall report to her and then a decision will be taken about all of you. What would you like her to do on a church holiday and in the morning, too—engage in mundane affairs? At such a time Miss Meropia likes to be quiet, she doesn't want to be disturbed, especially about money. Think for yourselves: when she comes back from church she sits down to meditate and when she raises her eyes to heaven, where do you think her thoughts are?

BUILDER. High up, no doubt, high up.

VILLAGE HEADMAN. So 'igh it fair makes you giddy to think on.

PAVLIN. There you are then! [*To the* HOUSEPAINTER] And you with your umber! You're a lot of village bumpkins, all of you! When will you learn some sense? Money is money, but all in good time. Here we're doing everything possible to avoid all wordly cares, and he comes clamouring to be paid for his milkfed bullcalf! Well, go on, all of you, to your appointed places with you!

[*The* PEASANTS *and* WORKMEN *go out. The* BUILDER, HOUSEPAINTER, CARPENTER *and* VILLAGE HEADMAN *take up their positions at the folding doors.* CHUGÚNOV *enters with briefcase.*]

CHUGÚNOV. [*Indicating with his eyes the people at the doors*] You've a lot of visitors to-day.

PAVLIN. [*Taking snuff*] A delegation, sir.

CHUGÚNOV. May I? [PAVLIN *offers him snuff-box and he helps himself*] I see you've divided the sheep from the goats: some—wait, others—come later!

PAVLIN. In the matter of money, sir, we are on the rocks.

CHUGÚNOV. It happens. A fair wind or a high tide, they say, will get you off again.

PAVLIN. May the Lord grant it so, sir. You can hardly expect a woman to have a good head for business.

CHUGÚNOV. Don't say that! Miss Meropia has business sense enough for half a dozen men.

PAVLIN. You can't compare her to a man, sir. If she had a man's brains, she wouldn't have sent for you. Every time she wants to bring an action in the courts, she sends for you.

CHUGÚNOV. You don't want any brains for an action in the courts. You can be as wise as an owl, but if you don't know the law . . .

PAVLIN. I understand, sir. But if she had any sense, she would keep away from the courts. Of course, it isn't my business to criticize my betters, but, I'm afraid I can hardly bring myself to admire her. Miss Meropia is just like that: if she picks a quarrel with any of her friends, she immediately goes to court. Think of it, sir. She has a very large number of friends and she is constantly picking quarrels with them. No wonder we never seem to get out of the courts.

CHUGÚNOV. I suppose you are right. She very often begins an action for no reason at all.

PAVLIN. Only unpleasantness for everybody all round, sir.

CHUGÚNOV. But we haven't actually involved anyone in any loss yet. No one ever dreams of complying with her demands and so far she hasn't won a single case.

PAVLIN. Exactly, sir. Think of the continual drain on the estate, paying damages and feeding solicitors' clerks!

CHUGÚNOV. What are you talking about? Who else will feed them? Don't they want to eat? Aren't they people like anyone else?

PAVLIN. I don't think so, sir.

CHUGÚNOV. But I am a solicitors' clerk myself, aren't I?

PAVLIN. I am aware of that fact, sir.

CHUGÚNOV. Very well, then, in that case you'd better keep a civil tongue in your head. I know how to deal with yokels like you, I owned 150 of them in the past.

PAVLIN. In the past, sir, but you don't any more now.

CHUGÚNOV. You're right there, I don't any more now. I was a gentleman once, but now I'm just a pettifogging lawyer and have to put up with all kinds of impudent talk from yokels.

PAVLIN. I can't help saying what's on my mind, sir, if you keep leading Miss Meropia astray. You can afford to give up all your litigation, sir, and be a gentleman again: you've such a good job!

CHUGÚNOV. Yes, I have a good job.

PAVLIN. Thanks to Miss Meropia's kindness, you are now the manager of Mrs. Kupavina's estate. What a fine job it is, sir! One can see you're not doing so badly out of it, either. You've built yourself a nice house, bought some horses, and, from what I hear, you've got plenty of cash, too.

CHUGÚNOV. So they've started wagging their tongues, have they? They're jealous, I shouldn't wonder.

PAVLIN. Why should they be jealous? Why shouldn't a man get all he can with God's help?

CHUGÚNOV. Why not, indeed? Let them talk. Do you think I care? I have tasted poverty. I know what it feels like to go begging from door to door. You remember my civil service uniform—don't you—the one I've only just discarded? It was worn to a thread and you could hardly tell whether it was a woman's frock or a uniform.

PAVLIN. Mrs. Kupavina is young and good-natured. She has no idea of business. A man with no conscience . . .

CHUGÚNOV. What's conscience got to do with it? What have you brought up my conscience for. Philosophy is hardly your subject . . .

PAVLIN. [*Glancing through the window*] Miss Meropia has arrived.

[*Goes out.*]

[KORNILY *in a white tie and white gloves enters from drawing-room, opens both folding doors and remains standing at the left side of entrance.* CHUGÚNOV *gets up from his chair and stations himself not far from the door of the drawing-room. At the folding doors, drawn up in a line, stand the* BUILDER, *the* VILLAGE HEADMAN, *the* HOUSE-PAINTER *and the* CARPENTER. MISS MEROPIA, *dressed in a black silk blouse, tied round the waist with a thick silk girdle, wearing on her head a lace kerchief, which half covers her face like a veil, and leaning heavily on an ebony stick with a large ivory handle rather in the shape of a crutch, passes slowly through the room, without looking at anybody, into the drawing-room. Everybody bows respectfully and bends down in turn to kiss her right hand. Two paces behind her follow* GLAFÍRA, *in a plain black woollen dress, and two* POOR RELATIONS, *also in black.* PAVLIN *walks on* MISS MEROPIA'S *left hand, leaning forward deferentially and carrying on his arm a kind of a black cloak.* KOR-NILY, *having let the procession pass, enters the drawing-room and closes the door behind him.*

VILLAGE HEADMAN. What a grand old lady! God bless her! Even the crutch is the same.

BUILDER. Do you remember it?

VILLAGE HEADMAN. When I was still one of her serfs . . .

BUILDER. She used to belabour you with it?

VILLAGE HEADMAN. Aye, and how she laid about me!

[*Enter* PAVLIN.]

PAVLIN. You've come at an unseasonable time, gentlemen.

CHUGÚNOV. Why? What's up?

PAVLIN. I daren't even make my report to her. [*To* CHUGÚ-

NOV] The servants are getting out of hand, sir. They can't or they won't boil up the milk properly. You keep on telling them that there must be a lot of skin on it, because Miss Meropia is very fond of skin. But they will not please her even in such a small thing. No wonder, she is so angry!

VILLAGE HEADMAN. What are we to do now like?

PAVLIN. Maybe you'd better come back in a week's time. The Lord may be more merciful then.

HOUSEPAINTER. What's the good of comin' again and again? It's just a blinkin' waste o' time!

PAVLIN. All right, that will do! You have had your say, now keep quiet, will you? Am I talking to you as a friend or not? Don't wait till I start swearing at you!

CARPENTER. Is that all? Is that what we're to take home with us?

PAVLIN. What else do you want? We haven't prepared a spread for you. [*To the* BUILDER] See you again one day, Mr. Storopilin. [*To the rest*] Well, God be with you, good people.

[*The* BUILDER, VILLAGE HEADMAN, HOUSEPAINTER *and* CARPENTER *go out.*]

PAVLIN. Lunch is being prepared for you in the dining-room, sir.

CHUGÚNOV. Let's have another pinch of your snuff. [*Helping himself*] Thank you.

PAVLIN. I'm afraid you'll have to wait a little, as Miss Meropia is expecting Master Apollonius.

CHUGÚNOV. Where is he?

PAVLIN. He spends all his time in one place, sir. It's a real scandal. Even the townspeople are beginning to shake their heads about it. He takes his gun, pretending to go hunting, but he goes straight to the village pub at Marsh Bottom. He is there all the time, sir, from dawn to dusk. And it is such a filthy place, too. It stands at the end of the village, on the highway, and it has a big sign with "Welcome" painted on it. It's a crying shame, that's what it is, sir. He is there for days, drinking and exchanging blows with the riff-raff of the village. Miss Meropia has sent the pantry-boy Vlas for him, with strict orders to bring him home.

CHUGÚNOV. And what is he going to do at home?

PAVLIN. Miss Meropia wants him to settle down. She wants to introduce him into good society, she wants him to go visiting with her to-day. She has even ordered new clothes for him.
CHUGÚNOV. Does she want to marry him off by any chance?
PAVLIN. That's the idea, sir.
CHUGÚNOV. Some bridegroom!
PAVLIN. Well, you see, sir, Mrs. Kupavina is a widow and Mr. Lynyayev is still a bachelor.
CHUGÚNOV. The dear lady seems to think of everybody.
PAVLIN. She does, indeed, sir. And how wonderfully she thinks everything out! Mrs. Kupavina is very rich, she ought therefore to marry a poor man, provided he is as young as Master Apollonius, for instance. Mr. Lynyayev, on the other hand, is also rich, but he is already getting on in years, and for him she has got a lady of a good aristocratic family, not very young, it is true, and her head, too, seems to be a bit unsteady, but she is so well brought up, sir, she is such a well brought up lady, sir, that you could hardly believe it possible. [*Glancing through the window*] There's Vlas with the young master.
CHUGÚNOV. I'll be in the dining-room.   (*Goes out.*)
[*Enter*: APOLLONIUS MURZAVÉTZKY, *wearing a black coat, buttoned up to the neck, a pair of breeches tucked into high boots, a peaked cap with a red band and a cockade;* VLAS *with gun, cartridge case, hunting bag and whip.*]
APOLLONIUS. [*Without removing cap*] Is auntie in her room?
PAVLIN. Yes, sir.
APOLLONIUS. What a beastly shoot. I'm fagged out, my dear fellow. But what else is there to do? I can't live without shootin'. I'll slip into my dressing gown and go to bed. [*He is about to retire to his room.*]
PAVLIN. No, sir. You are to wait right here. These are your aunt's orders.
          [APOLLONIUS *sits down at the window.*]
VLAS. I had to carry everything: master, harness and ammunition.
PAVLIN. [*Looking into hunting bag*] There isn't a bird in it, sir, not even a feather.

APOLLONIUS. Bad luck, my dear fellow, damn bad luck. I was unlucky from the start, I should have come back, really: a hare ran across my path. Every time I took aim—bang—it was either a spaniel or a miss.

PAVLIN. [*To* VLAS] Take it to Master Apollonius's room and put it down carefully.

APOLLONIUS. [*Opening window*] Hell, it's so stuffy here! [*Puts head out of window and begins to whistle*] Tamerlaine, you devil! You wait, I'll show you! Eh, you there, bring Tamerlaine here and fetch me my whip!

PAVLIN. No, sir, you can't do that here. Miss Meropia has strictly forbidden it. And what sort of Tamerlaine is it? Why do you call such a mongrel Tamerlaine? His real name should be Rover, but even that is too good for the likes of him. Spotty, that's the only name for him!

APOLLONIUS. A fat lot you know about dogs!

PAVLIN. I know his whole pedigree, sir. All he knows is filching eggs from the hen-run, that's all the training he has had. It's high time he was strung up on a tree, but why go even to that trouble with a dog like him? Wait till the autumn and then, by God's grace, the wolves will eat him up. He's too stupid to keep out of their way. We've even nicknamed him "The Wolf's Cutlet." As for you, sir, you'd better take off your cap, Miss Meropia may come in any moment now.

APOLLONIUS. [*Taking off cap*] Mind your own business! Know your place. I don't like wasting my time in talking to fools like you.

PAVLIN. Very good, sir.

APOLLONIUS. Damn it, I'm beginning to feel dashed funny! I wonder if I've caught a cold or something? I must have got my feet wet in that swamp. [*Shouts*] Eh, there, bring me some vodka!

PAVLIN. You're not at the Marsh Bottom pub, sir.

APOLLONIUS. Well, what about it? What if I'm not at the Marsh Bottom pub?

PAVLIN. Because here, sir, you won't get any vodka.

APOLLONIUS. Now, please, be a good pal, Pavlin, old boy. I beg you as a friend, as a good friend, do me the favour, will you?

PAVLIN. Ah, that's the way to ask, sir.
APOLLONIUS. I really don't know what's come over me, my dear chap. I'll be frank with you: I've a devilish thirst on me!
PAVLIN. Well, all right. What's one to do with you?
[*Goes out.*]
[GLAFÍRA *comes out of the drawing-room and goes to the door leading to the corridor.*]
APOLLONIUS. I say, old girl, won't you even look at me? Damn it, what lovely eyes you've got! I'd give my life for a glance from such eyes.
GLAFÍRA. What do you want?
APOLLONIUS. What do I want? What a funny question! I want to kiss you, of course, but . . .
GLAFÍRA. You are a fool.
APOLLONIUS. I beg your pardon.
GLAFÍRA. Good-bye. [*Is about to go.*].
APOLLONIUS. Wait a minute, will you? Tell me, is *ma tante irritée?*
GLAFÍRA. Your French is awful!
APOLLONIUS. Never mind, it'll pass in our county.
GLAFÍRA. I don't think she's exactly in raptures over you.
[*Wants to go.*]
APOLLONIUS. Wait a minute! Best regards . . .
GLAFÍRA. From whom?
APOLLONIUS. Lynyayev.
GLAFÍRA. Thank you. What's come over him? He has never been so civil before!
APOLLONIUS. I met him while out shootin'. Damn him, I borrowed some money from him. Are you two having an affair? Come on, old girl, confess! What are you looking so high and mighty for?
[GLAFÍRA *shrugs her shoulders and goes out. Enter:* PAVLIN *and* VLAS, *carrying a tray with a glass of vodka and some food.*]
PAVLIN. Quickly, sir, or, God forbid, Miss Meropia may come in!
APOLLONIUS. [*Drinks and eats*] What filthy vodka and what beastly food! Hell! [*To* VLAS] Get out!
[VLAS *takes tray and goes out.*]

PAVLIN. Be grateful for what you get, sir.

APOLLONIUS. Who do you think you are, head cook and bottle washer? Have you done me such a great favour or what? I ordered a drink and you brought it to me, that's all there is to it! You wouldn't have dared not to bring it!

PAVLIN. Very good, sir. I shall make a note of that.

APOLLONIUS. A country yokel and what a figure he's cutting! Too silly for words!

[MISS MEROPIA *enters.*]

MISS MEROPIA. What are you sprawling about in the chair for? Get up! Don't you see me? [*Raises her stick.*]

APOLLONIUS. [*Getting up*] I'm so sorry, auntie. I was sitting down because I'm not feeling up to the mark. I'm out of sorts, not in the best of spirits.

MISS MEROPIA. What do I care? [*To* PAVLIN] Close the door, and don't admit anyone till I tell you.

PAVLIN. [*Offering her the arm-chair*] Very good, ma'am.

[*Goes out.*]

MISS MEROPIA. [*Pointing to the chair*] Now you can sit down, when told to.

APOLLONIUS. Please, don't mind me.

MISS MEROPIA. Why should I mind you? But I can't bear to see you fidgeting like the devil in front of me. [*Banging the stick*] Sit down, will you? [APOLLONIUS *sits down*] How much longer will you go on tormenting and shaming me?

APOLLONIUS. What's the matter, auntie? I don't know what you're talking about.

MISS MEROPIA. I'm talking about your goings on in the pubs, your merrymaking with the farmhands, your quarrels and what not. For a Murzavetzky to behave like this is rank indecency.

APOLLONIUS. What a story! What a story! And you believe all the lies they tell about me?

MISS MEROPIA. What lies? Things have gone so far that people are ashamed even to tell me the truth. And what am I to expect of you? They chucked you out of the regiment . . .

APOLLONIUS. Really, auntie.

MISS MEROPIA. Shut up! I shouldn't have minded if it were for some silly prank or other. If you had squandered some

public money or lost it at cards I should at least be sorry for you, but for your fellow officers to chuck you out for some dirty little misdemeanour, for dishonouring their uniform!
APOLLONIUS. But, I say, auntie . . .
MISS MEROPIA. What a lovely present, what a pleasant surprise for your family!
APOLLONIUS. But, please, auntie, do let me say something in my defence, a few words . . .
MISS MEROPIA. You can't tell me anything worth listening to. You have nothing to tell me!
APOLLONIUS. But do let me, please.
MISS MEROPIA. All right, go on. Let's hear it!
APOLLONIUS. Fate, auntie, fate is a strumpet!
MISS MEROPIA. Is that all you have to say for yourself?
APOLLONIUS. Fate is a strumpet, I'm telling you. That's all there is to it.
MISS MEROPIA. [*Shaking her head*] Oh, Apollonius, Apollonius! How is one to be sorry for you or to care for you as one should? Only to look at you is enough to drive one crazy. Tell me one thing: can you take a good hold of yourself or not? Can you control yourself just for a bit?
APOLLONIUS. Of course I can control myself, auntie. How do you like that?
MISS MEROPIA. [*Not listening to him*] If only you'd behave yourself a little and try to keep up appearances, I'd get you some official job and a wife with a lot of money.
APOLLONIUS. Auntie, you're a dear! [*Kisses her hand*] Thank you.
MISS MEROPIA. But not a word about it to any living soul, do you hear?
APOLLONIUS. You needn't tell me that, auntie. I understand, I understand perfectly. I've been playing the fool, but only say the word and I shan't have another drop. Not a drop, I swear!
MISS MEROPIA. I don't believe a word of it.
APOLLONIUS. On my word of honour, auntie. The word of a gentleman!
MISS MEROPIA. I seem to have heard that before!
APOLLONIUS. All right, let's have a bet on it, auntie. Would

you like to lay a wager? I'm ready to take you on. That's a sporting offer, auntie!

MISS MEROPIA. I'd rather not bet. I prefer to keep you under lock and key. That should keep you out of mischief.

APOLLONIUS. [*Looking out of the window*] Anything you say, auntie.

MISS MEROPIA. In future you are only to leave the house with me. We shall go visiting to-day.

APOLLONIUS. [*Smiting his chest and yelling through window*] Tamerlaine! Tamerlaine! Jump! Jump!

MISS MEROPIA. Have you gone off your head? What are you doing? With his dirty paws through the window?

APOLLONIUS. Sorry! [*Yelling through window*] Down, down! Lie down at once, damn you!

MISS MEROPIA. Stop it, stop it! Sit down at once, sit down!

APOLLONIUS. But, auntie, you don't understand. You have to be severe with a dog or else you'd better give it away or drown it.

MISS MEROPIA. [*Banging her stick*] You numskull! Do as I tell you!

APOLLONIUS. Wait, auntie, I'll attend to you in a sec. [*Yelling out of the window*] Lie down, lie down, I tell you. Where's my whip? [*Yells*] Eh, there, bring me my whip!

MISS MEROPIA. [*Takes him by the hand and forces him to sit down*] It's you who need a whipping. What was I talking to you about? Did you listen to me at all?

APOLLONIUS. That dog has so upset me, auntie.

MISS MEROPIA. Listen to me, that's an order: go to bed at once and have a good sleep. In the evening I'll take you to see your bride-to-be. Try to make yourself smart, we're going to pay a visit to Mrs. Kupavina.

APOLLONIUS. Whoopie! I simply adore her, auntie. This is wonderful . . . this is . . . I simply don't know what to say, auntie. You're a dear. Thank you, thank you. [*He kisses her hand.*]

MISS MEROPIA. And now straight to bed!

APOLLONIUS. [*Goes to door and then comes back*] I want some money, auntie.

MISS MEROPIA. I don't think so.

APOLLONIUS. Then at least tell them to bring me something.
MISS MEROPIA. What do you want?
APOLLONIUS. A teeny-weeny bottle and a bite of something. Just imagine, auntie, a whole day on the marshes and not a drop to drink or a bite to eat!
MISS MEROPIA. And who was offering me a bet a short while ago?
APOLLONIUS. I will keep off it, auntie, I promise you, I will keep off it. But not all at once, you can't do it all at once, auntie. It's very dangerous, you know. There have been many cases of people who stopped drinking all at once and . . . I know of one such case when a fellow stopped all at once and, as he was sitting, without any more ado, he . . . They had no time to send for a priest even, auntie.
MISS MEROPIA. The Lord is merciful. I, somehow, don't think you'll die.
APOLLONIUS. [*Gives out a loud yell*] Oh! [*Puts hand on heart*] Oh-h-h! It's come, auntie, it's come!
MISS MEROPIA. What's the matter?
APOLLONIUS. It went right through me, auntie, from the heart to the solar plexus!
MISS MEROPIA. Never mind, it'll pass.
APOLLONIUS. [*Yells louder*] Oh-h-h-h! Like a dagger!
MISS MEROPIA. All right, go. I'll tell them, only it's for the last time, do you hear?
APOLLONIUS. I don't know if I'll be able to drag myself to my room. It doesn't take so long for a fellow to die, auntie. Not that I care a damn if I do, but without a priest, auntie, without a priest . . .

[*Staggers out.*]
[MISS MEROPIA *rings.* PAVLIN *enters.*]

MISS MEROPIA. See that Master Apollonius doesn't leave the house! Let somebody watch the hall continuously. It's an order, mind, and I shall hold you responsible for its being carried out.
PAVLIN. But, ma'am, if I may take the liberty of pointing out, Master Apollonius has been known sometimes to use the window . . .
MISS MEROPIA. Take away his clothes! Say you want them

to be cleaned and don't give them back to him. He won't run off in his dressing gown!

PAVLIN. If I may take the liberty of pointing out, ma'am, he has been known to run off even in his dressing gown, especially towards the evening.

MISS MEROPIA. Where does he get his money from?

PAVLIN. He borrows it, ma'am.

MISS MEROPIA. From whom?

PAVLIN. From different gentlemen, ma'am, from Mr. Lynyayev, for instance. If I may say so, ma'am, there isn't a gentleman who comes to our house he doesn't borrow from.

MISS MEROPIA. My patience is at an end! I shall marry him off, may the Lord forgive me, but I shall marry him off!

PAVLIN. Nothing could be better, ma'am.

MISS MEROPIA. What were all the people doing outside the house and in here?

PAVLIN. They came for their money. They've been waiting a long time, ma'am.

MISS MEROPIA. Well, they'll have to wait a little longer.

PAVLIN. They do rather make a nuisance of themselves, ma'am. They keep on worrying you.

MISS MEROPIA. Why should I be worried? I am never in want. I usually get enough for my needs. What are you gaping at me for? Yes, I mean it. Whatever I want, I get. If I want a thousand, I get a thousand, if I want fifty thousand, I shall get fifty thousand. You didn't forget to tell them—did you?—that I remembered those I owed money to in my prayers, but that I don't give another thought to those I no longer owe anything?

PAVLIN. I told them, ma'am, only they don't seem to appreciate your goodness. They're clamouring to be paid, ma'am. If I may say so, ma'am, they are such a rough lot and their ignorance is quite past curing.

MISS MEROPIA. And yet, Pavlin, there have been cases where my prayers have been answered by some piece of good fortune, big profits and so on. However, if they insist on getting their money, we shall have to give it to them.

PAVLIN. If only you could promise to pay them by a certain date, ma'am.

Miss Meropia. Why promise? I don't want to be bound by any promises. I shall. pay them, that's all I don't even know how much money I have or, indeed, whether I have any money at all and, anyway, I consider it sinful to pry into every hole and corner for it. When I want any money, when I really want it, that is to say, when I decide to pay them, the money will be found. All I shall have to do is to rummage round a little. That's the sort of miracle that happens to me. Do you believe me or not?

Pavlin. I dare not disbelieve you, ma'am.

Miss Meropia. So why all this talk? I don't want to worry about debts. Why be in such haste? How do we know, it may be they are being tempted through me?

Pavlin. Indeed, it may, ma'am.

Miss Meropia. Tell Chugunov I'll see him now.

Pavlin. Very good, ma'am. [*At the door*] Mr. Chugunov, Miss Meropia will see you now. [*To* Miss Meropia] He's coming, ma'am.

[*Goes out into hall.*]
[*Enter* Chugúnov.]

Chugúnov. Best wishes of the season, Miss Meropia.

Miss Meropia. Good morning, my dear Vukol. Sit down.

Chugúnov. Permit me to kiss the hand of my guardian angel. [*Kisses her hand and sits down.*]

Miss Meropia. I sent for you. I have some important business, Vukol, very important business to transact. For the past three nights I've been weighing it over in my mind very carefully and I'm not sure whether I can trust you with it or not.

Chugúnov. Would my conscience permit me to do anything against my guardian angel?

Miss Meropia. You have no conscience.

Chugúnov. I can't possibly have no conscience at all, ma'am. I must have some kind of conscience, surely.

Miss Meropia. [*Banging her stick*] You have no conscience.

Chugúnov. Well, just as you please, ma'am, just as you please. I can't presume to argue the point with you. One thing I will say, however, after God, you are my only . . .

Miss Meropia. Don't lie!

CHUGÚNOV. My conscience is clear so far as you're concerned.
MISS MEROPIA. And why? Because you're afraid of me. You know that I can get you sacked from your cushy job and even chased out of town, you have plenty to answer for, you know. And what will happen to you then? You'll have to go begging for some job of a clerk in some district office. Remember I can do it any time I like, even this very minute!
CHUGÚNOV. [*Gets up and kisses her hand*] I implore you as my guardian angel not to deprive me of your favours.
MISS MEROPIA. Sit down. [CHUGÚNOV *sits down*] This is what I asked you to come for. My late brother Viktor, father of Master Apollonius, had some business deals with the late Kupavin, the husband of Eulampe.
CHUGÚNOV. He was always borrowing money from old Kupavin. That's all the business transactions he ever had with him.
MISS MEROPIA. Yes, he borrowed money and Kupavin let him have it. Now, before he died, my brother began to build a paper-mill, but he didn't have enough money to finish it. Kupavin promised to advance him some, but he didn't.
CHUGÚNOV. That's so, ma'am.
MISS MEROPIA. But if Kupavin hadn't refused?
CHUGÚNOV. Then your brother would have built his paper-mill. Why not build it with somebody else's money?
MISS MEROPIA. Yes, he would have built it and, according to his calculations, he would not only have repaid all his debts, but would also have made fifty thousand pure profit. This means that it is Kupavin's fault that Master Apollonius is a pauper. I admit it is true that my dear brother liked to boast a little. I myself believed only half of what he told me. It may be, therefore, that I am wrong in believing that Mrs. Kupavina owes us fifty thousand; on the other hand, I might be wronging myself in thinking that she owed us only twenty-five thousand.
CHUGÚNOV. There is no harm in thinking, ma'am.
MISS MEROPIA. But I'm telling everybody I know, I've already spread the story all over the town, that the Kupavins

owe money to Master Apollonius, that they have, in fact, robbed my nephew.

CHUGÚNOV. Neither is there any harm in telling people anything you like.

MISS MEROPIA. "No harm." "No harm!" Will you tell me if it is impossible for me to get that money?

CHUGÚNOV. It is quite impossible for you to get that money, ma'am. No one can be forced to lend money to anyone. Kupavin may have refused to grant your brother the loan, but you can't claim it from his widow as a debt, for it is usual to build paper-mills with one's own money.

MISS MEROPIA. What are you croaking like a raven for? Do you think I'm a bigger fool than you? Do you think I don't realize that according to our laws, to those, that is, that are written down in your books, she owes me nothing? All right, you keep your laws and I'll keep mine. I don't care. I shall go on shouting at the top of my voice that my nephew has been robbed.

CHUGÚNOV. As you wish. No one can stop you from doing anything.

MISS MEROPIA. Do you think I'm doing that because I want to make a fool of myself? Or have I something in mind?

CHUGÚNOV. I suppose you must have.

MISS MEROPIA. I pin my hopes on people's consciences. I am still a great believer in people's consciences. Now, Eulampe Kupavina is a good woman, a woman with a highly fastidious sense of honour, she won't countenance any such talk about herself.

CHUGÚNOV. Do you really think she'll pay up?

MISS MEROPIA. No, I don't think she will. It's a lot of money and she can hardly be expected to pay it all. But I am ready to come to an arrangement with her.

CHUGÚNOV. How much do you hope to get from such an arrangement?

MISS MEROPIA. Nothing. All I want is that she should marry Master Apollonius, then we shall be quits. That's why I'm moving heaven and earth, that's why I'm going through fire and water, that's why I started all that talk about the debt.

Chugúnov. [*Rises to his feet in dismay*] My dear lady, my dear lady . . .

Miss Meropia. What are you in such a devil of a funk for?

Chugúnov. But . . . but this means that you, my dear guardian angel, will get hold of all her estate!

Miss Meropia. Certainly.

Chugúnov. But what's to happen to me then?

Miss Meropia. What do I care what happens to you? You can do what you like. You've had a good run for your money, haven't you? Got yourself a competence, didn't you?

Chugúnov. No, ma'am. Not at all, ma'am. Only a little bit, perhaps, but that's all. I want to buy a plot of land near the estate, three thousand they're asking for it.

Miss Meropia. Isn't that a bit too much of a good thing?

Chugúnov. I shouldn't desire anything more, ma'am. I'd have enough to last me for the rest of my days. I could afford even to give up my legal practice.

Miss Meropia. When it's all settled, I'll give you one thousand. You'd better do your best to get the other two thousand in the meantime. I don't care how you manage it, I don't want to be your judge, but you will get no more from me. I don't suppose if you embezzled it from Mrs. Kupavina, it would exactly ruin her.

Chugúnov. All I want is that you, my dear guardian angel, should not think badly of me, as for the others, I am not afraid of any of them. I can look after myself all right!

Miss Meropia. Well, that settles you. Now, you'd better listen to me.

Chugúnov. But I am listening to you, my dear guardian angel, I am listening to you!

Miss Meropia. In my opinion, no woman is worth a fig: cover her with gold and her price is still a farthing. Eulampe, rolling in money as she is now, no doubt thinks a lot of herself: no man is good enough for her.

Chugúnov. I'm afraid I can't tell you what's in her mind.

Miss Meropia. I am an old spinster. I don't know anything about men. It is quite possible that master Apollonius is no great catch, but, please understand, I am not even interested in that question. I want to do everything I can for my nephew, but I don't care a hoot what happens to her. So that if she shows fight, you and I, Vukol, will have to think of something to scare her.

CHUGÚNOV. Why, of course! We'll think of something.

MISS MEROPIA. Very well, you'd better start thinking straight away. Whose interests, do you think, ought you to have more at heart, mine or hers?

CHUGÚNOV. None but yours, ma'am.

MISS MEROPIA. Well, do something for me, your guardian angel, something really big, something to get this worry off my mind. My nephew will be the death of me!

CHUGÚNOV. All right. It is possible. Don't give it another thought, ma'am. Mrs. Kupavina trusts me implicitly. I can bring the whole thing to a satisfactory conclusion.

MISS MEROPIA. But what must we do?

CHUGÚNOV. We shall have to find some old accounts substantiating your claim. We shall have to see whether there isn't anything of the kind in the old ledgers. I'll have a good look round for it. Then Master Apollonius and myself will bring the matter before a justice of the peace and reach a satisfactory conclusion. As the manager of Mrs. Kupavina's estate, I am quite willing to acknowledge any debt in your favour, even one for one hundred thousand. As soon as Master Apollonius obtains the deed of execution, we shall be treading on *terra firma* and we'll be able to scare the fair lady out of her wits. Either marry or face ruin!

MISS MEROPIA. Hear, hear. That's all I want. But, of course, you understand, all this is still very much in the air. We shall most probably settle everything without having to resort to such violent measures. But if she prove stubborn, then don't blame me if . . . Why make any bones about it: for my own family I am ready to play fair or foul.

CHUGÚNOV. Let him who is without sin, cast the first stone, ma'am.

MISS MEROPIA. Has Eulampe any ready money?

CHUGÚNOV. Why shouldn't she have? She has plenty of cash about.

MISS MEROPIA. But that's strange. Has she forgotten it or what? I've told her again and again that her husband promised me one thousand for the poor. "I am not including that money in my will," he told me, "for when I die my wife will be sure to pay you." I believe I have even a letter to that effect from him. Did you look among my papers?

CHUGÚNOV. I've examined them about a dozen times, ma'am. I even took them home with me.

MISS MEROPIA. And there isn't anything?

CHUGÚNOV. Nothing at all, ma'am.

MISS MEROPIA. A pity. She daren't disbelieve me, but she might object all the same.

CHUGÚNOV. Well, one could . . .

MISS MEROPIA. Could what?

CHUGÚNOV. . . . find the letter, if you really want it.

MISS MEROPIA. But you've already looked for it.

CHUGÚNOV. I have, but not in the right place. I was only wasting my time. [*Takes out a letter and hands it to* MISS MEROPIA] Here's the letter, my dear guardian angel. I've found it.

MISS MEROPIA. [*After reading the letter through*] It certainly is in his handwriting. What's all this? Is it witchcraft?

CHUGÚNOV. Not witchcraft, ma'am! Shall I be guilty of such a sin? Shall I imperil my immortal soul?

MISS MEROPIA. Well, if it isn't witchcraft, then it is something which isn't much better: it's a forgery! For that they send you to Siberia. [*Gives letter back to* CHUGÚNOV.]

CHUGÚNOV. What things you do say, ma'am! Why say such awful things to me, my guardian angel? What kind of forgery is this? It's a clever piece of business, that's all. The late Kupavin promised to give you the money, well, what difference does it make whether he expressed his intention in words or in writing? If Mrs. Kupavina refuses to believe you and withholds the money, won't that be even a greater sin? Her late husband's wish wouldn't be carried out, the poor would get nothing and no prayers would be said for the salvation of his soul.

MISS MEROPIA. But if I deceived you, if he didn't promise me anything, what then?

CHUGÚNOV. Then, of course . . . [*He is about to tear up the letter*] It's easily done.

Miss Meropia. Wait! Wait! What are you doing? Give it to me! [*Takes letter.*]

Chugúnov. It's a pity it's so little, ma'am.

Miss Meropia. What's little?

Chugúnov. Little money. We might as well . . . In for a penny, in for a pound.

Miss Meropia. What are you talking about, you wicked man? Isn't that all he promised me?

Chugúnov. That's exactly what I mean, ma'am. It's a pity he promised so little, for when it comes to writing, it makes no difference whether you write a thousand more or a thousand less.

Miss Meropia. You're a real thief, Vukol, that's all. I'm out to help the poor and for their sake I might not always play fair, but you wouldn't turn a hair if you had to do a trick like that for your own profit. [*Conceals letter in pocket and shakes an accusing finger at* Chugúnov] My dear Vukol, keep your conscience clear whatever you do. Don't forget this is a criminal matter.

Chugúnov. It is a criminal matter, ma'am, it is.

Miss Meropia. Did you do it yourself?

Chugúnov. How could I do it myself? My hands are too unsteady. It's a nephew of mine . . .

Miss Meropia. Goretzky?

Chugúnov. Yes, my guardian angel. I was worried about the lad. I was beginning to think he wouldn't be any good for anything. He didn't attend school and he is hardly literate. I thought of training him as a surveyor, but it was just a waste of money. And suddenly such talent! Give him anything you like, and he'd copy it to a "t".

Miss Meropia. He'll land you in jail with this talent of his.

Chugúnov. I am sometimes a trifle apprehensive, ma'am, but I hate to get rid of him. Who knows, I may need him, if not for myself, then at least for somebody else . . . [*Glancing through the window*] Some visitors to see you, ma'am. I'd better go now. [*Kisses* Miss Meropia's *hand.*]

Miss Meropia. Good-bye, Vukol, and thank you.

CHUGÚNOV. If you need me again, my guardian angel, just let me know and I'll be at your service. [*Goes out.*]
[*Enter* PAVLIN.]
PAVLIN. Mr. Lynyayev and Miss Anfussa, ma'am.
MISS MEROPIA. Show them in.
[PAVLIN *goes out,* LYNYÁYEV *and* MISS ANFÚSSA *enter.*]
LYNYÁYEV. Good morning, my dear Miss Murzavetzkaya.
MISS MEROPIA. [*Exchanging kisses with* MISS ANFÚSSA] Good morning, you bad boy. Sit down, make yourselves comfortable. Where did you pick up this beauty?
LYNYÁYEV. Mrs. Kupavina thrust her on me. She'll be calling for her herself.
MISS MEROPIA. [*To* MISS ANFÚSSA] Would you like a cup of tea, my dear?
MISS ANFÚSSA. Well, I mean . . . Why not tea, you know . . .
MISS MEROPIA. [*To* PAVLIN, *who has remained standing at the doors*] Get some tea for Miss Anfussa.
[PAVLIN *goes out.*]
[*To* LYNYÁYEV] And if Mrs. Kupavina hadn't asked you to bring her aunt to me, I suppose you wouldn't have come.
LYNYÁYEV. I don't think I should have looked in on you this morning. We have no particular business to settle, have we?
MISS MEROPIA. Why call always on business? Why not pay a visit to an old woman and have a chat with her?
LYNYÁYEV. I'm afraid we seem to have only one subject of conversation, you and I, my dear lady, it's how to pull our fellow-men to pieces. I have no time for such talk to-day, I am in a hurry to get back home.
MISS MEROPIA. Why, of course, you're such a busy man, aren't you? I can imagine how important your business is! As soon as you get home, you'll drop down on a couch and stay there for hours. Don't you think I am aware of the fact that all the springs of your couches have given way from too much lying on and that they have to be constantly repaired?
LYNYÁYEV. I find a horizontal position rather inviting.
[PAVLIN *brings in tray with tea-pot cup and saucer and sugar basin.* MISS ANFÚSSA *pours herself out a cup of tea, takes a lump of sugar in her mouth and drinks.*]

Miss Meropia. [*To* Miss Anfússa] There's an occupation for you, my dear. Drink and enjoy yourself! [*To* Lynyáyev] You ought to be ashamed of yourself! Look, what a paunch you're getting!

Lynyáyev. I'm a very easy-going chap and my conscience doesn't trouble me, that's why I'm getting fat. I'm afraid, though, I shall soon grow thin again, something is worrying me.

Miss Meropia. That's something new, anyway. What's worrying you?

Lynyáyev. I have been fired with the ambition to catch a wolf, but I can't get on his scent.

Miss Meropia. For mercy's sake! Have you ever heard of a sheep catching a wolf?

Lynyáyev. There's a pettifogging rascal in our district who is making a devil of a nuisance of himself, not an assize without one or two actions from him, and actions of a most pernicious kind. He doesn't even hesitate to forge documents. I wish I could put him in the dock!

Miss Meropia. Look at him, what a hero! You'd better tell me why have you grown so shy lately, why have you stopped visiting your friends?

Lynyáyev. I am scared stiff.

Miss Meropia. What of? Are you a baby?

Lynyáyev. If I were a baby, I shouldn't be frightened. A baby has nothing to fear.

Miss Meropia. For goodness' sake what are you so afraid of?

Lynyáyev. Marriage.

Miss Meropia. Found something to be scared of. Do you find the life of an old bachelor so enticing?

Lynyáyev. Some men may not be afraid of marriage, but it terrifies me to death. I don't dare to darken the doors of any house where there are unmarried women about.

Miss Meropia. How is it you dare to come to see me? There are two unmarried women in my house, Glafira and myself.

Lynyáyev. But your house is a veritable nunnery, my dear lady, such humility, such serenity!

Miss Meropia. Well, we don't either of us wear our hearts

upon our sleeves for daws to peck at. So that's why you're so shy of people?

LYNYÁYEV. People? But are there any people around us?

MISS MEROPIA. Heaven have mercy upon us! What else do you think they are?

LYNYÁYEV. Wolves and sheep. The wolves devour the sheep and the sheep not only allow themselves to be devoured, but seem to like it!

MISS MEROPIA. And are unmarried women wolves, too?

LYNYÁYEV. They are the most dangerous of all! To look at her she looks like a young gazelle, her movements are so soft, her eyes so timid, but let her catch you off your guard even for a minute and she'll be at your throat! [*Gets up and takes his hat.*]

MISS MEROPIA. You see nothing but wolves, a scared crow is afraid of a bush. And what am I, pray? You'd better put me among the wolves. I may be a woman, but I'd hate to be a sheep in the same flock as you.

LYNYÁYEV. Good-bye. [*To* MISS ANFÚSSA] *Au revoir.*

[*Goes out.*]

MISS MEROPIA. [*To* MISS ANFÚSSA] What utter nonsense the man does talk! Has he said anything worth listening to? Is he often at your place, my dear?

MISS ANFÚSSA. Not very, but so, I mean . . . A neighbour, you know . . .

MISS MEROPIA. Making love to Eulampe, I suppose?

MISS ANFÚSSA. Well, I mean . . . How could he, I mean . . .

MISS MEROPIA. What is he doing?

MISS ANFÚSSA. Oh, you know . . . [*Dismisses it with a wave of the hand and yawns*] This and that, I mean . . .

MISS MEROPIA. He probably keeps on yawning and you, I suppose, are asleep most of the time. You're a bad watchman, my dear, I shall have to get you a good assistant.

PAVLIN. [*Opening the double doors*] Mrs. Kupavina, ma'am.

[MRS. KUPÁVINA *enters.*]

MISS MEROPIA. How are you, my dear rich lady? Thank you for doing me the honour of coming to see me.

MRS. KUPÁVINA. I am not such a rare visitor at your house, Miss Meropia.

MISS MEROPIA. [*Puts* MRS. KUPÁVINA *in her own chair*] Sit here, sit here, in the place of honour.
MRS. KUPÁVINA. [*Sitting down*] Thank you.
MISS MEROPIA. Well, tell me, how's everything?
MRS. KUPÁVINA. I'm bored, Miss Meropia.
MISS MEROPIA. Want to get married?
MRS. KUPÁVINA. Why should I be in such a hurry? I got sick of living under somebody else's thumb. I want to enjoy my independence for a bit.
MISS MEROPIA. Yes, of course. So that's what it is? But, you know, my dear, it is rather difficult to keep your state of single blessedness with so many gallants paying court to you.
MRS. KUPÁVINA. What gallants? I haven't met any yet.
MISS MEROPIA. Really, my dear, why throw dust in my eyes? I am an old bird, you can't deceive me with a bit of chaff.
MRS. KUPÁVINA. You seem to know more about me than I do myself.
MISS MEROPIA. And what about Lynyayev? What's Lynyayev doing at your house?
MRS. KUPÁVINA. Wrong, Miss Meropia. There you're absolutely mistaken. Why should I marry Lynyayev? To begin with, he's not so young, and then again, he's not the type of man that appeals to me.
MISS MEROPIA. He is too old for you. Even if you married him, he wouldn't be of any use to you. You'd be neither a married woman nor a widow. What kind of husband would he make? Neither fish, flesh nor good red herring, that's all about it.
MISS ANFÚSSA. Well, I mean . . . Not really, you know . . .
MISS MEROPIA. What do you know about it? I can't explain it to you, I'm a spinster myself. Start talking to women and, willy-nilly, you can't help committing a sin.
MRS. KUPÁVINA. No, I shall wait.
MISS MEROPIA. And I advise you to get married.
MRS. KUPÁVINA. Really?
MISS MEROPIA. Yes, get married.
MRS. KUPÁVINA. Who to?
MISS MEROPIA. Let me worry about it, my dear. God has given me enough commonsense for that.

Miss Anfússa. Yes, to be sure, I mean . . .

Miss Meropia. What are you interfering for? God has given some intelligence to some people, but he has overlooked you, so make the best of it.

Miss Anfússa. [*With a forlorn wave of the hand*] Well, I mean . . . Of course, you . . . naturally, but me, you know . . .

Miss Meropia. [*To* Mrs. Kupávina] You did not marry old Kupavin for love, but for his money, didn't you?

Mrs. Kupávina. But it was you . . .

Miss Meropia. What do you mean "it was you"! Don't you try to blame it on to me, my dear. You sold yourself, and that's not very nice. In fact, it is a great sin.

Mrs. Kupávina. But it was your doing, Miss Meropia. It was you who brought us together. I was too young to realize . .

Miss Meropia. Don't get in such a flutter about it, my dear. I'm not blaming you at all. All I'm concerned about is your own salvation. What must you do to clear your conscience? You must get to love a poor man, you must marry him, and you must bestow your riches on the man you love—that's the only way to make up for your past sin.

Mrs. Kupávina. It's easier said than done: get to love a man!

Miss Meropia. At your age, my dear, it shouldn't be so difficult to fall in love. Only don't be too choosy. You are young, very well, look for someone young; you want to keep your independence, to wear the breeches, all right, look for somebody who is poor and who will dance to your tune; you are not particularly bright yourself, so choose someone who is even more simple-minded than you and he won't get too high and mighty for you. Am I right or not?

Mrs. Kupávina. I agree with you entirely, but where am I to find such a man?

Miss Meropia. Let me find you one. The world isn't such a big place as all that. I shall find you one, don't you worry, my dear. Only let me warn you, if you want to be happy, don't try to be too clever, but rely on me. Do as I tell you, I shall do my best for you. I should never dream of going to such trouble about anyone unless I was fond of her.

Mrs. Kupávina. Thank you.

MISS MEROPIA. Ah, my dears, take advantage of my good heart while I'm still alive. When I die, I don't mind telling you, it's a devoted mother you'll be missing.

MISS ANFÚSSA. [*Wiping her eyes*] Well, of course, you know . . . Naturally, I mean . . .

MISS MEROPIA. [*To* MISS ANFÚSSA] What are you crying for? I'm not dead yet. [*To* MRS. KUPÁVINA] Well, my beautiful one, you have a good memory for your own affairs, but do you keep your husband's memory green?

MRS. KUPÁVINA. I do, Miss Meropia.

MISS MEROPIA. You do, do you? But you ought to see to it that others, too, remember him. Don't forget the poor, their prayers will be of great benefit to him.

MRS. KUPÁVINA. Yes, I see . . . You were telling me . . . I . . . I brought it for you.

MISS MERPOIA. Speak up, my dear. What are you mumbling for? I don't want your money. You don't seem exactly enthusiastic to do a good deed. It wasn't my idea, remember!

MRS. KUPÁVINA. I believe you.

MISS MEROPIA. It seems to me you haven't got perfect trust in me, or do you think I'm trying to cadge money from you? Look at that! [*She takes out letter from pocket*] Do!

MRS. KUPÁVINA. But I don't want to see anything. I believe you.

MISS MEROPIA. No, my dear, a stranger's heart is a deep well, it's too dark to see what's at the bottom. [*Gives her the letter*] What are you afraid of? Take it. [MRS. KUPÁVINA *takes the letter*] Who wrote it?

MRS. KUPÁVINA. My husband.

MISS MERPOÍA. And what does he say in his letter?

MRS. KUPÁVINA. Just as you were telling me.

MISS MEROPIA. Well, you believe me now, don't you?

MRS. KUPÁVINA. I never doubted you. [*Opens bag in which she puts in letter and takes out money*] Here you are.

MISS MEROPIA. What's that you're giving me?

MRS. KUPÁVINA. The money.

MISS MEROPIA. I don't want to touch it even. I hate to handle such abomination.

MRS. KUPÁVINA. You'd better count it all the same.

Miss Meropia. What for? It's not my money, why dirty my hands on it. If there isn't enough, you wouldn't have deceived *me*, but the orphans; if there is more, then somebody else will be offering a prayer for your husband's soul. I shouldn't be surprised if you asked me for a receipt, but I shan't give you any, my dear. Don't be afraid, though, I shan't ask you for the money again.

Mrs. Kupávina. Where shall I put it?

Miss Meropia. Put it on the table, in the Bible.

Mrs. Kupávina. [*Having put the money in the Bible*] Auntie, it's time we were going home.

Miss Anfússa. Well, I mean . . . I, of course, you know . . .

Mrs. Kupávina. Your nephew, I am told, has some claims on my husband's estate.

Miss Meropia. Why worry your pretty head about it, my dear? Is it your business that your husband robbed him? If you're a pauper, then you have to behave like a pauper, go about begging and spend all your days in pubs, trying to drown your sorrows. As for you, my dear, you'd better keep your money and stay rich. Or would you rather not? Well, anyway, I'll call on you soon and we'll talk it over.

Mrs. Kupávina. So good-bye for the present, Miss Meropia.

Miss Meropia. Good-bye, my dears. [*To* Mrs. Kupávina] You're a darling, Eulampe. Bless your dear heart. [*Whispers*] May you get a good husband, my dear. Do you know I love you as if you were my own daughter. [*To* Miss Anfússa] What are you wrapping up like that for? You're not going on a journey to Kiyev, are you?

Mrs. Kupávina. [*At the doors*] Good-bye!

Miss Meropia. [*At the doors*] Tell the coachman to be careful!

Miss Anfússa. We will, you know . . .

[Mrs. Kupávina *and* Miss Anfússa *go out.* Miss Meropia *takes the money out of the Bible, counts it and replaces some in the Bible, while putting the rest in her pocket. She then sits down in arm-chair and rings. Enter:* Pavlin *and* Glafíra.]

Pavlin. Did you ring, ma'am?

Miss Meropia. [*To* Pavlin] Listen carefully. I've changed my mind. I think I'd better pay everybody. Men are not angels, why tempt them? Have a look in the Bible. Can you find any money there?

PAVLIN. [*Opening Bible*] Yes, ma'am.

MISS MEROPIA. Take it. How much do we owe?

PAVLIN. About five hundred.

MISS MEROPIA. And how much have you got there?

PAVLIN. [*Counting the money*] Exactly five hundred, ma'am.

MISS MEROPIA. Very well. Pay them all. You can go.

PAVLIN. Very good, ma'am. Such wonders ought to be published in the newspapers. [*Goes out.*]

MISS MEROPIA. Glafira, I want you to do something for me.

GLAFÍRA. What is it, Miss Meropia?

MISS MEROPIA. I'll take you to Mrs. Kupavina to-day. Try to make friends with her, get as intimate with her as possible. She's not particularly clever and there is nothing I need teach you.

GLAFÍRA. Very well, Miss Meropia.

MISS MEROPIA. And should you find out that Michael Lynyayev is sweet on her, don't let him make any advances to her, but try to defeat his purpose, try to disparage him as much as you can and, what is important, praise Apollonius to the skies.

GLAFÍRA. I'll do it most willingly, Miss Meropia. It'll be a pleasure, I assure you.

MISS MEROPIA. And don't you cast your eyes on Lynyayev yourself! I have already chosen a wife for him.

GLAFÍRA. My ambition is of a different kind, Miss Meropia. I am dreaming of a convent cell.

MISS MEROPIA. Remember, that piece of cake is not for you.

GLAFÍRA. I am not thinking of bliss on earth.

MISS MEROPIA. [*Raising her eyes to heaven*] Oh, the she-devil! [*To* GLAFÍRA] It's I who am the she-devil. What are you staring at me for? Yes, I am a she-devil. What did you think I was? I shall never be able to obtain forgiveness for what I've done to-day, however much I pray. I have deceived a silly woman; it's like deceiving an innocent child. I shall fast and pray on bended knees for days. You'd better fast with me. Let's go to the chapel at once! You, too. You, too. [*She gets up,* GLAFÍRA *supporting her on the right*] Lead me. [*She walks as though all strength has gone out of her*] I have sinned, oh Lord, I have sinned!

ACT TWO

[*A tastefully furnished room in* Mrs. Kupávina's *country mansion. A lady's writing desk with all the appurtenances, in the background an open door, leading to a drawing-room; a door at either side.*]
[Mrs. Kupávina *comes out from side-door to right, followed late by* Chugúnov.]

Mrs. Kupávina. [*Sits down at writing desk*] Anyone in the drawing-room?

Chugúnov. [*From drawing-room*] I'm there, ma'am, playing snap with Miss Anfussa, we're amusing ourselves in our old age.

Mrs. Kupávina. Won't you come in, Mr. Chugunov? [Chugúnov *comes in*] Sit down.

Chugúnov. Thank you. [*Sits down.*]

Mrs. Kupávina. What's the business my late husband had with Miss Meropia's nephew?

Chugúnov. Your late husband seems to have had some unsettled accounts with his father.

Mrs. Kupávina. Miss Meropia goes about clamouring that we've robbed her nephew.

Chugúnov. Miss Meropia is a very severe lady, ma'am.

Mrs. Kupávina. What do they want from me?

Chugúnov. Why worry your head about it? What am I here for? Am I drawing my salary for nothing?

Mrs. Kupávina. I don't like all this talk. Please, do all you can to put a stop to it.

Chugúnov. Do you want it settled in a friendly way?

Mrs. Kupávina. I'm afraid I don't understand much about it, but, I suppose it is best to have it settled in a friendly way.

Chugúnov. Yes, ma'am. And what about money, should I require any?

Mrs. Kupávina. I have very little ready money.

Chugúnov. That's a great pity. You're a lady of property, ma'am, and yet you are so hard up for money. That's very strange, don't you think?

Mrs. Kupávina. But where am I to get the money from?

CHUGÚNOV. Good heavens, ma'am! You have only to ask me and you'll have as much money as you want.

MRS. KUPÁVINA. Then do me the favour, Mr. Chugunov, find me some money.

CHUGÚNOV. I shan't even have to look for it. Your name alone will bring you all the gold you want. I mean, all you have to do is to sign your name on a bit of paper and the money will be here.

MRS. KUPÁVINA. What have I to sign? I don't understand you.

CHUGÚNOV. Let me explain it to you. It's really very simple. Take this pen, please. As it happens I have a sheet of paper on me. [*Takes out bill of exchange.*]

MRS. KUPÁVINA. What a strange-looking paper!

CHUGÚNOV. Yes, they are making rather wonderful paper nowadays. Now, just write at the bottom here, "Eulampe Nikolayevna Kupavina, widow of Colonel Kupavin." [MRS. KUPÁVINA *writes*] That's all you have to do to get the money, ma'am. [*Blots it*] If I have to pay any money to anyone, all I have to do is to write on top here five hundred or a thousand and that's all there is to it.

MRS. KUPÁVINA. I see. I understand now. [CHUGÚNOV *tries to get hold of the bill of exchange, but each time* MRS. KUPÁVINA *glances at him, he jerks his hand away*] What's the matter?

CHUGÚNOV. I'm afraid it might get lost or something.

MRS. KUPÁVINA. Well, take it.

CHUGÚNOV. What did you say, ma'am? Did you say I might take it?

MRS. KUPÁVINA. Yes, of course, why not? What are you afraid of? Put it in your brief-case, if you like.

CHUGÚNOV. I'm not afraid of anything, ma'am, but aren't you? However, if you don't mind, I will take it. Thank you.

MRS. KUPÁVINA. What are you thanking me for?

CHUGÚNOV. Well, ma'am, for such a reward . . .

MRS. KUPÁVINA. What reward?

CHUGÚNOV. But your trust, ma'am, isn't that anything? Who in the whole county would give Chugunov a blank bill of exchange? Of course, mind you, we are all fallible, mortal men, poverty, a large family . . . They are spreading such tales about me, "Vukol Chugunov is a rogue, Vukol Chugunov can't be trusted with a penny," but you're different, ma'am. You...

MRS. KUPÁVINA. All right, all right! Only, please, come to some terms with the Murzavetzkys.

CHUGÚNOV. Who are the Murzavetzkys? They aren't worth your little finger, ma'am. Rogue, indeed! Well, let's say I am a rogue, but even a rogue has a heart! [*Beats his chest, in a choked voice*] Look at my tears, ma'am, they won't be shed in vain. Do you really think I could have the heart to play you false now? Let me assure you, ma'am, I shall find it very hard, not to say unpleasant!

MRS. KUPÁVINA. I believe I can hear someone in the drawing-room...

CHUGÚNOV. Visitors, I suppose, ma'am. I'll be in my office should you need me.

[*Goes out, left.*]

MRS. KUPÁVINA. [*Going up to drawing-room door*] Who're you talking to, auntie?

[*Enter* LYNYÁYEV.]

MRS. KUPÁVINA. Ah, it's you, Lynyayev!

LYNYÁYEV. How do you do? Have you been back long?

MRS. KUPÁVINA. No, I've only just come back.

LYNYÁYEV. And I was waiting for you at the Post Office. Why don't you look in there occasionally? You make me go two miles out of my way to bring your letters.

MRS. KUPÁVINA. I'm sorry. I wasn't expecting any letters. Have you brought any for me?

LYNYÁYEV. I have two letters from our mutual friend, Vassily Berkutov, one for me and the other for you. [*Gives her a letter.*]

MRS. KUPÁVINA. [*Puts letter on desk*] You've probably read yours already. What's his news?

LYNYÁYEV. But why do you put yours away? Don't you want to read it?

MRS. KUPÁVINA. I'm not in a particular hurry. Tell me what's in your letter.

LYNYÁYEV. But do read it, you'll learn good news. He'll be here to-day or to-morrow. I'm so glad, aren't you?

Mrs. Kupávina. Well, not so glad as you seem to be. *I* shan't run five miles to meet him.

Lynyáyev. Poor old Berkutov! Does he suspect what indifference awaits him here?

Mrs. Kupávina. I'm afraid I can't help that. I just can't get excited about it, that's all.

Lynyáyev. What have you been doing in town?

Mrs. Kupávina. I went there to give a thousand roubles to Miss Meropia.

Lynyávyev. You aren't joking, are you? Whatever for?

Mrs. Kupávina. For the poor, in compliance with my late husband's wishes.

Lynyáyev. But your husband never expressed such a wish, I assure you. He never thought of giving his money away to the poor. I tell you he couldn't stand that Murzavetzkaya. He always referred to her as a sanctimonious old so-and-so. Don't you realize that she's cheating you?

Mrs. Kupávina. You're always so unfair to dear Miss Meropia. When will you stop abusing her? She's a woman of such high character. Here, if you want proof, look for yourself! [*Gives him letter received from* Miss Meropia.]

Lynyáyev. [*Examines letter*] Say what you will, but it's a forgery!

Mrs. Kupávina. Really, Lynyayev, this is preposterous!

Lynyáyev. [*Heatedly*] I wish I knew the man she employs for this kind of thing!

Mrs. Kupávina. I wish you wouldn't talk like that! I refuse to listen to you!

Lynyáyev. May I keep this letter for a short time?

Mrs. Kupávina. Take it, only, please, don't let's have a public scandal and don't make Miss Meropia my enemy: I'm engaged in some important business negotiations with her.

Lynyáyev. You have no business of any kind with her, I assure you. I know your business very well.

Mrs. Kupávina. It isn't my business, but my husband's. He left some unsettled accounts with Murzavetzky, Miss Meropia's brother.

Lynyáyev. There were no unsettled accounts: this is again some trick to involve you in some costly legal action.

Mrs. Kupávina. Do cool down, Lynyayev. This has nothing to do with you, you know. I've already authorized Chugunov to settle everything as between friends. I've even signed some paper.

Lynyáyev. Good heavens, don't sign anything without consulting me beforehand. What have you signed?

Mrs. Kupávina. Don't make such a fuss! I've signed a paper, but there was nothing on it.

Lynyáyev. How do you know there was nothing on it?

Mrs. Kupóvina. Really? Haven't I any eyes?

Lynyátev. Your eyes will be of precious little use to you in this business. What you want is a lawyer.

Mrs. Kupávina. Don't be ridiculous! What do I want a lawyer for, if there was nothing on the paper?

Lynyáyev. How do you mean, nothing?

Mrs. Kupávina. Just nothing. A clean sheet of paper.

Lynyáyev. It's getting worse and worse. Don't you realize that you've been made to sign a blank bill of exchange? They can put any amount they like in the blank space and claim fifty thousand or even a hundred thousand from you!

Mrs. Kupávina. What nonsense! What a poor opinion you have of people, Lynyayev. Why, Chugunov thanked me with tears in his eyes for my confidence. He cried, I'm telling you, he cried!

Lynyáyev. Crocodiles, too, are said to shed tears, but that doesn't prevent them from swallowing a calf whole.

Mrs. Kupávina. So you think they're going to claim a hundred thousand from me?

Lynyáyev. If not a hundred thousand, then something very near it, trust them to let you off easily!

Mrs. Kupávina. What makes you think so?

Lynyáyev. Let me tell you a Russian fairy tale: "Once upon a time a gypsy climbed up a tree and began to chop the bough on which he was sitting. A Russian passed by and said, "Gypsy, you're going to come a cropper!' But the gypsy replied, 'How do you know that, are you a prophet?' "

Mrs. Kupávina. That is a stupid story, Lynyayev, too stupid for words. What man will cut down the bough on which he is sitting?

LYNYÁYEV. You'd be surprised! Every day I come across people who are doing just what the gypsy was doing and many is the time I have to be that prophet.

MRS. KUPÁVINA. I see what you're driving at. You're trying to get on your favourite hobbyhorse that women don't know anything, can't do anything and can't even live without some man to look after them. Well, I am going to prove to you that I am capable of looking after my own business without anyone's interference.

LYNYÁYEV. May the Lord help you! I hope, though, that you'll realize your mistake before it's too late, before you've managed to ruin your estate.

MRS. KUPÁVINA. Thank you for your good intentions, any way. Please stay to dinner.

LYNYÁYEV. Thank you, I will. May I take a nap in your summer house till then?

MRS. KUPÁVINA. Of course, there's plenty of time before dinner.

MISS ANFÚSSA. [*From the drawing-room*] Guests have arrived... It's, you know...

MRS. KUPÁVINA. Who is it? Miss Meropia?

MISS ANFÚSSA. [*From the drawing-room*] Yes, you know...

LYNYÁYEV. You'll have to excuse me. No one can force me to see that woman twice in a single day. May I go through here? [*Pointing to door, left.*]

MRS. KUPÁVINA. Do. Good-bye for the present.

[*Goes into drawing-room.*]

[LYNYÁYEV *goes through door to the left. From the drawing-room enter:* MRS. KUPÁVINA, MISS MEROPIA, APOLLONIUS, GLAFÍRA *and* MISS ANFÚSSA.]

MISS MEROPIA. Well, here I am with all my household bar the servants.

MRS. KUPÁVINA. I'm very pleased to see you.

MISS MEROPIA. Pleased or not, you can't very well show us the door. [*Pointing at her nephew*] He, too, insisted on coming.

APOLLONIUS. Please, auntie, please...

MISS MEROPIA. Hold your tongue! Why shouldn't you have come? You have a right to come here and she must show you the respect you deserve. You're not coming to waste your time or to make a nuisance of yourself. You have a right to ask her to settle your claim. Let her listen to what you have to say.

Mrs. Kupávina. With pleasure.

Miss Meropia. Hardly with pleasure, my dear. It's something that's crying to heaven, let me tell you!

Mrs. Kupávina. You'd better explain it to me.

Miss Meropia. It isn't my business, so why should I explain it to you? Let him explain, it's he who's been wronged. Talk it over between yourselves and, with God's help, you'll come to some kind of agreement. If you're sensible, my dear, you'll do what has to be done without bringing ruin upon yourself, but if you persist in being obstinate, then don't ask me for any favours. Charity, you know, begins at home.

Mrs. Kupávina. Won't you have anything?

Miss Meropia. Don't bother to entertain us. I've just dropped in to pay the compliments of the season. You know there is a fair not far from here?

Mrs. Kupávina. Of course, I know. There's going to be dancing on my lawn. But do have a cup of tea, won't you?

Miss Meropia. I can never refuse a cup of tea.

Mrs. Kupávina. Auntie!

Miss Anfússa. I, you know . . . It's ready, I mean . . .

Miss Meropia. You must be lonely by yourself, my dear. Miss Anfussa is not much company, so I brought you Glafira to be your companion for a few days.

Mrs. Kupávina. That is nice of you. I shall be glad to have her. Excuse me a minute. [*To* Glafíra] Please come with me! I'll show you to your room.

[Mrs. Kupávina *and* Miss Glafíra *go out through door to right.*]

Miss Meropia. [*To* Apollonius] How do you like her estate? Not bad, what?

Apollonius. It's a peach!

Miss Meropia. Win the widow's heart and it'll all be yours. Only for heaven's sake don't make a fool of yourself!

Apollonius. Really, auntie, me make a fool of myself?

Miss Meropia. Yes, you! Your words are brave enough, but, somehow, I can't trust your deeds.

Apollonius. Ten words, auntie.

Miss Meropia. What do you mean ten words?
Apollonius. I never waste more than ten words on women, auntie. Ten words and the girl's mine (*pointing to his ears*), head over ears!
Miss Meropia. Well, ten or more, so long as . . .
Apollonius. No, auntie, more than ten may not be safe. Damn it all, it's even dangerous!
Miss Meropia. Dangerous even?
Apollonius. On my word of honour, auntie! One has to have pity on them. They might get so infatuated that they might throw themselves into the river, and what then? Such an awful mess a fellow can get himself into!
Miss Meropia. Well, we'll see.

[Mrs. Kupávina *enters.*]

Mrs. Kupávina. [*To* Anfússa] Auntie, see to the tea, please.
Miss Anfússa. Yes, of course . . . I mean, it's . . . you know . . .
Miss Meropia. Come along, my dear, let me help you. I hate to have my tea brought to me by a servant. I like to sit down at the samovar myself.

[*Goes out through door to left with* Miss Anfússa.]

Mrs. Kupávina. Don't you want any tea?
Apollonius. Me, tea? Not for anything in the world. It's a woman's drink.
Mrs. Kupávina. Well, please yourself. Did you want to discuss your business with me?
Apollonius. Yes, passionately.
Mrs. Kupávina. You'd better see Chugunov about it. I asked him to deal with it.
Apollonius. Who's Chugunov? A mere lawyer's clerk. But you . . . you . . . No, say what you will, but it is different.
Mrs. Kupávina. But I can't discuss it with you. I don't know anything about it.
Apollonius. Who cares about business? What is business? Accounts and bills, stuff and nonsense, fiddle-daddle. What does that mean in comparison with the eternal, or, shall we say, a pickled cucumber? Sorry, I was talking nonsense. It's a rotten habit, trying to be witty. But that is beside the point.

Mrs. Kupávina. What do you want? I'm afraid I don't quite understand . . .

Apollonius. Vulgar souls can't think of anything but money, but high-minded people know that happiness is the only thing that matters, as a regimental scribe once said.

Mrs. Kupávina. But what kind of happiness are you after?

Apollonius. Me? Words fail me. No words can describe that happiness.

Mrs. Kupávina. What a pity! I shall never be able to find out then.

Apollonius. Heavenly eyes, languorous smiles, ruby lips, kisses, caresses, sweet nothings and so on and so forth, all this is nonsense. Let me be frank with you.

Mrs. Kupávina. Do me the favour.

Apollonius. You won't see me on my knees before you. No, I promise you. I have my pride.

Mrs. Kupávina. Really? I'm so glad.

Apollonius. But you must love me.

Mrs. Kupávina. Indeed? I didn't know that.

Apollonius. However, just as you please.

Mrs. Kupávina. I should think so, too.

Apollonius. I have my pride, I'm telling you.

Mrs. Kupávina. I heard you.

Apollonius. Hell! Do you know what? For certain reasons . . . I was going to tell you, but you wouldn't understand, I am no longer in the army. What matter? I did my best, but they didn't appreciate it, all right, to hell with them! I have been left no land and haven't acquired any . . .

Mrs. Kupávina. If my late husband really owed you something, you'll get it.

Apollonius. Don't mention it. You bore me. I beg your pardon, madam, I meant something else. You see . . . I'm a virgin. Auntie is an old maid and she doesn't understand the needs of a young unmarried officer, and, besides, she's as mean as . . .

Mrs. Kupávina. I told you that if my husband owed you anything you'll get it.

Apollonius. Again the same? This is really getting boring . . . You see, sometimes I have to do without the bare necessities, the most innocent pleasures. Say, for instance, tobacco. I'm ashamed to confess it, but just imagine, a gentleman and no tobacco!

MRS. KUPÁVINA. How much do you want?

APOLLONIUS. At the moment, just a trifle.

MRS. KUPÁVINA. How much?

APOLLONIUS. Of course, as a loan, you understand . . .

MRS. KUPÁVINA. Naturally, but how much?

APOLLONIUS. As much as you please. Not too much, though, a few . . . But, all the same, not a few pennies, you understand.

MRS. KUPÁVINA. [*Taking out a five-rouble note*] Will that do?

APOLLONIUS. That'll do perfectly. Thank you, a thousand thanks. In a day or two, on my word of honour!

MRS. KUPÁVINA. Excuse me, but I have to join the ladies.

[*Goes out.*]

APOLLONIUS. Rum? Hell, no. It doesn't agree with me. It's too dangerous. Let's try, [*snapping his fingers*] yes, why not? a drop of vodka!

[*Enter* MISS MEROPIA.]

MISS MEROPIA. Well? What are you trying to hide from me?

APOLLONIUS. Oh, just a little souvenir, auntie, something I asked for remembrance. Do you know what I need, auntie? I need freedom.

MISS MEROPIA. Don't talk nonsense.

APOLLONIUS. I need it, auntie, I do. For instance, if you don't let me out of the house this evening . . .

MISS MEROPIA. Where do you want to go? Not to the fair for a scuffle with some drunken peasants?

APOLLONIUS. What an idea!

MISS MEROPIA. Where then?

APOLLONIUS. [*Wiping his forehead*] I'll tell you later.

MISS MEROPIA. No, tell me now.

APOLLONIUS. [*Mysteriously*] Here.

MISS MEROPIA. Whatever for?

APOLLONIUS. For her final answer.

MISS MEROPIA. Final? Have you proposed to her already?

APOLLONIUS. Ten words, remember? You know, auntie, how I hate beating about the bush. I told her straight: will you be my wife? She's almost given her consent, but she wants me to call again this evening for her final answer. I can't very well let her down.

MISS MEROPIA. You're not telling me a lie, are you?

APOLLONIUS. Of course, not. Only not a word to her. She asked me particularly that it should remain a secret between the two of us.

MISS MEROPIA. But if it is true, do you realize how important it is for us?

APOLLONIUS. [*Seriously*] I know, auntie, I know how important it is.

MISS MEROPIA. I can't believe it, somehow. It's too good to be true. However, the devil is up to any kind of trick.

APOLLONIUS. I assure you, auntie, she's mine!

MISS MEROPIA. All right, I'll let you go. Only come back quickly, I'll wait up for you. I shan't be able to sleep a wink, you understand!

[*Enter*: MRS. KUPÁVINA, MISS ANFÚSSA *and* MISS GLAFÍRA.]

MISS MEROPIA. Thank you for your hospitality, my dear. I must pay another visit now. Good-bye, my dears. [*To* MRS. KUPÁVINA] I don't know when I shall be seeing you again.

MRS. KUPÁVINA. I'll come to see you myself.

APOLLONIUS. But I'll soon be calling on Mrs. Kupavina again, auntie. I have to.

MISS MEROPIA. Well, if you have to, you have to. [*To* MRS. KUPÁVINA] Treat him well, my dear. I shall know what your real feelings are towards me from the way you treat him: if you treat him kindly, you are my friend, if you disappoint him, you'll disappoint me. Good-bye, I can't discuss everything with you now.

[MISS MEROPIA, APOLLONIUS, MRS. KUPÁVINA *and* MISS ANFÚSSA *go out. Enter* GLAFÍRA, *sits down, takes out a small book and begins to read. Enter* MRS. KUPÁVINA.]

MRS. KUPÁVINA. At last I've got you to stay with me!

GLAFÍRA. Is that you? [*Puts down her book*] I wanted to stay with you a long time ago. I like the country because it gives one a chance to think of serious things.

MRS. KUPÁVINA. I hope you won't be in a hurry to leave me.

GLAFÍRA Thank you very much, but, I'm afraid, you'll

soon get bored with me. I am such a bad conversationalist and I like to be alone.

Mrs. Kupávina. I understand you had quite a gay time in Petersburg.

Glafíra. Yes, I didn't then realize the true meaning of life. Now I look at everything through more serious eyes, life's fitful fever has lost its attractions for me.

Mrs. Kupávina. When did you have time to change your views? You're still so young.

Glafíra. I am young, of course, but under the guidance of such a woman as my aunt, a woman who is almost a saint, I have in a short time succeeded in doing quite a lot for my soul.

Mrs. Kupávina. You've come at the right moment.

Glafíra. Why?

Mrs. Kupávina. I wanted someone to talk things over with. I haven't anyone here I can confide in. You don't mind my being frank with you, do you?

Glafíra. Not at all. I shall be glad to do anything for you. Tell me everything, or, perhaps, you'd better not. I can guess what's on your mind. You're a society woman, therefore, vain. You're in love, aren't you?

Mrs. Kupávina. You've almost guessed it.

Glafíra. I'm sorry for you.

Mrs. Kupávina. Why are you sorry?

Glafíra. Because it is a sin.

Mrs. Kupávina. Not a great sin, surely.

Glafíra. Well, that depends on the man you're in love with. Is he rich or poor?

Mrs. Kupávina. Rich.

Glafíra. Then it is a great sin.

Mrs. Kupávina. But I don't love him for his riches.

Glafíra. He'll be very pleased to get your money all the same. If you don't throw youself at him, he might marry a poor girl and make her happy. But if rich women get all the rich men, what are we poor girls to do? I'm sorry, I'm afraid I made a slip in saying "we." I don't want anything really, I'm quite satisfied as I am. I'm talking in general terms.

Mrs. Kupávina. What shall I do?

Glafíra. Take a good hold of yourself—give him up! And

if you can't do without love, then fall in love with a poor man, it's less sinful. You can easily fall out of love with him: just look at him more closely.

Mrs. Kupávina. Look at whom? Do you know him?

Glafíra. Of course I do.

Mrs. Kupávina. I don't think so.

Glafíra. You can't keep a secret. It's well known that you're in love with Lynyayev.

Mrs. Kupávina. But you're mistaken.

Glafíra. [*Quickly*] Am I mistaken? Did you say I was mistaken?

Mrs. Kupávina. Of course.

Glafíra. Then you're not in love with him?

Mrs. Kupávina. No! How did you come to think of it?

Glafíra. Tell me the truth! I implore you to tell me the truth!

Mrs. Kupávina. But, really, my dear, what is there to see in Lynyayev?

Glafíra. If that is so, then, please forgive me. Let's stop playing a comedy. Be in love with anyone you like and how much you like. What a rotten game I played with you? Don't you realize that I've been placed at your side as a spy and that I took on that part with pleasure?

Mrs. Kupávina. Why?

Glafíra. I thought you were my rival.

Mrs. Kupávina. So you're in love with Lynyayev?

Glafíta. In love with him? My dear, why should I be in love with him? But I want to marry him—he is my only hope, my last chance!

Mrs. Kupávina. But what do your behaviour, your dress, your sermons mean?

Glafíra. My dress, my behaviour, my sermons are just a mask. I'll be frank with you, only promise to help me.

Mrs. Kupávina. I promise.

Glafíra. It is true I led a gay life in Petersburg. My sister is married to a young man, a very clever young man. He made a big fortune out of nothing. We were surrounded only by well-to-do people: lawyers, bankers, stockbrokers. My sister and I lived in a kind of a daze: drove up and down the Nevsky Prospect, dressed up in silks, wore mink coats, had wonderful dinners at home and in restaurants, always in high society, at the opera, the French theatre, but more often at the operetta, picnics, carnivals, the sky was the limit! Such a life hasn't, of course, much to recommend it, but once you've tasted it, life in the provinces becomes unbearable, if only you knew how unbearable!

Mrs. Kupávina. What made you leave Petersburg?

Glafíra. I don't know what actually happened. Something quite unexpected for my sister and myself. My sister cried a lot about something, they had to sell everything they had, I was sent to Miss Meropia, and they disappeared somewhere, abroad I believe. Of course, I've only myself to blame, very much to blame: I should have found a husband there and then, it wouldn't have been so difficult at all, but I was so caught up in the whirl of society life that I lost my head like a silly schoolgirl. I shall never forgive myself for that.

Mrs. Kupávina. Why are you always dressed in black?

Glafíra. What else shall I wear? My old rags, long out of fashion? A plain black dress is at least original and attracts attention. In such a dress you're sure to make a bigger impression if you smile at someone or give him the glad-eye. A glad-eye is sure to have a greater effect if given from under an old-fashioned hat. But you can't go on wearing such dresses for long even if you have a good reason for it. To think that I shall have to wear such dowdy rags all my life is enough to make me scream.

Mrs. Kupávina. I'm surprised that Miss Meropia can't find you a decent husband: she is such a genius when it comes to helping her own relations.

Glafíra. She won't do anything for me. She has her own plans. She is a very clever woman, she'd be glad to marry me to a rich husband but only on condition that she managed my husband's affairs and got them into her hands completely, and even then she'd go on telling me that she'd conferred such a favour on me!

Mrs. Kupávina. Yes, I suppose you are right.

Glafíra. I can see through her and she can see through me. She knows perfectly well that if I succeeded in marrying a rich husband, she wouldn't see me again. However, I'm very grateful to her.

MRS. KUPÁVINA. What for?

GLAFÍRA. For teaching me a lot that's very useful, a lot that a poor girl ought to know of life.

MRS. KUPÁVINA. And what's that?

GLAFÍRA. She taught me how to practise deception, how not to waste a single word, how to behave with utter disregard for anybody, quite rudely, in fact, for rudeness in a sanctimonious woman is usually mistaken for frankness and even for simplicity. I have found my victim: it is Lynyayev. He is the only man whom I could manage, who could give me the kind of life I want, the kind of life I am accustomed to. Any other life would bore me to death, would be a sheer misfortune to me, worse than death. I am no enemy to myself, my dear, and that's why I shall do everything to marry Lynyayev. To marry him I am ready to use every subterfuge, every means at my disposal, lawful and unlawful. Well, I've told you everything. Please, forgive me if I've been too frank with you.

MRS. KUPÁVINA. Not at all, I quite understand your position. [*She regards* GLAFÍRA *in silence for a long time and then embraces her*] Oh, if I were as brave as you, my dear!

GLAFÍRA. If I were as rich as you! [*Looks straight into* MRS. KUPÁVINA's *eyes*] Will you be a darling and help me? You see me a poor girl now, but wait till you see me a rich married woman!

MRS. KUPÁVINA. I'll do anything for you, my dear. I'll be glad to. I should be glad to see a married woman with a will of her own. As for me, I lived under the ghoulish eye of my late husband and, I suppose, the same thing will happen to me again.

GLAFÍRA. Why such sombre thoughts?

MRS. KUPÁVINA. Well, such it seems is my fate, at least, to judge by the letter I received from my lover. That is what I wanted to talk over with you, my dear.

GLAFÍRA. Tell me what's the matter? How are things between you?

MRS. KUPÁVINA. Three years ago, when my husband was

still alive, our neighbour Berkutov stayed with us the whole summer.

GLAFÍRA. And . . .

MRS. KUPÁVINA. And . . . Don't judge me too harshly, my dear My husband was sixty-five. I fell in love with Berkutov. Of course, I was very careful. I don't think he even guessed that I was in love with him.

GLAFÍRA. I wonder.

MRS. KUPÁVINA. I don't know . . . perhaps. He stayed here one summer only and then he left for Petersburg. Since then I haven't seen him, but he sends me his regards and says all sorts of nice things about me in every letter he writes to Lynyayev.

GLAFÍRA. This is all so innocent!

MRS. KUPÁVINA. It is quite innocent, but, all the same, I am caught. About three months ago, Lynyayev began worrying me: write to Berkutov, write to Berkutov, ask him to pay you a visit during the summer, he won't refuse you.

GLAFÍRA. So, darling, you obediently wrote that letter?

MRS. KUPÁVINA. I did. I can't remember what I said, something too awful, I'm sure. I was silly, inexcusably silly.

GLAFÍRA. And you got a reply?

MRS. KUPÁVINA. That's the trouble: I did. His letter was so business-like, written in a kind of office-clerk's jargon. What he says, in short, is that, "I am much too busy to admire the beauties of nature, but if you want me to come, I'll come. In the meantime, make no changes on your estate, don't trust your manager, and don't sell anything, especially the forest."

GLAFÍRA. A serious-minded man and, I should say, a very clever one.

MRS. KUPÁVINA. Agreed, but who gave him the right to tell me what to do? Am I a minor? This is an insult. I didn't answer his letter and, to tell you the truth, I don't seem so keen on marrying him now. He'll be here to-day or to-morrow. I'll have a look, I'll see how he behaves. If I find that he wants to marry me, I'll be very nice to him, then I'll just laugh and let him go back to Petersburg empty-handed.

GLAFÍRA. Yes, it's quite a good plan, but you must carry it out properly.

MRS. KUPÁVINA. I'll do my best. I'm terrified of losing my freedom. Here's another letter from him. I haven't opened it yet, so you can see for yourself how indifferent I am. Lynyayev brought it to me.

GLAFÍRA. So Lynyayev has already been here? Good Lord, this means that I shan't see him again to-day and, may be, never. Please, ask him to come.

MRS. KUPÁVINA. I haven't got to ask him. He's in the garden, hiding from Miss Meropia. He's staying to dinner.

GLAFÍRA. That's fine! Do let's have champagne, I haven't tasted champagne for donkey's years. I'm sick of being a teetotaler.

MRS. KUPÁVINA. Certainly, my dear.

GLAFÍRA. I should like to ask you something else. Lend me some decent clothes. My present clothes are so horrible.

MRS. KUPÁVINA. Here's the key to my wardrobe. Help yourself to anything you like. You'll find a lot of new dresses which I haven't even put on. I've had hundreds of new dresses made, but I still dare not show myself in anything but mourning.

GLAFÍRA. Thank you, darling. That's so sweet of you. I'll only be a minute.

[*Runs off.*]

MRS. KUPÁVINA. [*Opens letter*] Let's see what he says. "I am carrying out your order and I am on the way to your estate. As soon as I made up my mind to see you again, a feeling of heavy impatience settled on me. I'm devastated that I shall be carried to you by an engine invented by an Englishman for the transportation of freight waggons. I want wings, the light wings of love. . . ." How nauseating! [*Goes on reading to herself*] It gets worse as it goes on. What's the matter with him? Does he really think I'm so silly that I shall believe all this nonsense. Very well, don't let me undeceive him. I shall catch him more easily that way!

[GLAFÍRA *appears in the doorway dressed only in a skirt with a kerchief thrown over her shoulders.*]

GLAFÍRA. I've found everything, silk stockings and shoes,

and everything fits me perfectly. [*Gives a dancer's high kick*] It is a shame to put some horrible peasant boot on such a leg!

Mrs. Kupávina. Darling, you are lovely! If he isn't made of stone, he's sure to . . . [*At the drawing-room door*] Auntie, tell them to serve dinner. Ah, and here's Lynyayev . . .

Glafíra. Wait for me. I'll be ready in a minute. Well, it's now or never!

[*Goes out through door to right.* Mrs. Kupávina *goes into drawing-room.*]

ACT THREE

[*Across the stage is a garden fence with a gate in the middle, by the gate is a bench, behind the fence can be seen the thickly wooded park of* Mrs. Kupávina's *estate. Early evening.*
Gorétzky *stands by the fence and is whistling to himself.* Chugúnov *comes out of the gate.*]

Chugúnov. What are you doing here? Go home! Go home at once!

Gorétzky. I don't want to go home. I was waiting to see you. I want you very badly. It's important.

Chugúnov. What do you want?

Gorétzky. I want money. Please, let me have a few banknotes.

Chugúnov. Money? No, sir. What do you want money for?

Gorétzky. I think it's about time I had some fun. I'm going to the fair. [*Whistles.*]

Chugúnov. What do you want to do at the fair? You'd better stay at home. And stop whistling! Keep indoors, don't show your nose outside.

Gorétzky. Don't you worry, uncle. They can't send me to jail without a trial. When they pass sentence on me I'll go, but not before!

Chugúnov. For God's sake, don't talk like that!

Gorétzky. I didn't say anything! What does it matter what I say? You'd better give me the money.

Chugúnov. Where shall I get the money?

Gorétzky. That's your business, not mine. I don't care where you get it. All I know is that I'm going to get dead drunk to-day. I'm going to be drunk for the next twelve days.

Chugúnov. Why twelve? How can you say now that you will be drunk for twelve days?

Gorétzky. I hope it won't be for longer. Come on, let's have it!

Chugúnov. How much do you want?

Gorétzky. Fifty roubles.

Chugúnov. Have you gone out of your mind?

GORÉTZKY. What'll happen to me after the fair I don't know, but at present I'm quite sane.

CHUGÚNOV. Who are you trying to rob? I ask you. Who are you trying to rob?

GORÉTZKY. You. Who else? I'm trying to get money out of someone who has plenty of it.

CHUGÚNOV. Who do you think I am, a banker?

GORÉTZKY. Don't pretend to be so bloody penniless, uncle. You can't kid me. I know you well. I'm a relative of yours, not a stranger. You are the manager of a very large estate. Look at it! Don't tell me you are not robbing your employer!

CHUGÚNOV. Robbing, robbing! You damn fool! You illiterate blockhead! All right, suppose I have money, do you think I'm going to give it to you?

GORÉTZKY. You'll be sorry, uncle. I can make things very hot for you.

CHUGÚNOV. [*Takes out wallet*] Here, take this and don't let me see you again. [*Gives him five-rouble note.*]

GORÉTZKY. What? Only five roubles? Is that all I am worth to you?

CHUGÚNOV. Well, here's some more. [*Gives him another five-rouble note.*]

GORÉTZKY. I want more, uncle. I want a lot more. You'd better buy me off or it will be worse for you.

CHUGÚNOV. It's you who are a robber, a real robber. You won't get another copper out of me.

GORÉTZKY. And if anyone offers me more, shall I sell you out together with that old witch Murzavetzkaya?

CHUGÚNOV. Don't shout like that. Mrs. Kupavina has guests. They might hear you.

GORÉTZKY. I don't care a damn. Let them hear me.

CHUGÚNOV. To blazes with you! I'd better get away from mischief.

[*Goes out.*]

GORÉTZKY. [*Shouts after him*] Listen to me, uncle, if they offer me more I shall sell you out. I don't care, I tell you. I said I was going to have a hell of a good time, and I am going to have it. If you don't give me enough money at a time like this, I'll do you in, so help me!

[*Goes out after* CHUGÚNOV.]

[MRS. KUPÁVINA, MISS ANFÚSSA, GLAFÍRA *and* LYNYÁYEV *come out of the gate.*]

LYNYÁYEV. [*To* MRS. KUPÁVINA] I can't understand what you want to walk through the wet grass for when you could sit very quietly in your room, or, if you insist on fresh air, on the balcony.

MRS. KUPÁVINA. I want to see the fair.

LYNYÁYEV. Please, don't go. I can't see anything thrilling in having to walk uphill for two miles to see some drunken peasants.

MRS. KUPÁVINA. You'd better confess that you're too lazy. There is no need for you to accompany me, you can stay here.

LYNYÁYEV. I don't mind going, but your servants will be there and we might interfere with their enjoyment.

MRS. KUPÁVINA. We'll watch from a distance, from the top of the hill. But you needn't come. I'll take my aunt with me.

LYNYÁYEV. All right, that's fine. However, maybe I'd better . . .

MRS. KUPÁVINA. No, no. You'd only be moaning and groaning all the way, wanting us to be sorry for you. We'll be all right without you. Auntie, let's go!

MISS ANFÚSSA. Well, I mean . . . Why not, you know . . .

MRS. KUPÁVINA. [*To* GLAFÍRA] You're staying here, too, darling, aren't you? Don't bother to come, if you don't feel like a walk.

GLAFÍRA. Yes, I think I'd better stay. The noise of the fair will only give me a headache.

MRS. KUPÁVINA. Wait for us here.

LYNYÁYEV. All right, we'll wait for you here.

[MRS. KUPÁVINA *and* MISS ANFÚSSA *go out.*]

LYNYÁYEV. You've put a new dress on, but you've kept your old modesty.

GLAFÍRA. Don't you like girls who are too modest?

LYNYÁYEV. Of course! It's nice, it's very nice.

GLAFÍRA. It may be nice, but it is also very boring.

LYNYÁYEV. But I am not asking you to entertain me. That is rather my duty, but I'm afraid I . . . I'm afraid all I can offer you is to be bored with me.

GLAFÍRA. I don't mind. Thank you very much.

LYNYÁYEV. Don't mention it.

GLAFÍRA. Why not? I think you deserve my gratitude.

LYNYÁYEV. Why?

GLAFÍRA. For a quiet time. Isn't that important? After spending an evening with you one can go to bed without a tremor of excitement and one can sleep the sleep of the just. I have never been in love, Mr. Lynyayev. I shall, I suppose, one day. I am of an age when I can expect to fall hopelessly in love any moment.

LYNYÁYEV. So you are just like the rest. And I thought that you . . .

GLAFÍRA. That I was incapable of falling in love? You won't find such a girl in the whole world, Mr. Lynyayev.

LYNYÁYEV. So you're afraid to fall in love?

GLAFÍRA. Of course, I am. Love can bring me nothing but suffering. I am a girl of some discernment and some taste and I could only fall in love with a decent man, and decent men are on the look-out for rich brides. That's why I am in hiding and keep away from society—I am afraid to fall in love. Don't think that because I am modest I can't love someone to distraction. Still waters run deep, you know, and I feel that were I to fall in love . . .

LYNYÁYEV. Don't, for heaven's sake, don't! I'm frightened.

GLAFÍRA. But I am not at all frightened of you.

LYNYÁYEV. Aren't you?

GLAFÍRA. Not at all! You will not try to turn my head. Besides, it's quite impossible for you to turn any girl's head.

LYNYÁYEV. [*Hurt*] Do you think so?

GLAFÍRA. Really, Mr. Lynyayev, what sort of lover will you make? Don't look hurt. You're a very nice man, everybody likes you, but it is quite impossible to fall in love with you. You are already getting on in years, you are fat and you probably spend all your time at home pottering about in a dressing gown and a nightcap. In a word, you're too much like a dear, old daddy.

LYNYÁYEV. You are rather cruel to me, you know. I am not at all like a . . .
GLAFÍRA. No, no! Don't deceive yourself, my dear Mr. Lynyayev. Give up all hopes of conquests, sir! [*She bursts out laughing.*]
LYNYÁYEV. But what are you laughing at?
GLAFÍRA. Excuse me, a funny idea just occurred to me. Suppose, thought I, you were to fall in love with me and began to pay me all sorts of compliments and even tried to make love to me, I shouldn't, you know, however much I liked and respected you, be able to keep a straight face. I should burst out laughing!
LYNYÁYEV. I must say the ideas that occur to you are so very playful!
GLAFÍRA. I'm sorry, I'm only playing the fool. You think it's strange that I should be so gay, but I haven't got much time left, you see.
LYNYÁYEV. Why not?
GLAFÍRA. I shall soon enter a nunnery.
LYNYÁYEV. Really? Or are you joking?
GLAFÍRA. No, I'm not joking. Good-bye, dear Mr. Lynyayev, don't think too badly of me! But, please, don't be angry with me for teasing you. I want to leave a good impression behind me.
LYNYÁYEV. As a matter of fact, you could leave a good impression behind you.
GLAFÍRA. How?
LYNYÁYEV. By doing me a little favour.
GLAFÍRA. I shall be very glad to.
LYNYÁYEV. Why "very"?
GLAFÍRA. Because you are a very nice man.
LYNYÁYEV. I want to find someone with a good handwriting. I could employ him for a short time.
GLAFÍRA. I'm afraid I can't help you there. My handwriting is quite good, but, frankly, I don't care for the job.
LYNYÁYEV. You've misunderstood me, or you don't want to understand me.
GLAFÍRA. If I were a man . . . But, really, Mr. Lynyayev, what will people say? However . . .

LYNYÁYEV. But no, no! You see, I know that Chugunov handles all Miss Meropia's official correspondence. I know his hand, but sometimes her documents are written in a very neat hand, not at all like Chugunov's.

GLAFÍRA. So you want to find one who can write as neat a hand?

LYNYÁYEV. What I want is to find out who that man is!

GLAFÍRA. Why not ask Chugunov?

LYNYÁYEV. He won't tell me.

GLAFÍRA. What have you in mind?

LYNYÁYEV. Don't you know?

GLAFÍRA. Perhaps I know more than you think.

LYNYÁYEV. Please, tell me who he is.

GLAFÍRA. I can't.

LYNYÁYEV. Why not?

GLAFÍRA. Because he is my lover!

LYNYÁYEV. It's getting worse and worse.

GLAFÍRA. I may have put it a little too strongly. What I mean is that he is in love with me. He writes me poems almost every other day. He is so sweet: he doesn't want a reply, all he wants is to pour out his heart to me.

LYNYÁYEV. But who is he? Please, tell me.

GLAFÍRA. Do you want to know him very badly?

LYNYÁYEV. Yes.

GLAFÍRA. I can not only give you his name, I can bring him to you in about ten minutes.

LYNYÁYEV. [*Rubbing his hands with joy*] Really?

GLAFÍRA. Only, you understand, I shan't do it for nothing.

LYNYÁYEV. Ask me anything you like, anything!

GLAFÍRA. I shall ask you only a small thing.

LYNYÁYEV. Anything, my dear girl, anything you like!

GLAFÍRA. Pretend to be in love with me and try to play the enamoured swain the whole evening.

LYNYÁYEV. But you won't laugh at me, will you?

GLAFÍRA. I shall probably, if you are very funny.

LYNYÁYEV. All right, for one evening I suppose I could just manage it. It won't be easy, mind, but a bargain is a bargain. But when will you bring him to me?

GLAFÍRA. Any time you like, even now. I saw him going

in the direction of the fair a few minutes ago. I'll go and fetch him. Wait for me here! Here's Mrs. Kupavina.

[*Goes out.*]
[*Enter* Mrs. Kupávina *and* Miss Anfússa.]

LYNYÁYEV. Why back so soon?

MRS. KUPÁVINA. I should have liked to stay a little longer, but I'm running away from someone.

LYNYÁYEV. I told you there would be drunks about. Who's pursuing you?

MRS. KUPÁVINA. Our friend Murzavetzky. Do take me home.

LYNYÁYEV. Miss Anfussa, be so good as to wait here for Miss Glafira. When she returns, tell her that I shall be here soon.

MRS. KUPÁVINA. And don't let Murzavetzky into the park. Tell him that I'm not at home, that I've gone out.

MISS ANFÚSSA. All right, you know . . . I won't, I mean . . .

LYNYÁYEV. Why stand on ceremonies with the dear boy? Why not have him thrown out?

MRS. KUPÁVINA. I can't do that. He'll tell Miss Meropia and I shall be in for a lot of trouble. I must treat him with kid gloves, or she'll gobble me up.

[Mrs. Kupávina *and* Lynyáyev *go out.* Miss Anfússa *sits down on the bench.* Apollonius *comes in.*]

APOLLONIUS. [*Whistles*] Tamerlaine, Tamerlaine, come here, sir! Damn the hound! I'll hang him. Yes, sir, that's what I am going to do with you. I shall hang you, sir. That'll be the end of you, sir. Beg your pardon, madam! Where are they? [*Straining his eyes in the growing darkness*] Ah, there they are. Both of them, I think. Everything seems to be blurred: one, two. No, two. Of course, two. [*Bows from a distance*] How do you do?

MISS ANFÚSSA. [*Turning away*] Don't, you know . . . Really, I mean . . .

APOLLONIUS. But really, Mrs. Kupavina . . .

MISS ANFÚSSA. But, you know . . . Where is she, I mean . . .

APOLLONIUS. Yes, my dear Eulampe, it's right here, in my heart. On my word of honour. [*Sighs*] Such excruciating pain . . .

Miss Anfússa. Well, you know . . . That'll do, I mean . . .

Apollonius. I quite agree with you, but what am I to do if I can't bear it any longer? I am in love with you . . . that's . . . that's all.

Miss Anfússa. You'd better, you know . . . Really, I mean . . .

Apollonius. Why don't you answer me? Won't you say anything? I'm here . . . at your feet . . . have pity . . . I might die. Please, answer me, my angel! Just one word.

Miss Anfússa. Really, you know . . . Be off, I mean . . .

Apollonius. Miss Anfussa, go away, pray. I'm not talking to you.

Miss Anfússa. Not to me, you know . . . Who to, I mean . . .

Apollonius. Who to? That's funny! Ha-ha-ha! Did you think I was talking to you?

Miss Anfússa. Well, you know . . . There isn't anyone else here, I mean . . .

Apollonius. Miss Anfussa, do be quiet, I mean, shut up! Eulampe, there are moments in a man's life when . . . What am I talking about? *One* moment is enough for a man . . .

Miss Anfússa. Oh dear, oh dear, you know . . . What am I to do, I mean . . .

Apollonius. You are silent, you let someone else speak for you—for a man with a sensitive soul this is . . . let me tell you . . . [*sighs*] . . . hard!

Miss Anfússa. But how can she, you know . . . If she isn't here, I mean . . .

Apollonius. [*Drawing near*] Who isn't here? Why isn't she here?

Miss Anfússa. Well, I mean . . . She just isn't here, you know . . .

Apollonius. [*Examining bench and* Miss Anfússa] But where is she?

Miss Anfússa. If she isn't here, you know . . . How should I, I mean . . .

Apollonius. [*Striking his forehead*] Good God! Good God!

Miss Anfússa. Well, you know . . . What's all the fuss about, I mean . . .

APOLLONIUS. What's all the fuss about? Why, I've been shamelessly deceived!

MISS ANFÚSSA. Who, you know . . . Would trouble, I mean . .

APOLLONIUS. But what's all this? Have my feelings been outraged or is it all a mirage?

[*Enter* LYNYÁYEV.]

But no, I shan't let her make a fool of me! No, sir!

MISS ANFÚSSA. [*Seeing* LYNYÁYEV] At last, you know . . . There he is, I mean . . . [*Gets up and goes towards gate.*]

APOLLONIUS. Come wind, come rain, I'll be here again.

MISS ANFÚSSA. Drivel on, you know . . . In wind and rain, I mean . . .

[*Goes out through gate.*]

APOLLONIUS. I shan't put up with it. I'll go . . .

LYNYÁYEV. Where?

APOLLONIUS. To her.

LYNYÁYEV. Alas!

APOLLONIUS. Why "alas"? What do you mean by "alas," sir?

LYNYÁYEV. You can't go to her. You won't be let in.

APOLLONIUS. I won't be let in, eh? We'll see! [*Wants to go through the gate.*]

LYNYÁYEV. [*Barring his way*] Listen, I'm going to give you some friendly advice: go home or you'll be sorry!

APOLLONIUS. What do you mean, I'll be sorry? Let me, sir, let me ask you . . .

LYNYÁYEV. [*Confidentially*] Men have been stationed in the park and, as soon as you enter, they will [*makes a sign*], you understand, don't you?

APOLLONIUS. What, what?

LYNYÁYEV. I have nothing to do with it. Mrs. Kupavina thought it necessary to make these arrangements.

APOLLONIUS. You can't frighten me. However, I don't care a damn if I don't see her to-night. It's she who'll be sorry. I wanted to settle everything quietly with her, but now, of course, it's too late, nothing doing!

LYNYÁYEV. Why quietly?

APOLLONIUS. But, damn it all, I'm sorry for her! She owes me fifty thousand!

LYNYÁYEV. Big money.
APOLLONIUS. I didn't want it. What do I want it for? All I wanted, old chap, was, so to speak, offer her my hand, just, you understand, in order to bring about a merger of our fortunes. Of course, I haven't really, you know, got anything, I mean . . . What am I talking about? I have a fortune and she has a fortune, so why all these demands and counter-demands?
LYNYÁYEV. It's a splendid idea, old boy, except that she doesn't want to marry you.
APOLLONIUS. All right, in that case I shan't show any mercy to her. Do you know, old chap, what I shall do to her? I shall fleece her, I shall absolutely fleece her!
LYNYÁYEV. Will you demand fifty thousand?
APOLLONIUS. Oh no, old chap, this isn't any longer a matter of fifty thousand. It's more like one hundred and fifty thousand! Her whole estate will be mine, it will be mine in a week!
LYNYÁYEV. That's fine, old boy! We shall be neighbours then. [*Presses* APOLLONIUS's *hand*] You'll come to see me, won't you? But now, I'm afraid, it's time you went home. Isn't that your carriage? I expect Miss Meropia has sent it for you.
APOLLONIUS. Yes, she's expecting me, I promised to bring her a final answer.
LYNYÁYEV. Well, what could be more final than that?
APOLLONIUS. But, you know, old chap, I'm really sorry for Mrs. Kupavina. She'll be crying her eyes out. Good-bye.

[*Goes out. He is heard shouting and whistling*: "*Tamerlaine, come here, sir!*"]

[GLAFÍRA *and* GORÉTZKY *come in from the opposite side.*]
GLAFÍRA. Let me introduce you, this is Claud Goretzky. [*To* GORÉTZKY] And this is Mr. Michael Lynyayev.
GORÉTZKY. [*Taking off his cap*] I've met you before, sir. [*To* GLAFÍRA] Miss Glafira, shall I break this fence for you?
LYNYÁYEV. What a strange request!
GORÉTZKY. Not at all strange, sir. How else can I prove . . .? Please, don't interfere, sir. [*To* GLAFÍRA] Shall I beat someone up for you? I'll gladly give anyone a jolly good thrashing just

to please you. I'd do anything in the world for you, Miss Glafíra!

LYNYÁYEV. [*Produces forged letter*] Ask him who wrote this?

GLAFÍRA. [*To* GORÉTZKY] Who wrote this?

GORÉTZKY. I can't tell you that! You'd better ask me something else.

LYNYÁYEV. But you said just now that you'd do anything in the world for Miss Glafíra.

GORÉTZKY. I would, but I was paid ten roubles not to tell.

LYNYÁYEV. I'll give you fifteen if you tell me.

GORÉTZKY. All right, I'll return the ten, I'll say it's too little. [*Takes the money*] Thank you, sir. [*Stuffs money in all his pockets*] I wrote this letter, sir.

LYNYÁYEV. You? In that case I shall want your help very badly. Will you come home with me to-night? I'll give you lots more money and plenty of food and drinks.

GORÉTZKY. I will, sir. Thank you very much, sir. [*To* GLAFÍRA] Let me do something really wicked for you, Miss Glafíra.

GLAFÍRA. But you've done it already.

GORÉTZKY. This is nothing. Besides, I was paid for it.

LYNYÁYEV. So don't forget. You're coming back with me to-night.

GORÉTZKY. Very good, sir. I'll be waiting for you in the office. Good-bye, Miss Glafíra.

[*Goes out.*]

GLAFÍRA. Well, are you satisfied?

LYNYÁYEV. I can't tell you how grateful I am. I feel so happy I could skip and dance like a child.

GLAFÍRA. I don't think it's so nice to be a child, try to be a young man.

LYNYÁYEV. How do you mean?

GLAFÍRA. Keep your promise.

LYNYÁYEV. What promise?

GLAFÍRA. To make love to me.

LYNYÁYEV. My dear young lady, I'm very awkward. What pleasure can it give you to watch a man of my age making a fool of himself?

GLAFÍRA. Why not try? Be a sport!

LYNYÁYEV. Well, what do you want me to do? Shall I tell you that your eyes are very beautiful?

GLAFÍRA. No, that's silly.

LYNYÁYEV. Or shall I make love to you in the Russian fashion, as our country lads and lasses do? It's all plain-sailing with them, no beating about the bush at all.

GLAFÍRA. Perhaps that would be going a bit too far. However, I'd rather have that than listen to your silly compliments. Poor man, you have to make love to me and you don't know how to! But don't worry. Let me help you. Let's begin by putting your cape round you. It's getting chilly. [*She wraps* LYNYÁYEV's *cape round him.*]

LYNYÁYEV. Thank you.

GLAFÍRA. Now, tell me have you ever been in love?

LYNYÁYEV. Why, certainly, I have.

GLAFÍRA. Did you say anything to the girls you loved?

LYNYÁYEV. I said quite a lot, but you must remember I was young then.

GLAFÍRA. Do try to remember what you said to them.

LYNYÁYEV. That's easy. I told one—she was a gorgeous blonde—that before we came into the world our kindred souls fluttered round the universe like butterflies in the moonbeams.

GLAFÍRA. And what did you say to the other?

LYNYÁYEV. And to the other—she was a ravishing brunette—I said that I'd provide her with a luxuriously furnished house in the country for the summer and that I'd buy her a pair of black stallions.

GLAFÍTA. Ah, how nice! You know, I'm beginning to enjoy this conversation. Go on!

LYNYÁYEV. I promised her mountains of gold, I told her that I couldn't live without her, I threatened that I would shoot or drown myself if she refused to be mine.

GLAFÍRA. And what did she say?

LYNYÁYEV. She said, "What do you want to drown yourself for? Marry me, and all your troubles will be over!" No, my angel, said I, marriage is much worse than drowning for me. "Well, if you feel like that," she said, "then go and drown yourself, because I shall never agree to bring mummy and daddy and the rest of my relations sorrowing to their graves."

GLAFÍRA. She was poor, wasn't she?

LYNYÁYEV. Yes.

GLAFÍRA. And so stupid.

LYNYÁYEV. Why? What would you have done in her place?

GLAFÍRA. I shouldn't have refused anything. I should have accepted the country house, and the horses, and the money and you would have married me all the same.

LYNYÁYEV. But that's quite impossible, I am firm as a rock in my resolution never to marry.

GLAFÍRA. Not at all. It's really very simple.

LYNYÁYEV. But how? Tell me, my dear girl, how would you have forced me to marry you? Go on, tell me!

GLAFÍRA. Let's sit down. [*They sit down on the bench*] All right. Now imagine that you are in love with me a little, just as much as you were with that brunette. Otherwise, of course, I could do nothing. [*She puts her feet up on the bench and leans against* LYNYÁYEV.]

LYNYÁYEV. Please, please, my dear young lady!

GLAFÍRA. [*Moving away from him*] I'm sorry.

LYNYÁYEV. That's all right. I only wanted to ask you, are you beginning to play your part or don't you regard me as a man?

GLAFÍRA. I'm feeling a little chilly.

LYNYÁYEV. Then, please, don't mind me in the least.

GLAFÍRA. [*Leaning against* LYNYÁYEV *again*] Well, you are in love with me. We live happily together. I am meekness and obedience personified. Not only do I carry out your desires, I anticipate them, and, in the meantime, little by little, I get you and your household into my hands. I learn to know all your habits, I make a study of your smallest whims, and, in the end, in quite a short time you suddenly discover that you can't live without me. I have become so much part of your daily life that you can't take a step without me.

LYNYÁYEV. All right, I admit this is quite possible.

GLAFÍRA. Well, one lovely morning I say to you, "Daddy, I

feel the need for prayer, do let me go to a convent for a day or two." At first you will, of course, raise all kinds of objections. I shall obey you without a word. Then, from time to time, I shall repeat my request without insisting on it and I shall keep on gazing at you with imploring eyes. You can't refuse me, but you keep on putting it off and, then, you just have to give in and you let me go. As soon as I'm gone everything in the house turns topsy-turvy, one thing goes wrong, another isn't to your liking, one day the coffee is bitter, another day dinner is late, your study hasn't been tidied and, if tidied, the papers and the books on your desk are not where you are accustomed to find them. You begin to lose patience, you begin to sigh, to pace your room, to stop dead in your tracks, to throw up your hands in despair, to talk to yourself. You catch yourself listening for any noises outside the house in the hope of my return, you run out on the porch to see if I haven't come back. But I keep on postponing, one day, two days, three days. At last your patience snaps, you can't bear the suspense any longer, you rush out of the house, you start walking up the road farther and farther, until you are two or even three miles from your house. Here I am at last! What happiness, what joy indescribable! Again your life becomes quiet and peaceful. Your eyes begin to beam with happiness and infinite tenderness!

LYNYÁYEV. [*Sighs*] Well, go on, go on!

GLAFÍRA. One morning when your tenderness knows no limit, I say to you with tears in my eyes: "Dear Daddy, I am ashamed to show myself among people. I have to hide myself from the whole world, bury myself alive for shame, but I am still so young, I still want to live!"

LYNYÁYEV. Of course, my dear, naturally!

GLAFÍRA. Good-bye, dear daddy, I say. I don't want any of your comforts, I don't care for any of your treasures . . .

LYNYÁYEV. Damn it, that's not fair!

GLAFÍRA. . . . I am going to marry someone else.

LYNYÁYEV. Whom?

GLAFÍRA. Well, even Goretzky.

LYNYÁYEV. What a wonderful husband for you!

GLAFÍRA. He may be poor, but at least he'll make an

honest woman of me. Anyway, all is finished between us. My mind's made up!

LYNYÁYEV. But, my dear girl, you can't throw me over like this, without any proper warning. You should have thought of it before.

GLAFÍRA. Darling daddy, I was afraid. Can't you see for yourself, this life is killing me, I am getting thinner and thinner every day, I may even die!

LYNYÁYEV. All the same this is a very dirty trick to play on me and, anyway, this is only play-acting.

GLAFÍRA. If you don't believe me, darling, then, of course I shall have to adopt another method. I shall be ready to sacrifice everything for you, even my life.

LYNYÁYEV. Ah, that's better!

GLAFÍRA. What can I do? Men are so strong-minded!

LYNYÁYEV. Anyway, old girl, I've had my way.

GLAFÍRA. Yes, you've had your way. Who am I to contradict you? However, on the same day, in the evening I decide to disappear unobserved. No one knows, that is to say, no one is going to tell you, where I am. One day goes by, then another. You send out scouts along all the roads, you engage private detectives, you yourself are rushing hither and thither, you lose your sleep, your appetite, you're going off your head. But a few minutes before you are about to lose your reason completely, you are told where I am. You rush to me with presents, jewels, tears, you're imploring me to come back to you, but I remain impervious to all your blandishments. You are crying, I myself am sobbing. I love you, I am sorry to part with you, but I stay put. At last I say to you, "Darling daddy, you like your bachelor life, you can't bear any other existence, all right, why not let's be married in secret. Then no one would know that you are married, you'll go on living your bachelor life, nothing will be changed —only my mind will be at rest, only I shall no longer have to suffer!" After a little persuasion, you accept the inevitable.

LYNYÁYEV. Yes, it is possible, it is quite possible, but, my dear, I should all the same have persisted in remaining a bachelor.

GLAFÍRA. All right, let's suppose that you win again. I

return to you, but the very next day, what happens? I have become the perfect society lady. My movements are so slow, so casual. And where did I get all those gorgeous dresses from?

LYNYÁYEV. Ah, so that's your game, is it?

GLAFÍRA. My upper lip curls disdainfully, my voice when I do condescend to speak to you, is harsh, peremptory, my gestures formal. How sweet and tender I shall be to strangers and how stand-offish to you. How overjoyed you'll be to get one kind word out of me! No more shall I gush over you, no longer shall I run all over the place to do your bidding. I shan't call you my darling daddy any more, but just Michael. [*Speaks drawlingly*] "Michael, please, be a dear and run down to the garden for me! I forgot my handkerchief on the bench!" And how you do run! This alone will force you to marry me. It's an old trick, but a tried one, and there are others.

LYNYÁYEV. This is all very well, but you can catch your man in this way only if he is really in love with you.

GLAFÍRA. Certainly. You needn't worry. You are absolutely safe, for you aren't in love with anyone.

LYNYÁYEV. I am safe and a jolly good thing, too. But if I were to fall in love, old girl, it would be with you alone!

[*Kisses* GLAFÍRA's *hand.*]

GLAFÍRA. What's that? What's this for?

LYNYÁYEV. Oh, nothing.

GLAFÍRA. If it's just "nothing," then it's an insult. You're feeling sentimental and you think that, as I am about, you can just start pawing me.

LYNYÁYEV. Not at all, my dear girl, didn't you yourself ask me to make love to you?

GLAFÍRA. Why, of course. I forgot all about it. All right, you can kiss my hand again.

LYNYÁYEV. Very well, I will. [*Kisses her other hand.*]

GLAFÍRA. It appears you, too, are beginning to play your part with zest.

LYNYÁYEV. I confess, I was a little afraid at first, but I must say I find it a very pleasant pastime.

GLAFÍRA. [*Sighs*] Yes, unfortunately it's only a pastime.

[MISS ANFÚSSA *comes in.*]

Miss Anfússa. Supper, you know . . . You're expected, I mean . . . Why at night? It's chilly, I mean . . .
Glafíra. [*To* Lynyáyev] Let's go.
Lynyáyev. I'll come presently.

[Glafíra *and* Miss Anfússa *go out.*]

What a dear girl she is, so pretty and clever! I must be careful, though. It doesn't take long. Spend two more evenings like that with her and you'll be thrown off your balance, one false stop and you're done for, they'll be putting the harness on you. It's a good thing she's going off to her nunnery or I should have to run from her as fast as my legs would carry me. I'll have a quick supper and then straight home, the further from temptation the better. She won't see me again, not for some time, at any rate. Later on, if I meet her again, it will be just "how d'you do" and "good-bye." You're lovely, my dear Glafira, but my freedom and quiet and my bachelor existence are dearer to me than your beauty.

ACT FOUR

[*A room in* Mrs. Kupávina's *country mansion, furnished in oriental style, french windows with long curtains opening onto a terrace, at either side two large windows covered with some transparent material; along the walls and under the windows soft couches; beyond the balustrade of the terrace a picturesque country landscape.*]
[*Enter* Mrs. Kupávina, Glafíra, *followed by a* Footman.]

Mrs. Kupávina. Your affair with Lynyayev seems to be getting along nicely.

Glafíra. I'm afraid it only seems so.

Mrs. Kupávina. He was so nice to you yesterday.

Glafíra. To order—it was all a prearranged joke.

Mrs. Kupávina. You seem to be losing hope, my poor darling.

Glafíra. Not altogether, I must meet him again, then I shall know for certain whether I could rely on him or not.

Mrs. Kupávina. You'll be able to see him again to-day. Goretzky brought a note from him. He is coming and, guess, with whom?

Glafíra. Why bother to guess? The light in your eyes tells me that you're expecting your future bridegroom.

Mrs. Kupávina. Yes, Vassily Berkutov has decided to make us happy, he has arrived from Petersburg.

Glafíra. When are you expecting them?

Mrs. Kupávina. This evening, of course. I shall have to dress up for such an occasion.

Glafíra. But Miss Meropia will probably send the carriage for me long before that.

Mrs. Kupávina. The carriage will wait.

Glafíra. She'll be cross.

Mrs. Kupávina. Let her be cross, you'll make it up with her.

Glafíra. It won't be so easy. She won't be in a hurry.
[Footman *enters.*]

Footman. Miss Meropia has sent the carriage, ma'am. The coachman gave me this letter for you.

[MRS. KUPÁVINA *opens letter and reads it to herself.*]
GLAFÍRA. I knew that would happen. What rotten luck! Again the black dress, again hypocrisy, again fasting.
MRS. KUPÁVINA. Is Mr. Lynyayev at home?
FOOTMAN. No, ma'am. He's gone to town.
MRS. KUPÁVINA. [*Uneasily*] What am I to do? This is so unexpected. . . . I am completely at a loss . . .
GLAFÍRA. What's the matter?
MRS. KUPÁVINA. Just listen to what Miss Meropia writes me. [*To the* FOOTMAN] Go tell the coachman to wait.

[FOOTMAN *goes out.*]

GLAFÍRA. Go on, read!
MRS. KUPÁVINA. [*Reads*] "My dear Mrs. Kupavina."
GLAFÍRA. The beginning sounds rather ominous.
MRS. KUPÁVINA. You'd better hear what's coming. [*Reads*] "You found it inconvenient to receive my nephew yesterday. If you were alone or lived in retirement, I should have said nothing, but you had visitors who were no whit better than he. He is of as good a family as Lynyayev and certainly no bigger fool than he. Either it was done thoughtlessly or some clever man induced you to do it. If you have forgotten everything you owe me and the innumerable favours I have done you, you ought at least to have remembered that I never forgive an insult. You have become so absorbed in your life of idle pleasure or so obsessed with some man that you are forgetting that there is a law action pending between you and Apollonius. In my simplicity of mind and kindness of heart I felt sorry for you as though you were a small, helpless child and I was anxious to settle everything peaceably, in a true Christian spirit, in a spirit of love and goodwill. But since you yourself seem not averse from slighting us and since you even seem to despise your benefactors, you must not be surprised if we demand a very large sum in settlement of our claim, a sum which you will not be able to raise by the sale of your entire estate. I shall press my claim without fear or favour and I shall be neither sorry for you nor shed tears on your behalf. Your former benefactress, Meropia Murzavetskaya." How do you like that?
GLAFÍRA. Isn't she trying to scare you?

MRS. KUPÁVINA. What a shock! I don't even know how to answer her. I shall have to wait till Lynyayev and Berkutov arrive and discuss it with them. You'll have to wait, too, to take back my reply.

[MISS ANFÚSSA *comes in.*]

MISS ANFÚSSA. They're here, you know . . .

MRS. KUPÁVINA. Are you quite sure, auntie?

MISS ANFÚSSA. Who else, I mean . . .

MRS. KUPÁVINA. I'd better go dress.

MISS ANFÚSSA. Of course, you know . . . You're not dressed, I mean . . . He's quite a stranger, you know . . .

MRS. KUPÁVINA. Ask them to wait.

MISS ANFÚSSA. Here they are, you know . . . They're coming across the park, I mean . . .

MRS. KUPÁVINA. [*To* GLAFÍRA] Come with me.

[MRS. KUPÁVINA *and* GLAFÍRA *go out.*]

MISS ANFÚSSA. [*After them*] You should have dressed earlier, you know . . . I warned you, I mean . . .

[*Enter* LYNYÁYEV *and* BERKÚTOV.]

LYNYÁYEV. Miss Anfussa, let me introduce you to a friend of mine, Vassily Berkutov.

MISS ANFÚSSA. I've seen him before, you know . . .

BERKÚTOV. How are you, Miss Anfussa?

MISS ANFÚSSA. Thank you, quite well, you know . . . My head sometimes, I mean . . . She asked you to wait here, you know . . . Soon, I mean . . .

LYNYÁYEV. Don't worry, Miss Anfussa, we'll wait.

MISS ANFÚSSA. She won't be long, you know . . . She's gone . . . I mean . . . We're very sorry, you know . . .

[*Goes out.*]

LYNYÁYEV. You'll hear from herself how they tricked her of a thousand roubles.

BERKÚTOV. Don't get so excited, my dear chap, don't get excited.

LYNYÁYEV. What do you mean, don't get excited? I can't help getting excited. This is forgery, pure forgery!

BERKÚTOV. Do calm yourself! I don't think it is forgery at all.

LYNYÁYEV. But Goretzky has confessed. What better proof do you want? A pity I got up so late and had no time to find out from him everything properly. Then you came and carried him off.

BERKÚTOV. I had a long talk with Goretzky. I took him to town. It appears he told you a lie. He wanted money and he told you a tall story. He purposely slandered himself, you see. And you, too! To take Goretzky's word!

LYNYÁYEV. Whatever you say, the thing's a fraud.

BERKÚTOV. In my opinion Miss Murzavetzkaya should be above suspicion. What kind of a world is it where everybody regards everybody else as a criminal?

LYNYÁYEV. You can expect anything from that old woman.

BERKÚTOV. People in the provinces smell crime everywhere, that's a well-known fact. You get bored without some scandal or other, you're always trying to undermine each other's reputations: you've nothing else to do.

LYNYÁYEV. But they are trying to rob Eulampe.

BERKÚTOV. You can think what you like, but, while I am here, leave her affairs to me. I beg of you, do me the favour, find yourself some other occupation.

LYNYÁYEV. I suppose you think even Chugunov a fine fellow?

BERKÚTOV. Well, what about Chugunov? Once a solicitor, always a solicitor. You can't twist him round your finger. All you high-minded and excitable lawyers seem to be preoccupied with questions of right and wrong, but, put you to the test and you won't be able to draw up a legal document properly. But the Chugunovs are men of the old school, they know their laws by heart. That's why they are so indispensable.

LYNYÁYEV. It's easy for you to talk. You are here on a short visit, but how do you expect me to live with such people? You'd better try it yourself.

BERKÚTOV. He who knows how to live will be able to live in peace with anybody and he who behaves like a child, as you do, will find life hard anywhere. I can live in peace with all sorts of people.

LYNYÁYEV. We'll see. Will you be staying here long?

BERKÚTOV. No. Later on I may settle here permanently, but now I'm too busy. I have important business in Petersburg. I came here to get married.

LYNYÁYEV. Who are you going to marry?
BERKÚTOV. Who do you think? Eulampe, of course.
LYNYÁYEV. Is everything settled then?
BERKÚTOV. Nothing is settled.
LYNYÁYEV. But if nothing is settled, why are you so sure?
BERKÚTOV. I can't see any reason why I shouldn't be sure. My dear chap, I had my eye on it a long time ago.
LYNYÁYEV. Do you mean you had your eye on Eulampe?
BERKÚTOV. No! On her estate, but, of course, also on Eulampe. What an income, what comfort, what a beautiful place! [*He points to the landscape outside the french windows*] Look at it, isn't it gorgeous? And there, on the left, by the river, what a beautiful little corner! As though nature herself has fashioned it for . . .
LYNYÁYEV. . . . a Swiss cottage.
BERKÚTOV. No, old chap, for a distillery. I admit, sinner that I am, that I've been thinking of it a long time. Kupavin, rather a doddering old man, you know, was sure to kick the bucket, if not to-day, then to-morrow, leaving behind him a fine estate and a pretty widow. I have had a very busy life, I'm beginning to think of retiring and what prospect is more inviting for a retired businessman than life on such an estate, with a beautiful wife at your side, some honorary position in the county . . .
LYNYÁYEV. We'll elect you as chairman of the landowners' association.
BERKÚTOV. We? But how many of you are there? You're constantly quarrelling among yourselves, you're split up into ten different parties, I suppose. I may as well accept your offer, then at least your party will be more powerful. You know what I've noticed? You don't seem to be any longer as strong a freethinker as you used to be. You provincials don't read enough. A large number of books and pamphlets in your line of thought has been recently published. I brought some of them with me. If you wish, I'll give them to you. Read one or two books and you'll have enough to talk about for five years.
LYNYÁYEV. Thank you. That's very kind of you. So all you want to make you happy is marriage?
BERKÚTOV. Yes, old chap, I want to get married as quickly

as possible. I know this estate like my own five fingers. It's in excellent order. I have to hurry up before it gets all tangled up in lawsuits. Kupavin was a wise old bird.

LYNYÁYEV. Not so wise after all. He seems to have gone out of his mind in his old age.

BERKÚTOV. You think so?

LYNYÁYEV. Yes, he spent a hundred thousand on the purchase of a forest.

BERKÚTOV. A wise bird! I am grateful to him for that!

LYNYÁYEV. But he left very little ready money. Eulampe is hard up.

BERKÚTOV. Good man! If he had left money, it would have been gone by now, but the forest still stands and is growing.

LYNYÁYEV. But what is one to do with it? No one wants timber now.

BERKÚTOV. Eulampe's forest is now worth half a million. In another fortnight the news will be out that a railway is to be built through that forest. I heard of it myself from an unimpeachable source. For the time being you'd better mind your p's and q's.

LYNYÁYEV. Damn it, that's clever! So that's what you're after! But I told you that she'd given a blank bill of exchange to Chugunov, a blank!

BERKÚTOV. Well, it could have been much worse.

LYNYÁYEV. How do you mean, "could have been"?

BERKÚTOV. If the blank had fallen into other hands.

LYNYÁYEV. But do you think Chugunov will make it easy for her?

BERKÚTOV. Chugunov, like the rest of the old-style rogues, doesn't see beyond his nose, his ambitions are so paltry. I've made inquiries, he's trying to buy a plot of land, they're asking three thousand for it. I suppose, that's all he wants.

LYNYÁYEV. Well, there doesn't seem to be anything in your way. You'll get married, of course, but I'm dying to see how you'll bring it off.

BERKÚTOV. I haven't the faintest idea myself, I'll see what happens. Of one thing I am sure, though, I'm going to see it through! Women are fond of thinking that they are free to dispose of themselves as they please. But when it comes to business they can't, as a rule, do a thing for themselves. It's the clever men who lead them where they list.

[*Enter* Mrs. Kupávina.]

Mrs. Kupávina. So sorry to have kept you waiting, gentlemen.

Lynyáyev. It's we who should ask to be forgiven for having arrived at such an inopportune time.

Berkútov. [*Kissing* Mrs. Kupávina's *hand*] My haste is forgivable, for I haven't seen you for such a long time. My impatience was so great . . .

Mrs. Kupávina. [*With a smile*] . . . that if you had wings . . .

Berkútov. . . . I should have arrived here earlier.

Lynyáyev. I must say, old man, you're a bit too heavy for Cupid.

Mrs. Kupávina. And I should think you have already spent all your arrows.

Lynyáyev. No, I believe he has kept one or two, in case . . .

Mrs. Kupávina. Only a few, I'm sure, and blunt ones at that.

Berkútov. That's why I have become so niggardly with them and am not shooting them all over the place.

Mrs. Kupávina. You shoot to kill, I presume?

Berkútov. At any rate, I am not throwing them away, that in itself is something, you'll agree.

Lynyáyev. May I take a stroll in the park? If I stay too long indoors after dinner . . .

Mrs. Kupávina. You get sleepy?

Lynyáyev. You've guessed it.

Mrs. Kupávina. Please yourself. My park is at your disposal.

Lynyáyev. Whose carriage is it in your yard?

Mrs. Kupávina. Murzavetzkaya has sent for Glafira.

Lynyáyev. So she's leaving?

Mrs. Kupávina. Are you sorry?

Lynyáyev. Not at all. Is she leaving soon?

Mrs. Kupávina. At once.

Lynyáyev. A happy journey. I hope she enjoys her trip to town.

[*Goes out.*]

Mrs. Kupávina. How long do you intend to stay here?

Berkútov. I'm sorry to say I'm here on a short visit. I came on business.

Mrs. Kupávina. Business?

Berkútov. I could have told you a lie. I could have said that I came here for the sole purpose of seeing you, of feasting my eyes on you, but, in the first place, you wouldn't have believed me . . .

Mrs. Kupávina. I might, you know.

Berkútov. Well, if that is so, I should have hated to deceive you. After an absence of two years, dare I hope that you will still find my presence agreeable? Your feelings may have changed, they probably have changed. You are now a rich and independent woman, to flirt with you is not quite honest. Besides, you yourself probably regard every one of your admirers as an enemy who wants to deprive you both of your independence and your money. Before it was different: you were not free and both of us were younger, too. [*With a sigh*] Ah, that was a glorious time!

Mrs. Kupávina. So you absolutely refuse to flirt with me?

Berkútov. Absolutely. And what about you? You would have liked to watch me squirm, to have a little innocent fun with me. Don't deny it! I can see it in your eyes. Well, I don't really mind. If you want to flirt, flirt with other men: you'll suffer from no scarcity of admirers. Let us talk things over as businessmen. I came here to find a purchaser for my estate.

Mrs. Kupávina. But it's a family estate!

Berkútov. What if it is a family estate? It's bringing me in very little, there's no earthly advantage in keeping it in the family, money will bring me in more interest.

Mrs. Kupávina. But does nothing bind you to your birthplace? Aren't you sorry to part with anything there?

Berkútov. I may be sorry, but it's bad business.

Mrs. Kupávina. Always business, business! Have you no heart?

Berkútov. My heart is getting colder as the years roll by, my dear Eulampe. I wondered if you wouldn't agree to buy my estate from me.

Mrs. Kupávina. I have no ready money, besides I am such a bad business woman myself.

Berkútov. Don't be so modest. Everything seems to be flourishing here, everything seems to be in such perfect order, everything looks so clean!

Mrs. Kupávina. Cleanliness is a woman's business and not a very tricky one, either. But I have no idea of the real position of the estate. There are some things which are beyond me. I must trust strangers to put them right for me and, of course, they may deceive me.

Berkútov. For instance?

Mrs. Kupávina. I have a certain business on my hands now which is worrying me a lot.

Berkútov. Tell me what is it, if it's not a secret.

Mrs. Kupávina. No secret at all. I wanted to ask your advice about it.

Berkútov. I shall be very glad to help you, if I have the time. What is it all about?

Mrs. Kupávina. It's a long story. You'd better read this letter. [*Gives him* Miss Meropia's *letter.*]

Berkútov. [*Having read letter, returns it*] I see.

Mrs. Kupávina. But what would you advise me to do?

Berkútov. You must find out how big the claim is and you must examine all the documents on which it is based.

Mrs. Kupávina. I believe it's a matter of twenty-five thousand. But what am I to do after that?

Berkútov. After that you'll have to pay up as quickly as possible so as not to bring it into court. In any event, you'd better get hold of about thirty thousand.

Mrs. Kupávina. But I have very little ready money.

Berkútov. That's bad.

Mrs. Kupávina. Are you trying to scare me?

Berkútov. Not at all. Why should I want to scare you? I'm merely doing my best to explain your position to you.

Mrs. Kupávina. And what is my position?

Berkútov. Your position is hardly an enviable one. You are a very rich woman, but these thirty thousand may bring your estate into such a state of disorder that you will never be able to put it right again.

Mrs. Kupávina. Why?

Berkútov. Because you'll have either to mortgage it ...

Mrs. Kupávina. That's a good idea!

Berkútov. But if you do that almost your entire income will go in paying the interest on the mortgage and you'll have very little for yourself.

Mrs. Kupávina. So I mustn't mortgage it?

Berkútov. In that case you'll have to sell part of your estate, the forest, for instance. You have about two thousand acres of woodland.

Mrs. Kupávina. Two thousand? Four thousand!

Berkútov. Somewhere else it would have meant a lot of money, but here, I understand, the price of timber is very low. The timber merchants will offer you about ten roubles an acre, which means that you would have to sell almost the whole of it and without the forest the estate is worthless. They may offer you more, but they'll ask for time to pay, they'll expect you to wait till the trees have been cut, but you want the money at once. This is your position.

Mrs. Kupávina. Yes, I can see it now.

[Footman *enters*.]

Footman. The surveyor is asking for you, sir. He says he must see you at once.

Berkútov. [*To* Mrs. Kupávina] Please, let me say a few words in your presence to Goretzky. I'm sending him to Vologda to survey the woods on my estate.

Mrs. Kupávina. Do. [*To* Footman] Show him in.

[*The* Footman *goes out*, Gorétzky *comes in*.]

Berkútov. [*To* Gorétzky] What do you want?

Gorétzky. My uncle has sent for me. He wants me to come at once. What am I to do, sir?

Berkútov. You don't know what he wants you for?

Gorétzky. He says he wants to see me on business.

Berkútov. [*After thinking it over*] You'd better go and do all he asks. In the meantime get everything ready for the journey. Your steamer leaves to-morrow. I shall want you in the morning. Try to see me before I call on Miss Murzavetzkaya. Don't talk too much and don't confide in anyone. Have you returned the fifteen roubles to Mr. Lynyayev?

GORÉTZKY. I'm going to give it back to him right now. Good-bye, sir.

[*Bows and goes out.*]

BERKÚTOV. Sorry, I am now again entirely at your service.

MRS. KUPÁVINA. Shall we continue our conversation? Please, try to think of something.

BERKÚTOV. With pleasure. I can't understand why you haven't settled everything yet with Murzavetzkaya. You see her often enough. You should have gone into the matter carefully and, without taking anyone's word for it, reached some kind of agreement, persuaded her to make some concession or got sufficient time to pay her without trouble. You seem to have no clear idea about your estate or your income or about the obligations in connection with your estate which have still to be met. You'll tell me, like the grasshopper in the fable, "How could I work, I was too busy singing!" All right, one can't ask much of you: you are inexperienced, your whole position is new to you. But didn't you have, with the exception of a pettifogging lawyer, any friend or even acquaintance who could help you to bring your business affairs in order? Couldn't you find anyone who could show a disinterested understanding of your business affairs and who could offer you some sound advice?

MRS. KUPÁVINA. I had one such friend.

BERKÚTOV. Well?

MRS. KUPÁVINA. I didn't listen to his advice.

BERKÚTOV. You didn't even answer his letter.

MRS. KUPÁVINA. A very strange letter in which . . .

BERKÚTOV. . . . there was all you needed: friendly sympathy and practical advice.

MRS. KUPÁVINA. Are you angry with me?

BERKÚTOV. [*With a smile*] No.

MRS. KUPÁVINA. Then show me that you aren't angry and give me some good advice.

BERKÚTOV. I shall consider it my duty to do so. But will you accept my advice? Give me your word that you will do as I tell you.

MRS. KUPÁVINA. I hate to bind myself by a promise without knowing . . .

BERKÚTOV. Don't be afraid. My advice is absolutely unselfish. All I have in mind is your own good.

MRS. KUPÁVINA. In that case, I promise. What do you advise me to do?

BERKÚTOV. Get married as soon as possible.

MRS. KUPÁVINA. [*In astonishment*] Get married? But to whom?

BERKÚTOV. To Apollonius Murzavetzky.

MRS. KUPÁVINA. Is that meant as an insult?

BERKÚTOV. Not at all. All I have in mind is your own good.

MRS. KUPÁVINA. How dare you even suggest this to me? Miss Murzavetzkaya's hints, I suppose, were a little too obvious?

BERKÚTOV. Why shouldn't they be obvious? Apollonius is a good-for-nothing scamp, but, at any rate, he is not ashamed of his shortcomings. He is a gentleman, he is young, he may get something from his aunt and you can hardly say that even with your fortune, he is no match for you.

MRS. KUPÁVINA. You are either joking or you want to insult me.

BERKÚTOV. Neither the one nor the other, I assure you. Any sensible man will tell you the same.

MRS. KUPÁVINA. So in your opinion the only thing for me to do is to marry Murzavetzky!

BERKÚTOV. Not the only thing, but the only worth-while thing, if you want to keep your estate without ruining yourself.

MRS. KUPÁVINA. [*Firmly*] So I ought to marry him? I ask you for the last time.

BERKÚTOV. Yes, marry him. I don't think you'll regret it.

MRS. KUPÁVINA. How indifferent you sound! Like a doctor, you pronounce your death sentence without pity.

BERKÚTOV. When one asks for medical advice, one doesn't expect pity, but skill and helpful advice.

MRS. KUPÁVINA. In view of our former relationship I should have expected . . .

BERKÚTOV. All devouring time consumes everything.

Mrs. Kupávina. From your last letter . . .

Berkútov. I feel I must apologize for my last letter to you. Intending to come here for a short visit and probably for the last time, I wanted to be friends with everybody and to leave a good impression after I'm gone. It's possible I went a bit too far and fell into the atrocious habit of using cliches.

Mrs. Kupávina. Is that all?

Berkútov. [*Coldly*] I'm afraid so. You haven't yet replied to Miss Murzavetzkaya's letter, have you?

Mrs. Kupávina. No, not yet.

Berkútov. You ought to answer it.

Mrs. Kupávina. I don't know what to say.

Berkútov. That shouldn't be very difficult. If you want me to help you, I'll be pleased to do my best. I shall be at Murzavetzkaya's to-morrow morning and I may mention your business to her. It may not be as terrible as it seems. Do you trust me?

Mrs. Kupávina. I should be grateful for your help.

[*Enter* Lynyáyev.]

Lynyáyev. I have walked all round the park, but I'm feeling sleepier and sleepier.

Mrs. Kupávina. I can suggest an excellent cure for your trouble. Mr. Berkutov and myself are going to another room to write a letter to Miss Meropia and you can take your forty winks here. My husband designed this room for that purpose. The windows are due north, all around you are trees, everything is quiet, soft couches . . .

Lynyáyev. All I want to be completely happy.

Mrs. Kupávina. No one will disturb you here. Go on, make yourself at home, be happy!

Lynyáyev. I'll do my best.

[Mrs. Kupávina *and* Berkútov *go out*.]

Say what you like, but a bachelor's life is very pleasant. If I were married, for instance, my wife would now have interfered with my rest. "Don't go to sleep, it's not good for you, you're putting on weight because of it, don't, darling, please!" And little does she reck how happy her "darling" is when he can have his sleep undisturbed, when his eyes close by themselves and off he drops into a delicious snooze. [*Lets himself down on the couch under the window.*]

[GLAFÍRA *appears from behind a curtain and regards him with a keen predatory look, like a cat who is about to pounce on a mouse.*]

LYNYÁYEV. And what bliss it is for a bachelor to open his eyes after awakening from a sound sleep. The first thought that comes into his mind is that he is his own master, that he is free! Yes, I am a confirmed bachelor and I thank the gods that be for it. I would not exchange my freedom for any caresses by a pair of soft little hands! [*Leans back slowly towards the head of the couch.*]

[GLAFÍRA *comes out from behind the curtain, puts one arm round his neck and looks him straight in the face.* LYNYÁYEV *sits up and looks terrified at* GLAFÍRA.]

GLAFÍRA. [*Putting a handkerchief to her eyes*] What have you done to me?

LYNYÁYEV. [*Gets up from couch and rubs his eyes*] Me? You'd better tell me what you are doing to me?

GLAFÍRA. I don't know. I seem to have gone mad. I can't remember anything. It's all your fault.

LYNYÁYEV. I don't know what you're talking about.

GLAFÍRA. It's your fault. I warned you . . .

LYNYÁYEV. But how is it my fault?

GLAFÍRA. I warned you again and again that I might fall violently in love any moment. I am such a nervous woman. And now it's happened. And you, you, knowing my passionate nature . . .

LYNYÁYEV. But I did it because you asked me to.

GLAFÍRA. I warned you, and you turned my head with your praises, you kissed my hands.

LYNYÁYEV. But it was all a joke, my dear girl, it was all a joke!

GLAFÍRA. I warned you that love could bring me nothing but suffering, didn't I? And you . . . I couldn't sleep the whole night. I've fallen madly in love with you.

LYNYÁYEV. I say, what frightful bad luck! I'm so sorry.

GLAFÍRA. I warned you that once I fell in love . . .

LYNYÁYEV. Yes, you did, but do get a hold of yourself, old girl!
GLAFÍRA. [*In despair*] You have ruined me!
LYNYÁYEV. I am sorry, old girl. I . . . I apologize. I didn't mean to. [*Wants to kiss* GLAFÍRA'S *hand.*]
GLAFÍRA. Don't touch me! I'm so nervous . . .
LYNYÁYEV. But do let me kiss your hand before we say good-bye to each other. I hope you will have a good journey.
GLAFÍRA. Please, leave me alone, don't touch me!
LYNYÁYEV. But just to say good-bye. At least, I'll know that . . .
GLAFÍRA. I'm so nervous . . .
LYNYÁYEV. . . . you don't despise me! [*Takes her hand.*]
GLAFÍRA. I warned you . . .
LYNYÁYEV. You're leaving, aren't you? Well, by all means, go, old girl! [*He kisses* GLAFÍRA'S *hand.*]
GLAFÍRA. Oh, I'm so nervous. Oh, oh! [*She shuts her eyes and throws her arms round* LYNYÁYEV'S *neck.*]
LYNYÁYEV. Wh . . what are you doing, old girl? Please, my dear, please . . .
GLAFÍRA. [*Opens her eyes*] Somebody's coming!
LYNYÁYEV. There's somebody on the terrace.
GLAFÍRA. Oh, oh! [*Shuts her eyes.*]
LYNYÁYEV. There's nothing to worry about, old girl, they won't come here.
GLAFÍRA. You've ruined me! What will people say? Where shall I go now? There's no other way out.
LYNYÁYEV. Please, not so loud or . . .
GLAFÍRA. Can they hear us? Please, hide me, hide me!
LYNYÁYEV. But where shall I hide you? Behind the curtains?
GLAFÍRA. They're coming! You've ruined me!
LYNYÁYEV. For God's sake not so loud!
GLAFÍRA. Oh, what have you done to me? [*Tightens her hold round his neck and shuts her eyes.*]

[MRS. KUPÁVINA *and* BERKÚTOV *appear through the french windows.*]

BERKÚTOV. What do I see? My dear fellow . . .

Mrs. Kupávina. Mr. Lynyayev, Mr. Lynyayev, so that's the kind of man you are!

Lynyáyev. [*In a voice choked with tears*] Well, what am I to do? I'll marry the girl!

[Footman *enters*.]

Footman. Your carriage is waiting, Miss.

Glafíra. Are the servants here, too? What have you done to me? What will Miss Meropia say?

Mrs. Kupávina. My poor darling, don't be so upset. You must stay with me.

Berkútov. Never mind, I'll be seeing Miss Murzavetzkaya to-morrow morning and I shall explain everything to her.

Lynyáyev. [*Almost in tears*] But I'm going to marry her! Please, tell Murzavetzkaya, that I'm going to marry Glafira.

ACT FIVE

[*Same as* ACT ONE.]

[PAVLIN, *enter* CHUGÚNOV.]

CHUGÚNOV. How are you, my dear Pavlin?
PAVLIN. How are you, sir? Haven't you come a bit too early?
CHUGÚNOV. I was told to be here early. May I trouble you for some of your snuff?
PAVLIN. [*Handing him the snuff-box*] Help yourself, sir.
CHUGÚNOV. Is Miss Meropia up already?
PAVLIN. Miss Meropia is now having her morning tea. Here she is herself. [MISS MEROPIA *comes in,* PAVLIN *goes out.*]
MISS MEROPIA. I see you're here already. Morning.
CHUGÚNOV. Good morning to you, madam. Did you have a good night?
MISS MEROPIA. [*Sitting down*] I slept quite well, thank you. Sit down, will you? [CHUGÚNOV *sits down*] I should have chased you out of town a long time ago.
CHUGÚNOV. But may I ask why, ma'am?
MISS MEROPIA. We're praying to God to save us from temptation, but you are the real tempter.
CHUGÚNOV. I don't think I have enough talent for such a role, ma'am. All I want is to please you, I don't want anything else.
MISS MEROPIA. I got her letter.
CHUGÚNOV. Yes, ma'am.
MISS MEROPIA. She'll be here to-day. The princess has been put in her place. She's scared stiff.
CHUGÚNOV. Will you make it up with her?
MISS MEROPIA. Never. I'm determined to get my revenge on her. I'll get my revenge even if I should never be forgiven for it. [*Bangs her stick.*]
CHUGÚNOV. How can you get your revenge? All you do is threaten her and threats cut no ice nowadays.
MISS MEROPIA. It is your business to do the devil's work. What have you got in mind? Tell me!

CHUGÚNOV. Why should I tell you, if you're so angry?

MISS MEROPIA. Tell me! You know how stubborn I am. If I ask you, you'd better tell me.

CHUGÚNOV. As you like, but I don't think you ought to make it up with her. How dares she insult her own benefactress!

MISS MEROPIA. Yes, yes, it's an insult, that's what it is.

CHUGÚNOV. Think of your position in the county. Master Apollonius may be everything they say he is, but he is still your nephew. This in itself is recommendation enough: a nephew of Miss Murzavetzkaya! Are there many such people as you?

MISS MEROPIA. Who do you think I am, a queen?

CHUGÚNOV. She invited him herself, ma'am. You're waiting for a reply, you're worried, and there her servants almost take him by the scruff of the neck and kick him out!

MISS MEROPIA. Exactly. [*Aloud*] Apollonius!

[*Enter* APOLLONIUS, *in sporting clothes, gun in hand.*]

CHUGÚNOV. Good heavens, look at him!

MISS MEROPIA. Where are you off to?

APOLLONIUS. There are snipe in the fields, auntie, and I'm going out shootin'.

MISS MEROPIA. Did Mrs. Kupavina invite you herself?

APOLLONIUS. Of course she did, auntie. I told you at the time.

MISS MEROPIA. But may be she didn't mean it. May be she asked you to come just out of politeness?

APOLLONIUS. Out of politeness! She fairly threw herself on my neck! I told her, "Don't do that! It isn't nice!"

CHUGÚNOV. So that's the kind of woman she is!

MISS MEROPIA. Apollonius is probably lying, but I suppose there must be a grain of truth in what he says.

APOLLONIUS. Every word of it is true, auntie, every word of it.

MISS MEROPIA. And what happened afterwards?

APOLLONIUS. Afterwards there was a real to do, auntie. Not only did she forbid me to come in, but she hid her servants in the park to waylay me. But for Tamerlaine it would have been farewell and adieu, fair ladies of Spain. You would never have seen me again, auntie. Tamerlaine is a lion, not a dog: he caught one by the throat, another by the throat, and the rest ran away. That dog is my true friend. [*Whistles*] Tamerlaine, come here, sir! Come here, my true friend! Come here, sir!

MISS MEROPIA. Stop it, stop it! You deafen me! For heaven's sake, go!

[APOLLONIUS *goes out into the hall.*]

MISS MEROPIA. What would you call such treatment, Vukol, eh?

CHUGÚNOV. It's disgraceful, ma'am. [*Takes snuff.*]

MISS MEROPIA. I'm going to have my revenge on her. I'll bide my time, but I shan't die in peace till I have my revenge. I'd give everything to get at her right now!

CHUGÚNOV. Now is the time, ma'am. She's probably having a good laugh with Lynyayev at you!

MISS MEROPIA. Don't incite me, you pettifogging rascal, don't incite me! I haven't asked you to come here for that!

CHUGÚNOV. How am I inciting you? Don't you know yourself that they are laughing at you?

MISS MEROPIA. A frivolous young woman with no sense in her head laughing at us as though we were fools and we, two wise old birds, sitting here and doing nothing!

CHUGÚNOV. Why nothing, ma'am. We can do quite a lot, quite a lot.

MISS MEROPIA. You devil incarnate! What dirty trick have you up your sleeve now? You'd better tell me at once.

CHUGÚNOV. [*Taking out a paper*] Show this to her, let her have a good look at it!

MISS MEROPIA. What's this? [*Taking letter*] A letter to Apollonius?

CHUGÚNOV. Read it, please.

MISS MEROPIA. [*Reads*] "My dear Apollonius, I owe your father, as a consequence of various business deals at different times, about thirty thousand roubles, as you can easily find out for yourself from your father's ledgers and accounts, if such are still in existence. But it is quite possible that, owing to the well-known negligence of your father, no proof of my debt can be found among his papers. As I have no intention of denying this debt and depriving you of what is due to you, I am enclosing all the necessary legal documents." . . . Oh, so that's your little game! I suppose, you've never thought of Siberia!

CHUGÚNOV. What's all this about Siberia! Everybody seems to be talking to me about nothing but Siberia and Siberia!

MISS MEROPIA. It's the kind of business you do, my dear man. That's why everybody is talking to you about Siberia!

CHUGÚNOV. [*Taking out bills of exchange*] And here are the bills of exchange.

MISS MEROPIA. So you've got them, too! You are a real devil, Vukol. Its' a wonder the earth doesn't open up and swallow you, Judas Iscariot, you! And what's that book?

CHUGÚNOV. That's an old ledger. I got it out from the box-room. It's damp and simply covered with stains. I put the bills of exchange into it for the night. Let them stay there until they get properly faded. The ink is still mighty fresh. That's the right place for them. [*Taking bills of exchange from* MISS MEROPIA] See, how clean they are?

MISS MEROPIA. Why should I look? It's the devil's work.

CHUGÚNOV. That's all the thanks I get! [*Places bills of exchange in ledger.*]

MISS MEROPIA. Isn't it the devil's work? Would a man ever think of it? Even if he did, he couldn't do it without the assistance of the devil.

CHUGÚNOV. I'm trying to please you and you go on reviling me. What a life!

MISS MEROPIA. Stop snivelling!

CHUGÚNOV. But it's true, isn't it? You'd better give the bills back to me. I'll destroy them.

MISS MEROPIA. Give them back to you, indeed! Tell me, you old office rat, what am I to do with them?

CHUGÚNOV. When Mrs. Kupavina comes, show them to her and talk sternly to her. "Pay up at once, or I'll put it into the hands of my solicitors!" She'll be entirely in your power and you'll be able to do what you like with her.

MISS MEROPIA. All right, all right. I'll put the fear of God into her, but don't think I shall go to court with these! They are forgeries, every one of them. [*Puts ledger on table.*]

CHUGÚNOV. But what forgeries! A sight for the gods! Ah, well. I could present them to the county court to-morrow morning and in the evening I'd get an execution. Why bother to write threatening letters? You are merely putting them on their guard against you. They may even get me disbarred.

MISS MEROPIA. Against his own employer! A fine manager you are!

CHUGÚNOV. But I've already made myself secure, got the money for the purchase of the plot of land. Why should I be sorry for her? You ought to insist on the full thirty thousand and give me twenty per cent commission.

MISS MEROPIA. How dare you talk to me like that? Who are you talking to? Are you trying to induce a woman of my social standing to involve herself in such dishonest deals? I feel like striking you over your bald pate for that! You deserve to be thrashed! [*Listening*] Somebody seems to have driven up to my house. I'll call you later.

[CHUGÚNOV *goes out.* PAVLIN *enters.*]

PAVLIN. Mr. Vassily Berkútov, ma'am.

MISS MEROPIA. Berkutov? Oh, yes, yes. I remember.

[PAVLIN *goes out,* BERKÚTOV *comes in.*]

BERKÚTOV. How do you do? You remember me, don't you?

MISS MEROPIA. Of course, I remember you. How could I forget you. Sit down, please. [BERKÚTOV *sits down*] When did you arrive?

BERKÚTOV. The day before yesterday, in the evening. You must forgive me, I wanted to call on you yesterday, but I was tired from my journey. While still in Petersburg I vowed to call on you without any delay on my arrival here, to pay my respects and to tell you that the news of your godly life and charitable deeds have reached even our capital.

MISS MEROPIA. Thank you, my dear.

BERKÚTOV. Besides, as a new arrival, I am anxious to learn what's been happening in the county. And from whom, dear lady, can I obtain a truer account or a more just appraisal of events than from you?

MISS MEROPIA. Who else but I would know of everything that's been happening here?

Easy Money.

BERKÚTOV. How are things at our rural councils, my dear Miss Murzavetzkaya?

MISS MEROPIA. How should they be? It's the old, old story of the pot calling the kettle black.

BERKÚTOV. But why don't they come to you for advice?

MISS MEROPIA. Who heeds an old woman like me? They think the world of themselves, they don't want my advice.

BERKÚTOV. Even assuming that they are not all fools, it surely must have occurred to them that it's only from you that they can obtain sound advice based on real experience and true knowledge of the life of the people and the needs of the county. If I were to take on some official job here . . .

MISS MEROPIA. Who's preventing you?

BERKÚTOV. I'm afraid I've still some unfinished business to attend to in Petersburg. Of course, if I were thinking of it, I should get myself elected to one of the more important positions in the county.

MISS MEROPIA. Why shouldn't you? We shall soon have elections for the President of the Noblemen's Chamber, the Chairman of the Rural Council . . .

BERKÚTOV. I merely mentioned it to assure you that, had I tried for some post here, I shouldn't have done it without having previously consulted you about it.

MISS MEROPIA. Listen to me, my dear Vassily, take the advice of an old woman, stand for election.

BERKÚTOV. I don't mind saying so I was in front of the queue when brains were given out and with my brains and your experience, my dear lady, we should soon be running the county.

MISS MEROPIA. I'm telling you, stand for election. What have you to be afraid of?

BERKÚTOV. I've nothing to be afraid of. I'm on the best of terms with everybody here. Although I can hardly bring myself to approve of the childish pranks of Lynyayev and his cronies, I don't think it worth while quarrelling with them.

MISS MEROPIA. Childish pranks they are indeed! You've got the right word for it.

BERKÚTOV. Of course, I shall always be a strong supporter of you and your party.

Miss Meropia. Let's enrol you as one of our members, as a new recruit to our ranks.

Berkútov. Thank you, I'll think it over. I shall always be glad to be of service to you. I have brought a few books of a religious character with me.

Miss Meropia. Could you lend them to me?

Berkútov. I'll make you a present of them. [*Getting up*] Permit me to take my leave. I'll call on you again, if I may, and not only once, I assure you. Your conversation is so stimulating. [*Bows.*]

Miss Meropia. I shall be delighted to see you.

Berkútov. By the way, I've been asked to clear up a little matter with you.

Miss Meropia. What is it, my dear Vassily? I shall be glad to do anything for you.

Berkútov. It doesn't really concern me. My neighbour, Mrs. Kupávina, wanted me to mention it to you. It isn't really important.

Miss Meropia. Not important? I am afraid she has misinformed you.

Berkútov. To begin with, she asks you to forgive her. She intends to call on you herself to-day.

Miss Meropia. That's better. She should have thought of it long ago.

Berkútov. As for the debt which her late husband owed your late brother and now your nephew, she doesn't seem to be sure whether her husband ever admitted such a liability.

Miss Meropia. He did, he admitted it himself.

Berkútov. Are you sure?

Miss Meropia. I have a letter in his own hand admitting everything.

Berkútov. Just a minute, Miss Murzavetzkaya, do you really believe it?

Miss Meropia. But why shouldn't I believe it if I am in possession of all the documents.

Berkútov. What scoundrels! What are they doing to you?

Miss Meropia. Who do you mean?

Berkútov. Your dear nephew and Co.

Miss Meropia. Please, don't forget yourself, sir. You are my guest!
Berkútov. You should drive him out of your house, you should get rid of all of them.
Miss Meropia. He's a gentleman! If he could only hear what you are saying! And what about me, sir? Am I not his aunt? Don't say another word, or . . .
Berkútov. Please, please, I can understand how you must feel about it. You have such a loving heart, you don't probably even suspect their villainy.
Miss Meropia. No, no, I won't listen to you! Please, do me a favour, not another word!
Berkútov. They don't care! What have they to lose? But to see a lady of your position in the dock! Why, the whole county . . .
Miss Meropia. [*In dismay*] How do you mean in the dock?
Berkútov. I'll explain it to you. It's no use beating about the bush, quite a number of people know it already. To-morrow it may reach the ears of the public prosecutor and an official investigation may be started. The chief culprit, Goretzky, has already made a full confession. I suppose he will be arrested shortly.
Miss Meropia. What is it all about?
Berkútov. They have forged bills of exchange in the name of the late Kupavin. It was done yesterday. I suspect your nephew, for, my dear lady, I really can't suspect you, can I?
Miss Meropia. Me? Of course not!
Berkútov. They have also forged a letter in Kupavin's name admitting his debt to your nephew and two bills of exchange. They got an old ledger out of the box-room and placed these forged documents there. [*Seeing the ledger on the table*] That kind of ledger. [*Takes ledger and opens it*] Here they are! Some accounts in the ledger have also been altered, a few stains taken out and a few blots put in. Wonderful workmanship! Direct evidence . . .
Miss Meropia. My dear Vassily, don't ruin me!
Berkútov. My chief task now is to save you.
Miss Meropia. Save me, save me! I shall never forget it. I should go down on my knees to thank you.

BERKÚTOV. Don't be alarmed. I'll do my best to quash any proceedings that might be started. I really am sorry to see you in such a fix. Why should you be made to bear the blame?

MISS MEROPIA. My dear boy, I hardly know what to say. I certainly am not to be blamed for anything.

BERKÚTOV. There is another letter by which Mrs. Kupavina was induced to give you a thousand roubles.

MISS MEROPIA. I'm afraid I can't remember. My memory has been failing me badly lately.

BERKÚTOV. I'll remind you. [*Taking out letter from pocket*] Here it is. You'll have to return the money.

MISS MEROPIA. But where am I to get that money? I have already distributed it among the poor. They are now offering prayers to God. You can't take it away from them.

BERKÚTOV. Of course, I quite understand that you were yourself deceived, but if this ever gets to the courts you'll have to return the money. However, don't worry about it now. Try to dismiss it from your thoughts.

MISS MEROPIA. I'd very gladly dismiss it, but I can't. You stun me and then you say don't worry about it.

BERKÚTOV. Try not to think of it. Let's talk of something else.

MISS MEROPIA. I am terrified of the assizes, my dear Vassily. I am simply terrified out of my wits.

BERKÚTOV. The whole thing will probably blow over. I have news for you: Lynyayev has proposed to Miss Glafira.

MISS MEROPIA. Who cares? My heart is still in my mouth. So she has caught him after all!

BERKÚTOV. Yes, and it was done very cleverly, too!

MISS MEROPIA. Serve him right! I have no pity for him. Oh, dear, my heart is still all a-flutter. You are still a bachelor, are you?

BERKÚTOV. I'm afraid so.

MISS MEROPIA. Why don't you get married?

BERKÚTOV. At first I was too busy and now I can't find myself a bride. Do find me one!

MISS MEROPIA. But whom? Oh, dear, oh, dear, it's gone to my temples now! Why not marry my neighbour, Eulampe Kupavina?

BERKÚTOV. I don't think she fancies me very much. I shouldn't mind myself.

MISS MEROPIA. Shall I be your matchmaker?

BERKÚTOV. Well, I don't think I need a matchmaker exactly, but I should be glad if you'd talk to her nicely and try to find out what she thinks about it and . . . just advise her.

MISS MEROPIA. You needn't teach me how to handle it. In such things I am not more stupid than you. Only get me out of this mess and . . . that thousand roubles . . .

BERKÚTOV. Do this thing for me and I'll do the other thing for you. Eulampe should be here any moment. Miss Glafira and Lynyayev are with her.

MISS MEROPIA. So you'd better excuse me for a minute, I'll go and make all the arrangements. I shall have to offer them lunch and coffee to greet the bridegroom. After all, he'll be my new nephew.

BERKÚTOV. Don't mind me in the least. I'd like to have a talk with Chugunov.

MISS MEROPIA. He's here, the jailbird. I'll call him to you. Vukol! Vukol! Here he is.

[MISS MEROPIA *goes out*, CHUGÚNOV *enters*.]

BERKÚTOV. How do you do, Mr. Chugunov?

CHUGÚNOV. How are you, Mr. Berkutov? When did you arrive?

BERKÚTOV. I've only been here a few days. I am very pleased to meet you. How's everything?

CHUGÚNOV. I've nothing to complain of, the Lord is merciful.

BERKÚTOV. I'm so glad. I am not taking up your time, am I? I should like to have a chat with you, just for a few minutes.

CHUGÚNOV. I'm entirely at your disposal, sir.

BERKÚTOV. I should like, my dear fellow, to gather a little information about this district.

CHUGÚNOV. Yes, sir. [*Takes out snuff-box*] Won't you?

BERKÚTOV. No, thank you, I don't take snuff. On the other hand, why not? [*Takes snuff*] What does it smell of?

CHUGÚNOV. Of jasmine, sir. I grow it on purpose. It's nice to have the flowers about in the house, on the window-sill, you know, and the scent, too, sir. Good snuff is not so easy to get nowadays. Before you could get snuff called "Love's Delight," that snuff, let me tell you, sir, was something . . . But what would you like me to tell you about our district?

BERKÚTOV. You see, people are beginning to talk about a Siberian railway. We, as local landowners, are naturally interested in this business and, provided there are no physical obstacles, such as hills, for instance . . .

CHUGÚNOV. No physical obstacles or hills of any importance at all, sir. Our county is rather flat. Only what are we to export to Siberia, sir, what kind of products?

BERKÚTOV. We have the products all right, my dear fellow.

CHUGÚNOV. What are they, sir? I should very much like to know.

BERKÚTOV. I suppose you must have read in the newspapers recently of the discovery of a large number of forged bills of exchange and other papers and, generally, of other cases of embezzlement. Well, you see, my dear fellow, such transactions usually have someone behind them: it's this man and others like him that we shall be exporting to Siberia.

CHUGÚNOV. I can see that you like to crack a joke, sir.

BERKÚTOV. No joke at all, my dear fellow, I assure you. To take only one case and in your town, too. A young man has just confessed to having forged several bills of exchange.

CHUGÚNOV. [*Shaking his head*] You astonish me, sir.

BERKÚTOV. Wait a minute, what's his name? Goretzky, I think.

CHUGÚNOV. Goretzky? Is that so? Yes, I seem to have heard of this young man.

BERKÚTOV. He says that he was forced to do it. He even let us have the originals which he had been told to copy.

CHUGÚNOV. Really, sir, people will do the most extraordinary things. They wouldn't even shrink from involving other people in their crimes, I'm afraid he'll find prison rather a tough place at his age.

BERKÚTOV. He has made a full confession. He even admitted that he had forged a bill of exchange made out in Mrs. Kupavina's name and Mrs. Kupavina tells me that a blank bill has been stolen from her.

CHUGÚNOV. Frightful!

BERKÚTOV. Listen to me, my dear fellow, have you got that bill? If you have still got it, you'd better return it as soon as possible.

CHUGÚNOV. Why should I? I am very grateful to you, Mr. Berkútov.

BERKÚTOV. What on earth for?

CHUGÚNOV. For having warned me in time. I can now destroy that bill. Let Goretzky say what he pleases, I don't know anything. I never saw such a bill in my life.

BERKÚTOV. It's a pity, a great pity, for, my dear fellow, you should at least have got something on that bill, if not the whole sum.

CHUGÚNOV. I should, no doubt, for, after all, you must admit that I acted honourably in this matter. To be given a blank bill of exchange, just like that! Anyone else in my place would have . . . Who would refuse to take advantage of such a piece of good fortune?

BERKÚTOV. Quite right, my dear fellow, quite right. Mrs. Kupavina deserves to be punished, so that she should be more careful in future.

CHUGÚNOV. To be sure she should be punished, sir. She oughtn't to be allowed to give blank bills to people, she could be robbed of her estate that way. I only made it out for three thousand, but not everybody would be so scrupulous about it as I.

BERKÚTOV. Make it a little less, my dear fellow. Write a receipt for part of it and Mrs. Kupavina will pay you the rest. Come on, get out the bill, here's pen and ink.

CHUGÚNOV. All right, sir. [*Produces bill, puts on glasses, takes pen*] What shall I put?

BERKÚTOV. Write, "Received two thousand roubles in cash on this bill."

CHUGÚNOV. But you're only leaving me one thousand, sir! It isn't much.

BERKÚTOV. Not at all, my dear fellow, even a thousand is much too much.

CHUGÚNOV. But think how honourably I dealt with her in this matter!

BERKÚTOV. Well, we're going to assess your honour for

what it's worth. Write, "Received two thousand five hundred roubles in cash on this bill."

CHUGÚNOV. But that will leave me with only five hundred! Really, sir, that is almost an insult!

BERKÚTOV. No! Not even five hundred. Write: "Two thousand five hundred and fifty." I'll explain to you presently why I have added another fifty. You will get the rest.

CHUGÚNOV. [*Writes as told and replaces bill*] Thank you very much, sir. I am very obliged to you, I'm sure.

BERKÚTOV. When your nephew told me all about your business and gave me the originals written in your own hand, my first thought was to go to the public prosecutor at once.

CHUGUNOV. But why to the public prosecutor, sir? What profit would you gain in getting yourself mixed up in such a business? It would only mean trouble for you and nothing more.

BERKÚTOV. Then I decided to talk things over with Miss Murzavetzkaya and with yourself first.

CHUGÚNOV. Quite right, sir. Hasn't the public prosecutor enough to do without us?

BERKÚTOV. And to make sure that your nephew does not let the cat out of the bag . . . He's such a rough diamond, you know . . .

CHUGÚNOV. A very uncouth lad, sir.

BERKÚTOV. I have sent him to Vologda to survey my woods there. He is on the way there now on a steamer. I gave him fifty roubles as travelling expenses, but my dear fellow, it was really your duty to provide him with travelling expenses. That's why I have subtracted fifty roubles from your five hundred.

CHUGÚNOV. Very good, sir. Are you going to spend a long time with us, if I may ask, sir?

BERKÚTOV. I don't know yet. It depends on my various business engagements.

CHUGÚNOV. If there is anything I can do for you, sir, please, keep me in mind, for old acquaintance sake.

BERKÚTOV. Certainly, my dear fellow, certainly!

CHUGÚNOV. Someone else has just arrived, sir. I'd better be going. Good-bye, sir.

[*Goes out.*]

[*Enter* MRS. KUPÁVINA *and* MISS ANFÚSSA, MISS MEROPIA *comes in from drawing-room.*]

MISS MEROPIA. [*To* MRS. KUPÁVINA] It's so nice of you to have come, my dear.

MRS. KUPÁVINA. I'm very sorry, Miss Meropia, to have given you so much cause for displeasure.

MISS MEROPIA. Let bygones be bygones, my dear.

BERKÚTOV. My dear Eulampe, I've carried out your request.

MRS. KUPÁVINA. Thank you.

BERKÚTOV. Miss Murzavetzkaya and her nephew consider themselves entirely satisfied and they have no more claims on you. Isn't that so, dear Miss Murzavetzkaya?

MISS MEROPIA. He's right, he's absolutely right, my dear. Employ a lawyer like him and you'll be sure to win your case.

MRS. KUPÁVINA. [*To* BERKÚTOV] This means that I owe everything to you. What is your fee?

BERKÚTOV. We shall settle it later, my dear Eulampe.

MISS MEROPIA. [*To* BERKÚTOV] You'd better go and have something. You have plenty of time. I suppose you've been up and about since morning and you must be hungry. And you, my dear Anfussa, do look after him for me. We shall join you soon.

MISS ANFÚSSA. Why not, you know . . . I'm feeling peckish myself, I mean . . .

[BERKÚTOV *and* MISS ANFÚSSA *go out.*]

MISS MEROPIA. Forgive me for being so severe with you, my dear. I did it out of love for you.

MRS. KUPÁVINA. I can't understand how I have wronged you. You send me such a terrible letter, full of threats . . .

MISS MEROPIA. I shall always treat you like that, my dear, always. You're to blame, you know. My heart aches for you. I should have scared you a little more.

MRS. KUPÁVINA. But why am I to blame?

MISS MEROPIA. Why? Why do you live by yourself? Why don't you marry someone? What's the good of such a life?

You're just getting yourself into one mess after another and letting your estate go to wrack and ruin. You can't rely on Chugúnov, can you?

MRS. KUPÁVINA. But you recommended him to me yourself!

MISS MEROPIA. How can you expect me to crawl into a man's soul? He seems to be as big a scoundrel as they make them.

MRS. KUPÁVINA. [*After a moment's reflection*] Say what you will, but I shall not marry him. I don't feel in any way attracted to him at all.

MISS MEROPIA. You don't feel attracted to whom?

MRS. KUPÁVINA. To Mr. Murzavetzky.

MISS MEROPIA. But who is forcing you to marry Apollonius? I thought you liked him, but if you don't, I don't care whether you marry him or not. You are a free woman, choose anyone you like?

MRS. KUPÁVINA. But whom shall I choose?

MISS MEROPIA. Think it over, my dear. You wouldn't mind marrying the right kind of man, would you?

MRS. KUPÁVINA. Why should I? I realize too well that I'm no good as a business woman.

MISS MEROPIA. [*Softly*] Is Berkútov staying here long?

MRS. KUPÁVINA. I don't think so, only a few more days. But he doesn't seem to care for me much.

MISS MEROPIA. I'm sorry to hear you say that, my dear. I thought he . . .

MRS. KUPÁVINA. No, no! I'm not going to throw myself at him.

MISS MEROPIA. But if he does care for you?

MRS. KUPÁVINA. No, he would like to marry someone much richer than me.

MISS MEROPIA. Of course, but you can never tell, he might just take it into his head to marry you.

MRS. KUPÁVINA. I don't know.

MISS MEROPIA. Of course, if he's only here for a few days and if he hasn't troubled even to be nice to you . . .

MRS. KUPÁVINA. He hasn't. He doesn't even dream of it.

MISS MEROPIA. In that case, I suppose, there's nothing to be done. Do you know if he has got someone in Petersburg?

MRS. KUPÁVINA. I should say he must have.

Miss Meropia. A German woman, I suppose. Anyway, let's just discuss it. There's no harm in talking it over. Suppose he did care, would you marry him?

Mrs. Kupávina. I really don't know what to say.

Miss Meropia. Don't be so bashful. You can tell me!

Mrs. Kupávina. What do you want to know for?

Miss Meropia. Don't you know the kind of woman I am? I'm dying to know everything about everybody and I just can't help poking my nose where I'm not wanted.

Mrs. Kupávina. All right, I don't mind telling you. I should like it very much . . .

Miss Meropia. Well, that's splendid! [*Aloud*] Vassily, come here, we want you!

Mrs. Kupávina. Please, don't . . .

Miss Meropia. Keep quiet, child. I was only anxious to find out how you felt about him. You're dear to me, why worry about the men? I know how to deal with them. You just watch me. Only remember: now that you've given your consent, don't go changing your mind again. Vassily!

[Berkútov *comes in.*]

Miss Meropia. My dear Vassily, you can kiss Eulampe's hand.

Berkútov. I'm always ready to do that.

Miss Meropia. May God bless you!

Berkútov. What do you mean by that, Miss Meropia?

Miss Meropia. I mean that I want you to marry. What's the use of being a bachelor? It's a crime against nature.

Berkútov. You are ordering me about, Miss Meropia.

Miss Meropia. You must forgive me, my dear boy, but I can see how lonely your life is without relations and without anyone to take care of you.

Berkútov. It's a good thing, my dear lady, that I am in love with Eulampe and that I have been in love with her a long time or you would have put us in a very embarrassing situation.

Miss Meropia. An embarrassing situation? You are mistaken [*banging her stick*], you're mistaken! I know better than any of you what's good for you, what's good for you, Vassily, and what's good for her. I can see through her, I can read her like a book, I can see right now that she loves you. And it's about high time you settled down, Vassily. Are you looking for a lot of money? If so, you ought to be ashamed of yourself. Look for a faithful heart!

BERKÚTOV. As you wish, dear Miss Meropia, as you wish.

MISS MEROPIA. You think that we provincials can't stand up to you who live in Petersburg, that we can't even provide you with a good wife. Well, here is one for you!

BERKÚTOV. [*With bowed head*] What do you say, Eulampe?

MISS MEROPIA. [*To* MRS. KUPÁVINA] Why aren't you saying anything? Well, let me say it for you: yes, I am very happy.

MRS. KUPÁVINA. I am an unsophisticated woman, I don't try to be clever, I dislike pretence. I couldn't disguise my true feelings from Miss Meropia and I can't disguise them from you.

BERKÚTOV. Thank you, my dear, for the happiness which you are bestowing on me. [*Kisses* MRS. KUPÁVINA'S *hand*] Please, employ me as your manager. You can't afford to lose any time.

MRS. KUPÁVINA. Yes, darling.

[*Enter* CHUGÚNOV.]

BERKÚTOV. [*To* MRS. KUPÁVINA] Here's one of your creditors. You owe him some money on a bill of exchange.

MRS. KUPÁVINA. I owe nothing to Mr. Chugúnov.

CHUGÚNOV. You gave me a bill of exchange for my services and industry, ma'am.

MRS. KUPÁVINA. I always paid you your salary in cash.

CHUGÚNOV. It must have slipped your memory, ma'am, it must have slipped your memory.

BERKÚTOV. It is true, Eulampe, one does easily forget things. Mr. Chugunov deserves to be rewarded: he is such a painstaking man. Come to-morrow and you'll get what is owing to you. You can thank Mrs. Kupavina.

CHUGÚNOV. I shall bring all my children with me, ma'am. I'll tell them all to thank you.

[*Enter* PAVLIN.]

PAVLIN. Miss Glafira and Mr. Lynyayev.

[*Goes out.*]
[*Enter* LYNYÁYEV *and* GLAFÍRA.]

MISS MEROPIA. Already inseparable?
GLAFÍRA. Why not, auntie? Michael is such a darling and I can't bear to leave him even for a moment.
MISS MEROPIA. Well, future Mrs. Lynyayev, welcome under my roof! Sit down.
LYNYÁYEV. Miss Meropia, I hope you'll pardon me for having been in such a hurry to propose to Miss Glafira without asking your permission first.
MISS MEROPIA. It's your look out, my dear man, don't blame me.
LYNYÁYEV. I'm not blaming you, I'm asking you to excuse me.
GLAFÍRA. He wants to thank you. [*To* LYNYÁYEV] Speak up, Michael.
LYNYÁYEV. [*With a sigh*] Yes, ma'am, thank you . . .
GLAFÍRA. What he likes most in me is my meekness. [*Tossing her shawl to* LYNYÁYEV] Please, Michael, hold my shawl. [*To* MISS MEROPIA] My humility [*To* LYNYÁYEV] Hold it properly, don't crush it. [*To* MISS MEROPIA] My modesty. And I owe all this to you, auntie. [*To* LYNYÁYEV] You are so silent, Michael, I have to do all the talking for you.
LYNYÁYEV. Yes, I'm very grateful to you, Miss Meropia, very grateful.
MISS MEROPIA. One thing I should like you to remember, my dear boy, it was none of my doing, you did it of your own free will. That pair I have really brought together and for them I shall be answerable to God. As for you two, you've made your bed, so lie on it.
LYNYÁYEV. [*To* BERKÚTOV] Are you also getting married? And so quickly, too! My congratulations!
GLAFÍRA. [*To* MRS. KUPÁVINA] So you've made up your mind at last, my dear. Well, accept my congratulations.
MRS. KUPÁVINA. Yes, I used to dream of freedom, but I've come to the conclusion that for a woman to be happy she must be dependent on a man.
MISS MEROPIA. Don't slander women, my dear! There are all kinds, there are those who can manage not only their own affairs, but even those of a whole county; you could even put them at the head of an army. And there are all sorts of men:

there are fine fellows like him [*pointing at* BERKÚTOV], but we've also heard of others who seem to like women to treat them like servants . . .

LYNYÁYEV. Yes, there are wolves and sheep in the world, wolves and sheep. [PAVLIN *brings in coffee.*]

GLAFÍRA. [*Accepting a cup*] Michael, be a dear and hold my umbrella. [*Laughs*] Oh, how clumsy you are! You let everything drop out of your hands.

MISS MEROPIA. [*To* BERKÚTOV] Are you going to spend the winter here?

BERKÚTOV. No, I think that Eulampe will prefer to spend it in Petersburg.

MRS. KUPÁVINA. Yes, of course.

MISS MEROPIA. [*To* LYNYÁYEV] And you?

GLAFÍRA. We shall spend this winter in Paris.

LYNYÁYEV. Yes, in Paris.

BERKÚTOV. But next summer we shall come here to be under your wing.

LYNYÁYEV. We, too . . .

GLAFÍRA. No, no, Michael, we haven't decided yet. I am thinking of spending the summer in Switzerland.

LYNYÁYEV. No, we haven't decided yet.

BERKÚTOV. Thank you, Miss Meropia, for your friendly welcome and for the interest you've taken in my affairs. Please, accept this trifle from me. [*Gives her a little box*] You'll find an aquamarine rosary in it. Ladies and gentlemen, I haven't been here long, but I have already been able to appreciate the rare qualities of this wonderful woman and I hope that all the best people in the land will show due respect to Miss Murzavetzkaya. We must set an example to others and we must show them how to respect and reverence old age.

CHUGÚNOV. [*Wiping his eyes*] It's true, it's true, every word of it.

MISS MEROPIA. Thank you, Vassily, thank you. [*Kisses* BERKÚTOV's *brow*] Well, my dear boy, I've seen all sorts of people in my life, but none to compare with you. [*Softly*] Now, I've settled your business, what about mine?

BERKÚTOV. Everything will be all right. Chugúnov will tell you.

MRS. KUPÁVINA. Shall we go? Good-bye, Miss Meropia. Glafíra and I are so anxious to go round the shops. Please, let her come back to me.

MISS MEROPIA. My dear child, I shall be only too glad for you to take her off my hands.

GLAFÍRA. Michael, you will be coming with us.

LYNYÁYEV. But there is only room for two in Eulampe's carriage.

GLAFÍRA. I know, Michael, but you can sit on the box! Let Miss Anfussa go home in your carriage. Miss Anfussa! [MISS ANFÚSSA *comes out*] You take Michael's carriage!

MISS ANFÚSSA. All right, you know . . . Good-bye.

LYNYÁYEV. But if I should sit on the box, there would be no room left for the coachman! Besides, do you want me to be jolted for twelve miles to the estate?

GLAFÍRA. Do as I tell you, Michael! It's very good for you. You're getting fatter and fatter. You really ought to do something about it, or what will you look like in Paris?

[MRS. KUPÁVINA, BERKÚTOV, LYNYÁYEV, GLAFÍRA *and* MISS ANFÚSSA *go out*.]

CHUGÚNOV. [*By the window*] To Paris and to Petersburg. Think of the money they'll be taking out of the county!

MISS MEROPIA. Well? A fine business man you've turned out to be. Thank you. You nearly dragged into the mud a respected and universally honoured name.

CHUGÚNOV. You can have me hanged, but what's done is done.

MISS MEROPIA. Well, what did Berkútov say to you, you old office rat!

CHUGÚNOV. Everything's in apple-pie order. He even sent my nephew to Vologda so that he wouldn't talk.

MISS MEROPIA. There's a real man for you! I shall not easily forget him, and you, too, you'd better remember him well!

CHUGÚNOV. He is a real man all right, but let me tell you this:—Why did Lynyayev call us wolves? What kind of wolves are we? We are mere chickens, you and I, pigeons pecking at a grain here and a grain there and always running about with empty bellies. It's men like him who are the real wolves. It is they who swallow a whole meal at one gulp!

[APOLLONIUS *is heard shouting at the top of his voice, off stage: "Tamerlaine! Tamerlaine!" He rushes in presently, looking the picture of despair.*]

APOLLONIUS. No, auntie, no! This time I shall not survive it!

MISS MEROPIA. Never mind, my poor darling, never mind.

APOLLONIUS. [*Collapses into a chair*] No, auntie, no. My best friend . . .

MISS MEROPIA. Well, what can be done about it?

APOLLONIUS. I've lost my best friend, auntie. Where are my pistols?

MISS MEROPIA. Good heavens, think of the sin you'd be committing!

APOLLONIUS. I don't care. I'm going to blow my brains out. My pistols are already loaded, auntie.

MISS MEROPIA. My poor boy, I didn't realize how much you cared for . . .

APOLLONIUS. Yes, auntie, I've lost the best friend in the world. Outside the town, in broad daylight . . . the wolves have got Tamerlaine!

MISS MEROPIA. Fie, for shame! And I thought . . .

CHUGÚNOV. Outside the town, in broad daylight! A lot have got *you* to moan about! What's so sensational about that? Here under our very noses the wolves have devoured not a Tamerlaine, but your bride-to-be with her rich dowry and Michael Lynyayev with his estate, and your aunt and I have only just managed to escape by the skin of our teeth. There's something sensational, if you like!

CURTAIN

NOTES

Even a Wise Man Stumbles, which was first performed in 1868, is one of the most popular plays in Ostrovsky's large repertory. It is also a play in which the characters lose their essentially Russian features and are above everything else general types of humanity as common in London as in Moscow. Even the fortune-teller Manefa whom modern Russian critics are fond of describing as "that sad phenomenon of Russian life" is not such an exclusively Russian phenomenon. It is to be found in every corner of the world.

To describe this play as "a brilliant satire on Moscow upper class society" is also to limit its scope unfairly. It is rather a satire on humanity at large and as such its appeal is universal.

Ostrovsky was very brief in his descriptions of the characters of this play. Mamayev is merely described as "a rich gentleman," Krutitzky as "an old man, a very important gentleman," and Gorodulin as "a young, important gentleman." Of these three, Krutitzky is, as a rule, taken to be a retired general and performed as such on the Russian stage. He is the classical Colonel Blimp, immortalized by Ostrovsky over half a century ago.

Glumov, the hero of this comedy, is also a universal type of a clever young man who lives on his wits and is undone by his own cleverness. His name, in accordance with Ostrovsky's custom of selecting names which describe his characters (a custom shared by English playwrights from Ben Jonson to Sheridan), suggests the English equivalent of "Sneerwell." Russian critics thought it improbable that so clever a reprobate as Glumov should forge the instrument of his own undoing by keeping a diary of his misdeeds. But, as a modern Russian critic points out, one of the severest of these critics, the famous Russian reactionary Suvorin, himself kept a similar diary which exposed his own political activities in a very bad light.

This comedy was first performed in Petersburg on November 1, 1868, and in Moscow on November 6th of the same year. It has become one of the most famous plays in the

NOTES

repertory of the Moscow Art Theatre. Stanislavsky, who played Krutitzky, gave a very original interpretation of this character. In his autobiography, *My Life in Art*, Stanislavsky describes his conception of Krutitzky in these words: "Who would ever think that I found the make-up and the general image of the role of General Krutitzky in the appearance of an old house, standing somewhat askew in an outer courtyard and seemingly swollen and overgrown with mossy sidewhiskers! From this house ran out little men in undress uniforms with many unnecessary papers and projects *à la* General Krutitzky under their arms. All this together brought me in some mysterious way to the make-up of my role in Ostrovsky's comedy."

Easy Money. Ostrovsky translated Shakespeare's *The Taming of the Shrew* in 1865. Five years later his brilliant version of Shakespeare's comedy was published. The problem of transplanting Katharine and Petruchio to Russia and giving them a modern setting was not an easy one, but by solving it in such a masterly fashion Ostrovsky has created one of the finest comedies in the world repretory of plays. What attracted Ostrovsky to *The Taming of the Shrew* was the fact that it was a comedy that dealt with the intimate details of family life, a *genre* which Ostrovsky made his own. But, as a modern Russian critic points out, Ostrovsky was also interested in the two protagonists of the Shakespearean comedy as human types and in the psychological problems which the clashing of interests of two strong-willed individuals exert upon each other. Vassilkov and Lydia, however, are not copies of Petruchio and Katharine. Quite the contrary, as individuals they differ from Shakespeare's hero and heroine almost as much as the Moscow of Ostrovsky differed from Shakespeare's Padua.

A comparison between the two plays, not to my knowledge made before, reveals a number of highly interesting facts, some of them technical, such as the general outline of the plot, but others more directly bound up with incidents in Ostrovsky's comedy.

NOTES

To begin with, both Petruchio and Lydia are animated by the same desire of marrying for money. Petruchio tells Hortensio—

> I come to wive it wealthily in Padua,
> If wealthily, then happily, in Padua.

And Petruchio's servant, Grumio, underscores his master's intentions:

> "Nay, look you, sir, he tells you flatly what his mind is: why, give him gold enough and marry him to a puppet or an aglet-baby; or an old trot with ne'er a tooth in her head, though she has as many diseases as two and fifty horses: why, nothing comes amiss so money comes withal."

These are exactly Lydia's sentiments in marrying Vassilkov.

Glumov's intrigue to spread the rumour that Vassilkov owns goldmines and so entice Lydia and her mother into casting their net for a desirable husband seems also to be an echo from Shakespeare's comedy. Hortensio tells Petruchio that Katharine is so "intolerably curst and shrewd and froward"

> That, were my state far worser than it is,
> I would not wed her for a mine of gold.

This reference to a mine of gold quite possibly suggested to Ostrovsky a minor, but essential part of the plot of his play.

Less evident, though far from improbable, is the likelihood that a reference by Grumio to Petruchio's method of taming Katharine by throwing "a figure in her face and so disfigure her with it, that she shall have no more eyes to see withal than a cat," has led Ostrovsky to invent the scene with the bills in Act III. What Vassilkov actually does is "to throw a figure" at Lydia's face and force her complete, if only temporary, submission to his will.

Again, Petruchio's declaration to Katharine:

> Now, Kate, I am a husband for your turn;
> For, by this light, whereby I see thy beauty,

> Thy beauty that doth make me like thee well,
> Thou must be married to no man but me;—

is re-echoed almost in the same words by Vassilkov to Telyatev and, later on, to Kuchumov and Glumov as well in the closing scene of Act I.

Also Petruchio's assertion—

> O! the kindest Kate.
> She hung about my neck, and kiss on kiss
> She vied so fast, protesting oath on oath,—

describes exactly Lydia's behaviour to Vassilkov.

Of the other characters in Ostrovsky's comedy, Kuchumov seems to be the only one whom Ostrovsky found in Shakespeare's comedy. Gremio is the Elizabethan counterpart of Ostrovsky's aged philanderer. Like Kuchumov, Gremio promises—

> Myself am struck in years, I must confess:
> And if I die to-morrow, this is hers,
> If whilst I live she will be only mine.

Finally, to complete this textual comparison of the two plays, Petruchio's words—

> And as the sun breaks through the darkest clouds,
> So honour peereth in the meanest habit,—

are re-echoed, though with a purely satirical intent, by Telyatev's "virtue shines through even the meanest rags."

To turn from the textual to the more general points of contact between these two plays, it is noteworthy that in no other play of Ostrovsky are there so many references to England, the English people and English institutions. Vassily, Vassilkov's valet, who so admires the English worker that he insists on dressing like one, is, besides, the closest approach to a Shakespearean clown to be found in Ostrovsky's plays. He possesses a mind of inconsequential stupidity which is the hallmark of Shakespeare's clowns.

Glumov, the hero of *Even a Wise Man Stumbles*, plays here only a subsidiary role. His career is left rather hanging in the air in the first comedy and is wound up here by Ostrovsky who, having anticipated our age by inventing a Colonel Blimp, prophetically makes Glumov a *secretaire intime* or gigolo to a rich woman.

Easy Money was first performed in Petersburg on April 16, 1870, and in Moscow on October 6th of the same year. It was an instantaneous success in both capitals and since then it has become one of the favourite classics on the Russian stage.

Wolves and Sheep is the most biting satire ever written by Ostrovsky, but it is not only a satire on capitalism and the new type of clever business man produced by it, it is also a satire on humanity at large which, according to Lynyayev, is divided into wolves and sheep, "the wolves devour the sheep and the sheep not only allow themselves to be devoured, but seem to like it."

The plot of this play was suggested to Ostrovsky by a famous trial of the head of a woman's convent, Mother Superior Mitrofaniya, who had appropriated the funds of her convent for her own needs. Except for the episode of the thousand roubles which Miss Meropia obtains from Mrs. Kupavina by deceit, there is, however, little similarity between the plot of this play and the dishonest dealings of Mother Superior Mitrofaniya.

In this play, too, the names of some of the characters suggest their moral make-up. Murzavetzkaya suggests the common Russian word *merzavetz* which means scoundrel. Chugunov, Miss Meropia's dishonest accomplice, suggests the Russian word *chugun* meaning cast-iron.

This play was first performed in Petersburg on December 8, 1875, and in Moscow on December 26th of the same year. It is also one of the most popular of Ostrovsky's comedies and has supplied numerous Russian actors and actresses with parts that made them famous. The part of Glafira, in particular, is considered by Russian critics to be one of the most brilliant women parts on the Russian stage. One Russian critic sums her up in the words: "She is life itself." "By throwing off her nun's clothes," the same critic writes, "she

NOTES

seems to throw off her whole hypocritical past and her assumption of the part of a society woman is full of such gusto that it infects even the most phlegmatic spectator. And the scene in which she catches the simpleton Lynyayev—is it not the very perfection of stage craft which allows an actress to put every possible shade of meaning in the psychological subtleties of her dialogue?"

As for Lynyayev's part, the famous Russian actor Lensky has, in the words of another critic, "created dramatic history on the theme of the transformation of a happy-go-lucky bachelor into a dispirited model of a henpecked husband."

All Ostrovsky's plays are usually divided into short scenes, in accordance with the tradition followed by Molière. In the present translation this tradition is disregarded and the scenes are run together in accordance with modern usage.

D. M.

THE END